What People Are Saying about Rediscovering God's Church

If you desire to grow spiritually and relationally, *Rediscovering God's Church* is an absolute must-read. Derek Prince is one of God's precious and extraordinary gifts to today's church. The Lord is still using Derek to help inspire and instruct the Lord's church. Be blessed beyond your recognition!

—*Kirbyjon H. Caldwell*
Windsor Village United Methodist Church
Author, *The Gospel of Good Success*

I had the delight of personal acquaintance with Derek Prince, dating back to the 1960s when he was based in British Columbia. Just a few years before his passing, I had the privilege of spending quality time with him in India, where he was born. Whatever Derek Prince wrote was very helpful. His scholarly research and anointed teaching are evident in this new book. It's a valuable contribution to all of us.

—*Don Gossett*
Evangelist and Author of over two dozen books,
including *What You Say Is What You Get*

With *Rediscovering God's Church*, Whitaker House makes available [Derek Prince's] key teachings on church transformation for application to today's congregations... While admitting to a measure of idealism, Prince dares the church to move into the future with biblical resolve, acting as "God's redemptive agent in the world."

—*Chris Maxwell*
Christian Retailing magazine

First Corinthians 4:20 tells us that we have many teachers but not many fathers. Derek Prince's ministry is a spiritual legacy that not only teaches the multitudes, but also releases the "Spirit of the Father." I was graced with the opportunity to minister with Derek Prince at a conference in England. I sat in awe as I listened to the revelation of God's Word through him. At the same time, there was a strong awareness that I was not just in the presence of a "teacher" but an "apostolic father." Derek's ministry has begotten many through the gospel. This continual birthing has paved a path for the next generation. I am honored to be a part of that generation. His pioneering anointing has released a spiritual DNA that produces a legacy of sons and daughters who understand the pattern of God for the church in the last days. I pray that the *ecclesia* or "called out ones" will catch the vision of this book and continue to carry the torch. I believe that *Rediscovering God's Church* is a blueprint from God concerning the order that He established for His end-time church.

—*Kimberly Daniels*
Spoken Word Ministries
Jacksonville, Florida

Rediscovering
GOD'S
CHURCH

Derek PRINCE

Rediscovering GOD'S CHURCH

WHITAKER
HOUSE

Rediscovering God's Church

Derek Prince Ministries–International
P.O. Box 19501
Charlotte, North Carolina 28219-9501
www.derekprince.org

ISBN-10: 0-88368-812-3
ISBN-13: 978-0-88368-812-0
Printed in the United States of America
© 2006 by Derek Prince Ministries–International

1030 Hunt Valley Circle
New Kensington, PA 15068
www.whitakerhouse.com

Library of Congress Cataloging-in-Publication Data
Prince, Derek.
Rediscovering God's church / by Derek Prince.
p. cm.
Summary: "Describes God's original blueprint for the church and how today's church can fulfill this calling"—Provided by publisher.
ISBN-13: 978-0-88368-812-0 (trade hardcover : alk. paper)
ISBN-10: 0-88368-812-3 (trade hardcover : alk. paper)
1. Church. I. Title.
BV601.P75 2006
262—dc22   2005035894

2 3 4 5 6 7 8 9 10 11 12 13 **UJ** 14 13 12 11 10 09 08 07 06

Contents

Introduction by Derek Prince Ministries............ 9

Part 1:
God's Vision for the Church

Chapter 1: God's Portion Is His People.............. 13
Chapter 2: Transformation: God's Program
            for the Church................................. 18

Part 2:
The Nature of the Church:
Seven Pictures of the Church in Ephesians

Chapter 3: Picture #1: The Assembly................. 25
Chapter 4: Picture #2: The Body of Christ 36
Chapter 5: Picture #3: The Workmanship 45
Chapter 6: Picture #4: The Family 53
Chapter 7: Picture #5: The Temple.................... 63
Chapter 8: Picture #6: The Bride...................... 73
Chapter 9: Picture #7: The Army...................... 91
Chapter 10: The Seven Pictures and
             Their Application 104

Part 3:
The Structure of the Church

Chapter 11: The Universal Church..................... 113
Chapter 12: The Local Church 132
Chapter 13: Apostolic Teams and Elders:
            The Two Legs of the Body.............. 166
Chapter 14: Apostles and Elders,
            Not Bureaucracy 180
Chapter 15: Reproduction, Not Succession......... 196

Part 4:
The Leadership of the Church

Chapter 16: Mobile Ministry: Apostles 209
Chapter 17: The Marks of a True Apostle 234
Chapter 18: Mobile Ministry: Prophets 249
Chapter 19: Mobile Ministry: Evangelists 274
Chapter 20: Mobile Ministry: Teachers 290
Chapter 21: Resident Ministry: Pastors 303
Chapter 22: Pastors: Ruling, Teaching,
             Shepherding 322
Chapter 23: Resident Ministry: Deacons 348

Part 5:
The Lifestyle of the Church

Chapter 24: The Daily Life of
             the Local Church 359
Chapter 25: The Corporate Gathering 381

Part 6:
The Future of the Church

Chapter 26: Your Kingdom Come 393
Chapter 27: A Glorious Church 419

About the Author 429

Introduction

by Derek Prince Ministries

ack in the 1930s, so the story goes, the telephone rang in the rector's office of the Washington, D.C., church occasionally attended by President Franklin Roosevelt. The voice on the phone breathlessly inquired, "Please tell me: Do you expect the president to be in church this Sunday?"

"That," the rector explained patiently, "I cannot promise. But we expect God to be there, and we suspect that will be incentive enough for a reasonably large attendance."

We don't know if Derek Prince was familiar with that anecdote, but those of us who knew him intimately are confident he would have enjoyed it immensely and agreed with the sentiment wholeheartedly. You see, Derek loved the church. And, as much as any teacher of modern times, he understood the greatness to which the body of Christ is called and destined.

In one of his many radio broadcasts over the years, Derek summed up his approach to the church in this way:

I believe that God is concerned with the restoration of two peoples to whom He's related by a covenant, which He has declared He will never break. The first, historically, is Israel. The second is the church.

If you are new to Derek Prince, you need to know that he was one of the truly great Christian minds of the twentieth century. He was born a British citizen, but he lived large swaths of his life in Israel and the United States (eventually becoming a U.S. citizen). He was educated at England's prestigious Cambridge University, where he was a contemporary of C. S. Lewis. And, for a time, he held a fellowship in ancient and modern philosophy there.

Don't be put off by those impressive intellectual credentials, however. Millions around the world, in hundreds of nations, have found the teaching of Derek Prince to be inspiring, uplifting, enlightening, and always accessible.

Thus, the book you now hold in your hands is a treasure. On its pages, you'll find an extraordinary depth of revelation about the nature, role, structure, and destiny of the church—local and universal. And, as you read, you'll also gain fresh insights into your place and part in God's plan for history.

Part 1:

God's Vision for the Church

Chapter 1

God's Portion Is His People

ne of the grandest themes of Scripture is the church—the object of God's affection, the future bride for His beloved Son.

Christ's redemptive mission on earth is a love story, played out on the stages of time and eternity, and filled with drama, pathos, love, struggle, and triumph. God's intention is to provide for His Son a perfect companion for all eternity.

The church is also God's redemptive agent in the world. But His challenge is the very people who comprise the church. He must get us, in our unruly condition, to become the perfect bride of His only Son.

The Mirror of God's Word

Scripture compares God's Word to a mirror that reveals our inward spiritual condition so that we may see ourselves as God sees us: all the way to the end result—not only as we should be, but as we will be.

> *The LORD does not see as man sees; for man looks at the outward appearance, but the LORD looks at the heart.*
>
> (1 Samuel 16:7)

If we look into this mirror before we have been reconciled to God through Jesus Christ, it shows us our unclean and sinful condition. Once we have been reconciled to God and cleansed from our sin, it shows us what we have become as God's new creation in Christ. We experience in a personal way these truths of Scripture:

> *Therefore, if anyone is in Christ, he is a new creation; old things have passed away; behold, all things have become new.* (2 Corinthians 5:17)

> *For we are His workmanship, created in Christ Jesus for good works, which God prepared beforehand that we should walk in them.* (Ephesians 2:10)

God's final objective is not just redeemed people; His goal is a special people.

In this book, we will look into the mirror of God's Word so we can learn what we are like in God's sight as His collective people. We will examine the seven pictures of God's people as revealed by the apostle Paul in the book of Ephesians. From there, we will explore the structure, leadership, lifestyle, and future of the church.

God's Redemptive Purposes

God's purposes in redeeming His people to Himself are found in the book of Exodus:

> *And Moses went up to God, and the Lord called to him from the mountain, saying, "Thus you shall say to the house of Jacob and tell the sons of Israel: 'You yourselves have seen what I did to the Egyptians, and how I bore you on eagles' wings, and brought you to Myself. Now then, if you will indeed obey My voice and keep My covenant, then you*

shall be My own possession among all the peoples, for all the earth is Mine.'" (Exodus 19:3–5 NASB)

There are two primary objects of redemption as revealed in these words of God to Israel.

A Direct, Personal Relationship with God

First, notice what God said about the actual act of redemption: *"You yourselves have seen what I did to the Egyptians, and how I bore you on eagles' wings, and brought you to Myself"* (verse 4). This Scripture reveals that God brings the redeemed to Himself. His first purpose of redemption is to bring His redeemed people into a direct, personal relationship with Him. It is surprising how few people in the Old Testament period seemed to grasp this concept. They were interested in the Law, the material blessings, and the Promised Land. They were looking at *things*, which is why most of them missed out on a wonderful, direct, personal relationship with God. Even today, many people do not seem to fully understand that the primary purpose of God is to *bring us to Himself.* Everything else is secondary.

His Own Possession

The second purpose of redemption is for God to make the redeemed into His own possession. The phrase translated as *"My own possession"* in Exodus 19:5 (NASB) is from a Hebrew word for which the exact meaning is unknown. Other translations use the phrases *"a special treasure to Me"* (NKJV), *"my treasured possession"* (NIV), and *"a peculiar treasure unto me"* (KJV). The indication is that God wants to make us something *personal, peculiar, special.* It is rather exciting that we do not know the exact meaning of the original Hebrew term because it leaves open so many possibilities. But we do know that it is something beautiful, far above the level of what we could imagine or think for ourselves. That is why He redeemed us.

A New People

God *invests in people*. He is much more concerned about people than about things. This truth is illustrated beautifully and simply in Deuteronomy 32:9: *"For the Lord's portion is His people."* God's purpose centers on His redeemed people—His portion in all that has happened and is happening in the world. Yet we must clearly understand that His ultimate goal is not only to redeem individuals; it is also the creation of a special *people*, a single, new, organic *whole*—something vastly different from what existed among peoples before God intervened through redemption.

Contemporary Christianity places most of the emphasis on the individual and his or her relationship with God. While this is very important, the final objective of God is not just redeemed individuals; His goal is a *special people*.

In His prayer to His Father, Jesus revealed to us tremendous insight into the particular stage in God's purposes in which we are living today:

> *I do not pray for these alone, but also for those who will believe in Me through their word; that they all may be one, as You, Father, are in Me, and I in You; that they also may be one in Us, that the world may believe that You sent Me. And the glory which You gave Me I have given them, that they may be one just as We are one: I in them and You in Me; that they may be made perfect* [or complete] *in one, and that the world may know that You have sent Me, and have loved them as You have loved Me.* (John 17:20–23)

Jesus' ultimate vision is to blend individuals from every race and background into visible unity. The world sees things in time and space; it does not see mystical realities of a spirit realm. If we are going to reach the world with God's redemptive message, we must be visible—something the world can see and appreciate. Thus, we cannot hide or downplay our Christianity, because God's purpose is to bring His people to become *visibly* united. And this unity will be irrefutable testimony to the entire world that God indeed sent Jesus. As we come to be a true reflection of God's redemptive people, others will also be drawn to Him in personal relationship, and will join us in becoming His own special treasure for all of eternity.

Chapter 2

Transformation: God's Program for the Church

I n order for God to make us into the kind of people He intends us to become, there must be a process of transformation. When God first redeems us, we are only beginning the journey toward all that we ought to be and that God intends us to be. I marvel at God's faith in even taking on this project of transforming people like me!

The Process of Transformation

As an example of how the process of transformation works, take a look at the call of Jesus to His first disciples:

> *And Jesus, walking by the Sea of Galilee, saw two brothers, Simon called Peter, and Andrew his brother, casting a net into the sea; for they were fishermen. Then He said to them, "Follow Me, and I will make you fishers of men." They immediately left their nets and followed Him.*
>
> (Matthew 4:18–20)

This simple scene does not contain a lot of complicated psychology, but just the essence of what has to happen. There are two main components to Jesus saying, *"Follow Me, and I will make you fishers of men."*

Total Commitment

First, Jesus requires *total* commitment. "Leave it all; follow Me. I'm not telling you where we're going; you just have to follow Me in faith. Put your life in My hands and let Me take care of the consequences." That is essential. God cannot really work His purposes until His people are fully committed.

Then, Jesus says, "I'm not telling you where we're going, but I am telling you what I will make of you. I will make you fishers of men." The important thing with every one of God's redeemed people is not what we are right now, but what God wants to make of us. If we yield to the Lord, He guarantees the finished product. But first we must commit ourselves to God's purpose, and then He begins to work in us to make us into what He wants us to be.

The same principle is inherent in the teaching of Paul:

> *I beseech you therefore, brethren, by the mercies of God, that you present your bodies a living sacrifice, holy, acceptable to God, which is your reasonable service. And do not be conformed to this world, but be transformed by the renewing of your mind, that you may prove what is that good and acceptable and perfect will of God.* (Romans 12:1–2)

As we saw in Matthew 4:18–20, the first step to God's transforming process within us is *total commitment to God*. Paul expressed this truth in the words, *"Present your bodies a living sacrifice."* He was thinking in terms of the Old Testament sacrifices of animals, such as sheep and bulls, which were killed and then placed as an offering on God's altar. Once they were placed on God's altar, they no longer belonged to the person who offered them; they belonged to God alone. Paul was telling us Christians that we have to offer our own bodies to God in exactly the same way. Once you have placed your body on the altar, it no longer belongs to you; it belongs entirely to God. But there's one major difference: Your body won't be killed first; it'll be placed live on the altar! Now *that's* total commitment.

Transformation from Within

Commitment to God leads us to think in a higher way. When our minds become *renewed*, our values change and our priorities are altered. Things take on a different meaning. That is something God does only for the committed. When we are transformed by the renewing of our minds, we are able to discern and approve God's will. We *can* find out what He really wants. He has a wonderful plan for each of us individually and for His people collectively, but He reveals His plans only to those who are committed.

> *But we all, with unveiled face, beholding as in a mirror the glory of the Lord, are being transformed into the same image from glory to glory, just as by the Spirit of the Lord.*
> (2 Corinthians 3:18)

Remember, God's Word is a mirror that shows us what we are *inwardly*. This mirror is an essential instrument in the process of transformation. Notice that the above Scripture is written in the plural. It is not just for individuals; it's for us *all*. It shows us what God intends for all His believing people collectively. Without this view of God's people as a single whole, we tend to get lost in our own needs and problems and blessings, and we miss the larger, overall plan and purposes of God. "We fail to see the forest for the trees," as the saying goes.

Transformation: God's Program for the Church

Transformed from Glory to Glory

As we reflect on the mirror of God's Word, we behold the glory that God is going to work in *us*. As we behold this glory by faith and continue looking in the mirror of God's Word, the Spirit of God transforms us into the likeness of what we see—but only if we look *by faith* into the mirror. If we do not look in the mirror, the Spirit of God cannot work on us. This is not just one single transformation, but *"from glory to glory"*! Each time we arrive at a certain level, God shows us there is a higher level and urges us to move upward.

This transformation depends on two things. First, it depends on our looking by faith into the mirror of God's Word. Second, it rests on the work of the Holy Spirit when we look into the mirror. Each one of us must look regularly into the mirror of God's Word to check on our own personal spiritual condition and relationship to God.

So here is the order of transformation: commitment, then transformation from within, which leads to the revelation of God's purpose.

> *For our light affliction, which is but for a moment, is working for us a far more exceeding and eternal weight of glory, while we do not look at the things which are seen, but at the things which are not seen. For the things which are seen are temporary, but the things which are not seen are eternal.*
> (2 Corinthians 4:17–18)

Paul said that we go through affliction as part of the process of transformation. But the affliction will benefit us and will work out God's purposes for us—*if* we continue to focus on the unseen things and not on the visible circumstances and situations swirling around us.

The things that are seen, Paul said, are temporary; the unseen things are eternal. The way we see the unseen eternal realities of God's purposes for us is to look by faith in the mirror of God's Word. When we do that, the Holy Spirit reveals the destiny God has for us—where He is taking us, and what He desires to produce in us and from us. As we keep on looking by faith, not taking our eyes off the mirror, the Holy Spirit continues to change us into that which we have apprehended by faith. Each time we newly apprehend truth by faith, we experience a further transformation. This is the process that takes us truly from glory to glory!

> *Looking into the mirror of God's Word is an essential part of the processs of transformation.*

Part 2:

The Nature of the Church: Seven Pictures of the Church in Ephesians

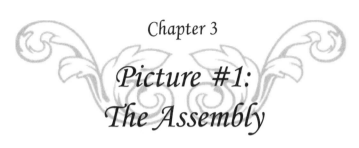

Chapter 3

Picture #1:
The Assembly

"[God] put all things under *[Jesus']* feet, and gave *[Jesus]* to
be head over all things to the church."
—Ephesians 1:22

n the next few chapters, we will be examining seven
pictures of God's people from Paul's epistle to the
Ephesians, the first being the assembly.

The Greek word translated "church" in Ephesians 1:22 is
ecclesia, from which we get such English words as ecclesiol-
ogy. The noun *ecclesia* is derived from a verb that means "to
call out." The concept is a group of people that is formed by
being called out from a larger group of people. It is also a
group called out for a special purpose, which applies to the
church. We are called out of the world through faith in Jesus
Christ for a special purpose of God.

In the contemporary secular Greek of New Testament
times, the word *ecclesia* had a very specific meaning. It meant
a "governmental assembly." It is used in that way three times
in the nineteenth chapter of Acts, where we read about an
uproar that broke out in the city of Ephesus because of Paul's
ministry.

Note the use of the word "assembly" in Acts 19:

Some therefore cried one thing and some another, for the assembly [ecclesia] was confused, and most of them did not know why they had come together. (verse 32)

The people were holding an unorganized, unauthorized meeting, and the town clerk rebuked them and told them they had no right to hold a meeting there in that way. Then the clerk added,

But if you have any other inquiry to make, it shall be determined in the lawful assembly [ecclesia]. (verse 39)

The word is used again in verse 41:

And when he had said these things, he dismissed the assembly [ecclesia].

Thus, the root meaning of the word we habitually translate as *church* actually means "a legal or governmental assembly."

In this chapter, I am going to stick to the word *assembly* in translating the word for church. This meaning has been obliterated by many modern translations, but *the governmental assembly* is the first picture of God's people in the mirror of God's Word.

Qualifications to Enter the Assembly

In the Greek assembly in Ephesus, many people were excluded: slaves (who comprised nearly half of the population), women, and all visitors and temporary residents. The assembly was reserved only for free citizens residing in Ephesus.

Picture #1: The Assembly

What are the qualifications to be in the assembly of the Lord Jesus Christ? Jesus Himself told us:

> [Jesus] *said to them, "But who do you say that I am?" Simon Peter answered and said, "You are the Christ, the Son of the living God." Jesus answered and said to him, "Blessed are you, Simon Bar-Jonah, for flesh and blood has not revealed this to you, but My Father who is in heaven. And I also say to you that you are Peter, and on this rock I will build My church, and the gates of Hades shall not prevail against it."* (Matthew 16:15–18)

Peter came out boldly and proclaimed to Jesus, *"You are the Christ* [Messiah], *the Son of the living God."* This revelation did not come by Peter's natural reasoning or logic. It came from God the Father through the Holy Spirit. It did not reveal Jesus of Nazareth as the carpenter's son, whom he already knew, but it revealed Jesus in His divine, eternal nature as the Son of God, the Messiah.

I believe that millions today have been given membership to churches when they have not received this basic revelation. Thus, the church cannot function in its full authority because its members don't even qualify to enter the assembly!

The language of Jesus in the above passage is very emphatic: *"You are Peter, and on this rock I will build My church."* All the emphasis is on the word *"My."* My church, *My* assembly. Jesus was saying, in effect, that there are many assemblies. Each city and state has its assembly. Nations have their assemblies. But Jesus said, "I am now building *My* assembly." There is a relationship between *build* and *My.* If Jesus doesn't build it, He will not own it. He owns only what He builds.

Once, a preacher was speaking on the gifts of the Holy Spirit. At the end of his message, a lady came up to him and said, "Brother, we don't have these gifts in our church." He said, "Well, they have them in the church of Jesus Christ. Which is your church?" That's an important and far-reaching question. Which is your church? Is it *His* church?

There are four elements that constitute the procedure for admission to the assembly of Jesus Christ: Confrontation, Revelation, Acknowledgement, and Confession. We can never enter the assembly to rule until we have had a life-shaking, personal encounter with Jesus, as Peter had before his proclamation of who Jesus is. And we cannot know the truth about Jesus unless it is revealed to us.

> *The church as an assembly is a group called out for a special purpose of God.*

Since Jesus made Peter the example, let's use what transpired between the two of them to illustrate the procedure:

There is a *direct confrontation*: Peter met Jesus face-to-face. There was nobody between them, no mediator, no middleman.

There is a *revelation granted*: The revelation was granted by God the Father through the Holy Spirit. Without that revelation, Peter could not have known who Jesus truly is.

There is an *acknowledgement of the revelation*: Peter acknowledged the revelation when he responded to Christ's question.

There is a *confession of the revelation*: Peter confessed, out loud, *"You are the Christ, the Son of the living God."*

Picture #1: The Assembly

The Church as Zion

In Scripture, the title that is regularly used for the assembly of God's people when they meet in divine order is *Zion*. Let's examine what the Scripture says about Zion and our relationship to Zion as believers:

> *But you have come to Mount Zion and to the city of the living God, the heavenly Jerusalem, to an innumerable company of angels, to the general assembly and church of the firstborn who are registered in heaven, to God the Judge of all, to the spirits of just men made perfect, to Jesus the Mediator of the new covenant, and to the blood of sprinkling that speaks better things than that of Abel.*
>
> (Hebrews 12:22–24)

Notice that this is not a future event. The writer did not say, "You are soon going to come." He said that you have already come! Not physically, of course, but spiritually, we are already part of the total governmental assembly of God. Although part of it is in heaven and part of it is on earth, we are all *one* assembly. Included in that assembly are *"thousands upon thousands of angels in joyful assembly* [or festal array]*"* (NIV). It's a supremely dignified, glorious assembly.

I recall an incident that occurred at a commanding officer's parade during my years in the military. Everybody had to polish all their pieces of brass and their boots, and stand at attention. There was a military band, and everything was precise and official and dignified. There was an air of *authority*. That is the picture here of Zion, and we are part of it!

Through our faith in Jesus Christ, we are part of the great governmental assembly that governs the entire universe. The Head of that assembly, under God the Father, is Jesus Christ.

We, as the church (God's people, the assembly), are the representatives of God's authority in the earth.

Our Earthly Authority

One of the Old Testament verses most quoted in the New Testament presents the tremendous authority of the assembly of the Lord:

> *The LORD said to my Lord, "Sit at My right hand, till I make Your enemies Your footstool."* (Psalm 110:1)

In Mark 12:35–37, Jesus applied the above reference to Himself. *"The LORD"* is God the Father. *"My Lord"* is David's Greater Son, the Lord Jesus Christ. This verse refers to a statement the Father says to the Son after Jesus' death and resurrection, when He has ascended and taken His place at the Father's right hand. God the Father says to Jesus Christ the Son, *"Sit at My right hand."* All authority in heaven and in earth has been given to Jesus until God makes all His enemies His footstool.

The New Testament clearly reveals that Jesus is *right now* seated at God's right hand. (See, for example, Romans 8:34; Ephesians 1:20; Colossians 3:1; Hebrews 1:3; 1 Peter 3:22.) Jesus Christ is on His throne right now. And here is how His authority is to be executed on earth:

> *The LORD shall send the rod of Your strength out of Zion. Rule in the midst of Your enemies!* (Psalm 110:2)

I believe that all three Persons of the Godhead are represented in the first two verses of Psalm 110. In the first verse, we read that God the Father says to Jesus the Son, *"Sit at My right hand."* Then, in the second verse, we see that God the

Picture #1: The Assembly

Holy Spirit stretches forth the scepter of Christ's authority from Zion, the assembly of His people, and says, *"Rule in the midst of Your enemies!"* Sometimes, we are so conscious of the enemies that we forget that Christ is *already* ruling. His enemies have not all been subdued under His feet yet, but He is ruling supreme in the midst of His enemies—right now, through us! The Holy Spirit extends the scepter of Christ's authority over the nations, kings, and rulers of this earth. And He does this out of the assembly of God's people who are met in divine order through prayer, the ministry of the Word, and the gifts of the Spirit.

Jesus rules *"out of Zion,"* which is the picture of God's people meeting in divine assembly, divine order, and divine authority. God the Father says to God the Son, "All authority is Yours. From now on, You're ruling." But His rule is exercised by the Spirit "out of Zion," the assembly of God's people. *We* are that rod stretched forth in the Lord's hand representing His authority in whatever sphere we operate! Oh, if we would only grasp the solemnity and power of that truth.

> *The essential feature of the assembly is governmental authority.*

Most Christians accept the fact that Jesus is going to rule someday. But it is vital to know that He is ruling *right now*. When you fully grasp that fact, it will drastically change the way you live. Through our prayers, intercession, and fasting, through our proclamation of the gospel and our committed lifestyle, we are being utilized by Christ to "rule in the midst of His enemies."

31

Christians are like the rod of Moses in the story of Israel's deliverance from Egypt. The rod is a symbol of authority. The final deliverance of God's people could not take place before Moses learned to use his rod. Likewise, the completion of the destiny of God's people will not take place until we learn to "use the rod," or to function in a unified, governmental way as the assembly, the governing body of God—not in the age to come, but now.

After giving a strong exhortation about right relationships in the church, Jesus said,

> *Assuredly, I say to you, whatever you bind on earth will be bound in heaven, and whatever you loose on earth will be loosed in heaven. Again I say to you that if two of you agree on earth concerning anything that they ask, it will be done for them by My Father in heaven. For where two or three are gathered together in My name, I am there in the midst of them.* (Matthew 18:18–20)

In this passage, notice that the initiative is not with heaven, but with earth. When we agree on earth, heaven does the work. When we bind or loose on earth, it is bound or loosed in heaven. Our agreeing and binding and loosing are made effective as we gather together in a *unified* assembly. Heaven takes notice of our requests and our petitions and makes them effective. We have incredible authority as the ruling assembly of God!

I knew a young pastor in Denmark who was facing the problem of divorced people wanting to remarry. He had refused to marry one couple but consented to marry another, and he was being criticized for it. He was not sure if he was doing the right thing, so he took time off to seek the Lord on the issue. He prayed, "Lord, why didn't You make clear in the New Testament Your standards for marriage and divorce and remarriage?" The Lord answered him, "If I'd given you a set of rules, you would have just used them legalistically to bring people into bondage, and you would have shown no mercy." So the pastor said, "Lord, if You'll just show me what *You* would do, then I'll do that." The Lord responded, "On the contrary, if you'll decide what *you* will do, I'll do that."

That is precisely what Matthew 18 says: Whatever you bind, I'll bind; whatever you loose, I'll loose; if you agree, I'll do it. God has placed the responsibility on us, the assembly. He says, "You make the decrees, and I'll enforce them. You make the decisions, and I'll see that they're carried out."

Your Giftings

Another very important point about the assembly is that it functions only when we recognize each other's gifting.

> *As each one has received a gift, minister it to one another, as good stewards of the manifold grace of God. If anyone speaks, let him speak as the oracles of God. If anyone ministers [or serves], let him do it as with the ability which God supplies, that in all things God may be glorified through Jesus Christ, to whom belong the glory and the dominion forever and ever. Amen.* (1 Peter 4:10–11)

What has God made you? What is your office, your function? Every person has a gift (Greek, *charisma*). We must be sensitive to—and minister to one another through—our *charisma*, whether our gifts are speaking, serving, teaching, or anything else.

In my opinion, leadership is also a charisma. The gift of leadership is very recognizable. The ability to lead is something that God places upon a person by the Holy Spirit for a purpose. Or your charisma might be a particular service. One of the great missing ingredients in Christian life today is serving others.

We need to be much more sensitive to the charisma of our brothers and sisters in the church. We should recognize their offices, functions, and places in the assembly.

> *And we urge you, brethren, to recognize those who labor among you, and are over you in the Lord and admonish* [or correct] *you, and to esteem them very highly in love for their work's sake.* (1 Thessalonians 5:12–13)

Spiritual authority can operate only by voluntary recognition. It cannot be imposed; it must be submitted to. Without submission, there is no spiritual authority.

The work of those in spiritual authority is to admonish the believers, straighten them out, correct them, tell them when they are doing wrong. It takes a true friend to do that. There is nothing more sobering than having somebody tell you, "I accept your authority." People who look to me for leadership place a tremendous and very solemn responsibility upon me.

I want to challenge you to a more serious commitment to the church. No one would ever act casually and without discipline in a legal setting, such as a courtroom, and yet many Christians do so in the church assembly, which is a higher court than any earthly assembly. Attend church consistently and punctually, dress appropriately, serve in some capacity, and appreciate the fact that you are a part of an important institution. Give the assembly your very best in attitude and service.

The Essential Feature of the Assembly and God's Requirement

With each of the seven pictures of the church, I will give you a twofold application: I will point out both the essential feature of each picture and what is required of us as God's people.

The essential feature of the assembly is governmental authority. God has deposited much governmental authority in His assembly. What is required of us in order to exercise God's authority is *respect for God's order.* We cannot govern others if we cannot govern ourselves.

Have you ever attended a conference or meeting where the leader was trying to call the meeting to order, but everybody kept on talking, paying no attention to him? Members are independently carrying on their own conversations and are busy with their own agendas—not to mention showing disrespect for the authority of the leader—so that nothing can be accomplished. Who would want to put a group like that in charge of anything? Yet I wonder if this is the picture of the church that many of our critics have.

We will not be fit to govern the world until we have learned to govern ourselves. Yet God *has* destined us to govern ourselves and also to be the instrument of His government in the earth. What a challenging image we see in the mirror, and what a position we must rise to!

Once you establish a heart of dedication to the assembly, you must pursue the next aspect of relationship to the church: membership in the body of Christ.

Chapter 4

Picture #2:
The Body of Christ

*"And [God]...gave [Jesus] to be head over all things
to the church, which is His body, the fullness of Him
who fills all in all."*
—Ephesians 1:22–23

uilding on the image of the church as God's governmental assembly of believers, the second picture is
that of His body, the body of Christ.

We relate to the world we live in through our bodies. It
is in the body that we get things done in a world of time and
space. Similarly, Christ relates to the world through us, His
body. We are the instruments by which He works out His
redemptive purposes in the world.

> *Therefore, when Christ came into the world, he said: "Sacri-
> fice and offering you did not desire, but a body you prepared
> for me; with burnt offerings and sin offerings you were not
> pleased. Then I said, 'Here I am—it is written about me in
> the scroll—I have come to do your will, O God.'"*
>
> (Hebrews 10:5–7 NIV)

Picture #2: The Body of Christ

This passage pictures Jesus coming to the earth not to introduce the Law (which had already been introduced by Moses), but to save us by being the sacrifice for our sins. In order to do that, He had to have a body with which to provide a sacrifice.

When put together, these two phrases, *"a body you prepared for me,"* and, *"to do your will, O God,"* tell us that the function of the body is to be the instrument used to accomplish God's will. This displays the twofold aspect of Christ's body: First, the physical body of Jesus became the sacrifice for our sins on the cross; and second, the body of God's collective people continues and completes His ministry on the earth.

The New Testament presents several pictures of believers as the body of Christ. Paul wrote in Romans,

> *Just as each of us has one body with many members, and these members do not all have the same function, so in Christ we who are many form one body, and each member belongs to all the others.* (Romans 12:4–5 NIV)

This body is not a group of separated, isolated individuals. We belong to one another.

In 1 Corinthians, Paul amplified this picture of the body of Christ:

> *The body is a unit, though it is made up of many parts; and though all its parts are many, they form one body. So it is with Christ. For we were all baptized by one Spirit into one body—whether Jews or Greeks, slave or free—and we were all given the one Spirit to drink.*
> (1 Corinthians 12:12–13 NIV)

The word emphasized in the above passage is *one*: *"They form **one** body....We were all baptized by **one** Spirit into **one** body.... We were all given the **one** Spirit to drink."* The emphasis throughout is the *unity of the body*. Paul continued,

> *Now the body is not made up of one part but of many. If the foot should say, "Because I am not a hand, I do not belong to the body," it would not for that reason cease to be part of the body. And if the ear should say, "Because I am not an eye, I do not belong to the body," it would not for that reason cease to be part of the body. If the whole body were an eye, where would the sense of hearing be? If the whole body were an ear, where would the sense of smell be? But in fact God has arranged the parts in the body, every one of them, just as he wanted them to be. If they were all one part, where would the body be? As it is, there are many parts, but one body. The eye cannot say to the hand, "I don't need you!" And the head cannot say to the feet, "I don't need you!"*
>
> (1 Corinthians 12:14–21 NIV)

In our relationships toward one another, the word I believe applies best is *interdependent*. The essence of Paul's teaching is that every member needs all the other members. None of us is independent; we cannot do without one another. Therefore, we cannot say to other believers, "I can get along without you. It doesn't matter what happens to you; I'm all right." That attitude is neither permissible nor correct because God has sovereign control over the body. The eye, though it is a wonderful, refined, delicate instrument with more than three million moving, working parts, cannot say to that rather prosaic member, the hand, "I don't need you." Even more remarkably, the head cannot say to the feet, "I don't need you." The head is right at the top, the feet are down at the bottom, and the whole length of the body separates them. Yet they clearly need each other in order for the body to operate with optimum efficiency.

What is significant is that, in a certain sense, the head typifies Jesus. Therefore, Jesus would not say to the lowest part of His body, "I don't need you." Rather, He needs us because we are His body, the instruments He uses to get things done in this world.

The weakest members are actually the most important. No outward part of the body is more frail and sensitive than the eye, yet perhaps none is more important. Notice how carefully nature has protected the eye. It gets all that protection and honor not because it is strong, but because it is weak. Here is the way that the body has been knit together. The strong has to protect the weak. We cannot ignore or despise any member of the body of Christ. This is a vital lesson.

When I was a missionary in East Africa, people would come to my door every day from six in the morning until ten at night. I got tired of telling them that I could not do the many things they requested, even in my own field of education. Sometimes, when I had reached the point of real irritation, it was as if the Lord was saying to me, "Now, take care, because you are talking to one of My children." I would have to stop and remember that I had no right to be irritated, impatient, or contemptuous of any child of God. This is true of the members of the body. We need one another, we depend on one another, and we are compelled to honor one another. When one member suffers, the others suffer with it. When one member is honored, the others are honored with it. So it is with the universal body of Jesus Christ, the church.

The Complete Body

From [Christ] *the whole body, joined and held together by every supporting ligament, grows and builds itself up in love, as each part does its work.* (Ephesians 4:16 NIV)

This verse pictures the finished product. Though there are many joints and ligaments that hold us firmly intact, all of us together who are united in Christ are one body. As we are held together in this single, organic unity, the body builds itself up. But, to build itself up, the body depends on each part to do its work. One unhealthy part affects the health of the rest of the body.

What is required to keep all the parts healthy in our relationship with Christ? The words *obedience, submission,* and *willingness* come to mind, but the word I choose is *availability.* The members must be available to the Head. No matter how strong and useful my arm is, it's no good to the head unless it is available to do what the head wants. The same goes for every other part of my body. There is a saying that the only kind of ability God looks for in a person is *avail*ability.

Holding fast to the Head, from whom all the body, nourished and knit together by joints and ligaments, grows with the increase that is from God. (Colossians 2:19)

The *"joints"* are the interrelationships between the various members of the body, through which God's supply comes. My relationship with you is my "joint" with you. It is crucial to understand that our needs are supplied through the joints, or relationships, within the body.

"Ligaments" are needed to keep the joints together. A *ligament* is committed, covenant love—love that is committed

to another person, like a man to his wife ("for better, for worse," "in sickness and in health"). If I disagree with my wife's doctrine, do I go find another wife? Of course not. When a man is committed to a woman by marriage, it is in spite of disagreements, tensions, and problems. Any marriage that is committed only while there is no tension or problems will not last. What is needed is something that will hold the people together in spite of the tensions and the problems. What is the answer? *Covenant commitment*: a deep, permanent, individual commitment.

We do not get our needs met through the Head alone, but through the network of joints and ligaments throughout the body, which are all linked in various ways to the Head. The Head may have made full provision for every need of every member, but the members will not have their needs supplied unless they are rightly related to the other members through the Head.

Since spiritual "nourishment" is supplied through both joints and ligaments, we cannot say, "I'll get everything I need from the Lord alone." The Lord hasn't arranged the body in that way. He has arranged the body so that we must have many of our needs met from our fellow members.

It is remarkable that, on the cross, Jesus did not suffer one bone being broken. Yet the Bible says that all His bones were out of joint. (See Psalm 22:14.) This is how it is with the church; but by God's grace, the bones hold together even if the relationships within the body need a lot of work!

Discovering Your Place

It is important to discover your real place in the body. As I wrote earlier, I have found that the most practical pattern for discovering one's place is found in Romans 12:

I beseech you therefore, brethren, by the mercies of God, that you present your bodies a living sacrifice, holy, acceptable to God, which is your reasonable service. And do not be conformed to this world, but be transformed by the renewing of your mind, that you may prove what is that good and acceptable and perfect will of God. (verses 1–2)

Let's examine the four steps laid out in these verses.

1. Present Your Body

Again, this passage speaks of *"a living sacrifice,"* in contrast with the sacrifices of the Old Testament where the sacrificial offering was killed and placed on the altar. The call to be a living sacrifice raises a deep and far-reaching question that we must each resolve: Who owns your body? Settle the question of your body's ownership. If you own it, then the Lord does not. If the Lord owns it, then you do not. Have you ever really presented your body to the Lord and renounced your claim of ownership over it? If not, the time has come.

2. Renew Your Mind

Once you present your body, the second phase of discovering your place in Christ's body occurs: *You begin to think differently.* Natural, unregenerate man is self-centered. He always asks, "What will this do for me? What will I get out of this? Will I enjoy this? Will this promote me?" But we cannot find God's will until our entire way of thinking has been changed. Scripture says that a carnal mind is at enmity with God, and He does not reveal His will to His enemies but only to His friends. (See Romans 8:7.)

3. Discover the Will of God

As your mind is renewed, you start to discover the will of God, and you begin to enter into His will for your life. In fact, the further you go in the will of God, the better it gets! As the verse states, it is first *"good"*—something that you can intellectually accept as positive. The next stage is *"acceptable,"* in which you really settle in and embrace the will of God. Finally, it becomes *"perfect"* in the sense that you cannot imagine anything more fitting or pleasing!

It is only the renewed mind that finds the will of God. Many Christians stumble and grope through life, never really finding God's will, because they have never been renewed in their minds.

4. Put Away Independence

I believe that a primary emphasis of the Holy Spirit to God's people today is that we must give up our aggressive individualism and negative, incorrect attitudes toward our fellow believers. Again, not one of us can say to any of the others, "I don't need you." God's purposes will not be complete until the body is complete—until all the members are united, with every part doing its job, and the body is growing together in health and glorifying Him.

All of us together who are united in Christ are one body.

I am an independent person, but I am not a "lone ranger" Christian. I have always been closely associated with a local church wherever I have lived. In fact, I shudder to think what would have become of me over the years if I had not been a true part of the body. I was part of a home cell group in the 1970s when one of our group's members lost a child in an accidental drowning. When a person is in shock, he cannot even articulate his deepest needs. I saw firsthand how the body of Christ rallied around that family, meeting every need without being asked.

Of course, for this type of body ministry to be truly effective, the body must know the person, as our group did, so it can corporately swing into appropriate action.

I have surrendered two beloved wives to the Lord in death: Lydia in 1975, and Ruth in 1998. The grief through which I passed would be difficult to express, but the love of my brothers and sisters got me through those times. Anyone present at the memorial service for my wife Ruth will remember my first words, spoken through the tears that became very much a part of my life: "I am not crying because I am sad, but because I never knew there was so much love in the world!" The messages of comfort and love from around the world, received from people I had never met, were an overwhelming blessing to me. Those with whom I walked daily simply rose up, took care of me, and walked me through those painful months. I could never have done it alone, and fortunately I did not have to.

I feel sad for those who rob themselves of "body life" through rebellion or independence. They are missing out on the love that God expresses organically through Christ's body. I would never have known fully the love of God had I not passed through grief in the arms of the body of Christ. Don't make the mistake that many have of finding themselves alone and without the resources of the body when they deeply need them. Don't say, "If tragedy comes my way, I can make it alone!" Once trouble begins, it is too late to start building relationships within the body. Find your place now, and nurture close friendships with your fellow Christians. Not only do you need them, but they also need you!

Chapter 5

Picture #3:
The Workmanship

For we are His workmanship, created in Christ Jesus for
good works, which God prepared beforehand that
we should walk in them.
—Ephesians 2:10

e have taken a look at the first two pictures of what God intends His people to become: the assembly of God and the body of Christ. We have a serious role to play in the governmental assembly that exercises spiritual judgment and authority in the earth; and we flow together in unity, joined to our brothers and sisters as members of the same body. One function is *governmental*, the other is *relational*.

God's Creative Masterpiece

The third picture is *the workmanship*. The English translation of Ephesians 2:10 does not fully bring out the real significance of this picture. The Greek word translated *"workmanship"* is *poiema*. The Latin version is *poema*, from which we get the English word *poem*. The *Jerusalem Bible* uses the phrase *"work of art."* In other words, this word is taken from the field of art and creativity. I like to translate it as, "We are God's creative masterpiece," which more properly conveys Paul's meaning.

When you ponder all that God has created, it is breathtaking and humbling that God would choose people like us to be the materials for His creative masterpiece.

> *The more you allow God to cut away, the better your vision is revealed.*

Think for a moment of what is involved in a creative work of art. For example, consider the art of sculpture. There are so many examples of beautiful sculpture in Greek antiquity. When the right tools are used with great skill and patience, the practical outworking follows the inner vision. The sculptor creatively envisions within a block of marble something to be revealed. He arms himself with a chisel, and his inner mental vision of what he wants to produce, and begins to chip away at the stone. Gradually, the form emerges, which is the expression of the artist's inner vision.

When I was working with Elizabeth Sherrill on my wife Lydia's book, *Appointment in Jerusalem*, I produced the manuscript after two years of labor. Elizabeth said, "Now go through it and take out about 20 percent." If you have ever worked for two years on a book, you know what that means!

She quoted to me what Michelangelo said about his statues: "Every stroke of the chisel reveals a little bit more of the plan." The more you cut away, the better your vision is revealed. Likewise, as God goes on cutting and cutting and cutting, you might wonder, "Lord, is there going to be anything left of me?" But every stroke of His chisel reveals more perfectly the plan of the Master Artist.

We could also consider the art of painting. The essence of painting includes the blending of form and color in the right proportions to produce a scene or an object. The painter's blending of the shapes, colors, and forms can help us see aspects we may have missed when we looked at the actual scene or object. So it is with us. God works on us, blending and shaping and positioning us, and then He unveils us to the world, which is then able to see something in us it did not perceive before.

Consider another example of creative work, that of poetry. I have always been particularly interested in poetry. I have even written a few poems myself. In essence, poetry is artistry with words. It is the blending together of words to evoke a picture, make an impression, or create an impact. Each word must be the precise word set in just the right place and perfectly related to the words around it. In the same way, God wants to make us collectively into a poem, with each one of us being carefully selected and placed in the right position in relation to all the others around us.

We are God's poem, His creative masterpiece, *"to the intent that now the manifold wisdom of God might be made known by the church* [God's people] *to the principalities and powers in the heavenly places"* (Ephesians 3:10).

Paul's statement is astonishing. It is breathtaking to know that God chose us, His redeemed people, to demonstrate His manifold wisdom to the entire universe—in time and eternity—and to the unseen heavenly realms! The word *manifold* is a vivid word that I translate as "many-sided." Each one of us demonstrates a unique refraction of the overall, multifaceted wisdom of God, and we all blend into a harmonious whole!

Where did God go for the material to make this greatest creative masterpiece, His church? He went to the scrap heap! To the broken pieces of lives that had been marred by sin. To the pile of broken families, sick bodies, and corrupted minds.

In Ephesians 2:10, in a very beautiful, yet practical, way, Paul told us that we were created to do the good works that God prepared in advance for us to do. This verse tells us that we are not merely to be ornamental; we are also to be *useful*. We are to fulfill a function. We are not just to stand around and be interesting and spiritual. God has a good *work* for each believer to accomplish! Our assignment is to find those good works and to walk in them.

There is no room for improvisation. None of us is free to write the score for his own life—God has already written it. We find our place in that creative masterpiece when we yield to God. Then we discover something ready for us to do that we might never have dreamed. If someone had told me years ago that I would someday become a teacher of the Bible, I would have laughed. My friends would have laughed louder still because there was nothing in me at that time that gave the faintest indication of what God planned to make out of me.

The Essential Feature of Workmanship and God's Requirement

The essential feature of the picture of the masterpiece—the *poiema*—is the demonstration of *God's creative genius*. God has been a creator right from the beginning, and He's still creating today. He created the heavenly bodies, the stars, the seas, the mountains, the animals, and the flowers. And when He finished all that, He said, "My greatest masterpiece is still to come." *We* are that masterpiece—the ultimate revelation of God's creative genius!

Yieldedness

What is required of us as members of His *poiema* is summed up in one word: *yieldedness*. If we are a word in a poem, we just take our place. If we are a piece of clay in the Potter's hand, we just let Him mold us. If we are part of a block of marble, we just let Him chip away at us. We don't argue with Him or tell Him how to do His work. We don't ask, "God, do You really know what You're doing with me?" The key is yieldedness. As we willingly surrender ourselves fully into His hands, He will shape us into His marvelous work.

> But now, O Lord, You are our Father; we are the clay, and
> You our potter; and all we are the work of Your hand.
>
> (Isaiah 64:8)

Once we put ourselves in God's hands, it is up to Him to make of us what He wants.

Merge-Ability

What does it require of us toward each other to fulfill this picture of God's creative masterpiece? I had to invent a word to describe our responsibility: *merge-ability*, the ability to merge with others. Other appropriate words might be *blending* or *cohesiveness*. What we are individually is not the most important thing; it is what we become *together* that is the final goal. For that, we must demonstrate a willingness to lose our individual identities to attain a greater whole.

49

When God wants to shape us, change us, and mold us, He uses pressure. When we are experiencing pressure, we want to say, "God, I can't stand it any longer!" But He says, "I'm doing it to make you not the way you want to be, but the way I want you to be." All of us who love the Lord will experience the pressure of His hands in the days that lie ahead. The wheel is going to spin faster and faster. The pressure may grow more intense. But as long as we stay in His presence and remain pliable, we will emerge as the vessel He wants us to be.

> *But indeed, O man, who are you to reply against God? Will the thing formed say to him who formed it, "Why have you made me like this?"* (Romans 9:20)

Romans 9 is one of the more difficult theological chapters of the Bible because it deals with God's sovereign predestination. Paul talked about the potter making a vessel for *"dishonor"*—something that is unclean—and a vessel for *"honor"* (verse 21). Predestination says, in essence, that God determines what He will make out of every piece of material. He determines whether He will make a garbage can or a flower vase. We do not have the choice; it is God's decision. This is, of course, not the entire picture, which must be balanced by other truths. We do have free will. But, while we don't know exactly how our freedom to choose and predestination work hand-in-hand, God knows what choices we will make.

In Bill Gothard's seminar on Basic Youth Conflicts, he gives an example of a girl with a deep inner problem. She could not find real peace, release, or satisfaction because she was angry with God for making her too tall. It is not unlike people to think in that way about things over which they have no control. We don't have the final say in such matters, as we are reminded by the apostle Paul:

> *Does not the potter have power over the clay, from the same lump to make one vessel for honor and another for dishonor? What if God, wanting to show His wrath and to make His power known, endured with much longsuffering the vessels of wrath prepared for destruction, and that He might make known the riches of His glory on the vessels of mercy, which He had prepared beforehand for glory, even us whom He called, not of the Jews only, but also of the Gentiles?*
> (Romans 9:21–24)

God uses some vessels to show His wrath upon. The example Paul used in Romans 9 was Pharaoh. God said to Pharaoh, *"For this very purpose I have raised you up, that I may show My power in you"* (verse 17).

If you discover that you are a vessel of glory, you can say, "Praise the Lord; it's not my doing. It's His choice." For, *"it is not of him who wills, nor of him who runs, but of God who shows mercy"* (verse 16). As difficult as it may be for some to accept, we need to get back to that neglected part of God's truth.

The essence of this particular picture is that, in some ways, we are passive. The clay cannot give the orders or make the decisions. If this was the only picture of God's people, it would be incomplete. But our understanding of what it is to be God's people is also incomplete without this picture. Modern Western culture probably needs a much clearer vision of what it means to be willing clay in the hands of a loving Potter.

I have met many people who have never accepted themselves as God's workmanship or masterpiece. God cannot fully use you until you accept yourself as God has made you. Simply have faith that the best is yet to come! The most exciting developments within my ministry began when I was in my late fifties, after several decades of often obscure, exacting labor. I have always stayed true to the call God gave me long ago, through a message in tongues and its interpretation, to be "a teacher of the Scriptures in truth and faith and love, which are in Christ Jesus, for many." The "many" did not appear until much later in my life, but the ministry came to pass.

We are His workmanship, created for a significant task. We are important to His plan, and we must be confident concerning whom He is making us into!

Chapter 6

Picture #4: The Family

For through Him we both have access by one Spirit to the Father. Now, therefore, you are no longer strangers and foreigners, but fellow citizens with the saints and members of the household of God [or members of God's family].
—Ephesians 2:18–19

s we continue looking by faith into the mirror of God's Word to find out what kind of people we are in His sight, God truly wants us to understand how central we are to the outworking of His purposes in the earth.

We now turn to the fourth picture taken from Paul's epistle to the Ephesians: the family. In this list of seven pictures of God's people, the fourth is in the center. I believe this is appropriate because the family is central to our understanding of God's people. In the New Testament, His people are very seldom referred to by the title Christians or even believers. The most common title used is brothers, emphasizing membership in one spiritual family.

For through Him we both [Jews and Gentiles] *have access by one Spirit to the Father.*　　　　　(Ephesians 2:18)

Notice again that all three persons of the Godhead are represented here: Through Jesus the Son, we have access to the Father, by one Spirit. The next verse reveals the wondrous result:

> *Now, therefore* [because we have access to the Father], *you are no longer strangers and foreigners, but fellow citizens with the saints and members of the household of God.*
> (Ephesians 2:19)

The word *"household"* would be best represented in contemporary English by *family*. Because Christ has gained us access to the Father, we have become members of God's family.

Relationship to the Father

God's family is determined by relationship to the Father. In New Testament Greek, there is a very close similarity between the words *father* and *family*. The word for father is *pater*; the word for family is *patria*, which is derived from *pater*. This relationship is brought out clearly in Paul's prayer:

> *For this reason I bow my knees to the Father of our Lord Jesus Christ, from whom the whole family in heaven and earth is named.* (Ephesians 3:14–15)

There is a direct play here on the words *"Father"* and *"family."* From God the Father (*pater*) the whole family (*patria*) in heaven and earth is named. Family comes from fatherhood. So, again, having God as our Father makes us members of His family.

This truth is further brought out by the writer of Hebrews:

Picture #4: The Family

For it was fitting for Him [God the Father], *for whom are all things, and through whom are all things, in bringing many sons* [believers] *to glory, to perfect the author* [the Lord Jesus] *of their salvation through sufferings. For both He who sanctifies* [Jesus] *and those who are sanctified* [the believers] *are all from one Father; for which reason He* [Jesus] *is not ashamed to call them brethren, saying* [quoting from the Old Testament], *"I will proclaim Thy name to My brethren, in the midst of the congregation I will sing Thy praise."* (Hebrews 2:10–12 NASB)

There is a beautiful revelation in this passage. God has made us His sons through Jesus, and Jesus Himself is the only begotten Son of God the Father; therefore, Jesus acknowledges us as His brothers because of our relationship to the Father. Jesus never did anything without the Father leading the way. Jesus did not call us "brothers" until the Father called us "sons." Once His Father called us sons, then He acknowledged us as His brothers.

> *The central concept of the family is obedience.*

There are two main features of this particular revelation that emphasize the idea of fatherhood: The primary, decisive feature is a shared life-source. When we all share the same life-source, we are members of the same family. The Father is the source of every family, heavenly or earthly. A family is not a denomination or a label, nor is it an organization or an institution. A family is a family because it has a shared life-source.

Second, God's fatherhood has relational implications in two directions: vertical and horizontal. The vertical is the relationship that each of us has to God as Father. The horizontal is the relationships we all have to one another as members of the same family. The vertical relationship to God is primary, but it also gives us a horizontal responsibility to one another. We cannot claim to be God's sons if we do not acknowledge His other sons as our brothers!

These two relationships, the vertical and the horizontal, within the family of God are beautifully exemplified by the opening words of the Lord's Prayer:

> *In this manner, therefore, pray: Our Father in heaven, hallowed be Your name.* (Matthew 6:9)

Two very important words occur right at the beginning of this prayer: *"Our Father."* In the original Greek it is actually "Father our." So the first word is *Father*, which is the decisive word. Jesus is saying, "Keep in mind that, through Me, you become children of God. Always approach God as your Father. Don't come to Him only as God, because He is God over everyone. Come to Him as your loving heavenly Father, with whom you are now in right relationship."

The second word is *our*—not "my" Father, but "our" Father. What does this mean? In coming to God as "our" Father, we acknowledge that He has many other children. You are not an only child. All of God's other children are your brothers and sisters. This acknowledgment rules out self-centeredness on our part.

There is so much in those two simple, introductory words to the Lord's Prayer.

In John 14, when Jesus was talking to the disciples about the Father, one of them said, *"Lord, show us the Father"* (verse 8). This grieved Jesus, and He said,

Picture #4: The Family

Have I been with you so long, and yet you have not known Me, Philip? He who has seen Me has seen the Father; so how can you say, "Show us the Father"? (John 14:9)

Just before that, in John 14:6, Jesus said, *"I am the way, the truth, and the life. No one comes to the Father except through Me."* People often quote that Scripture, but they very rarely complete it. Jesus said, *"I am the way"*; but a way is not an end in itself. A way is meaningless unless it leads us somewhere. Where does Jesus, the Way, lead us? To the Father! We have not fulfilled the purpose of God if we merely find the way. What we have to find is *the end* of the way! The primary mission of Jesus Christ is not to bring us to Himself, but to bring us to the Father.

For Christ also suffered once for sins, the just for the unjust, that He might bring us to God. (1 Peter 3:18)

God's purpose is to gather in a great family of sons patterned after the pattern Son, Jesus. Everything is working together for good along the line of that purpose, to make us sons conformed to the image of Jesus Christ.

And we know that all things work together for good to those who love God, to those who are the called according to His purpose. For whom He foreknew, He also predestined to be conformed to the image of His Son, that [the Son] might be the firstborn among many brethren.
(Romans 8:28–29)

The Central Concept of the Family Is Obedience

The central concept that these passages evoke concerning our relationship to God as our Father is *obedience.*

For it was fitting for Him, for whom are all things and by whom are all things, in bringing many sons to glory, to make the captain of their salvation perfect through sufferings.
(Hebrews 2:10)

The *"Him"* spoken of in this passage is God the Father; the *"captain"* of our salvation is Jesus; and the *"many sons"* are we, the believers.

The writer of Hebrews told us that the captain of our salvation was made perfect through sufferings. Jesus was morally perfect, but in personal development He wasn't perfect until God brought Him to maturity. He grew up as the pattern Son under the discipline and discipleship of the Father, who brought Him to full personal development. He then became the pattern for all sons on their way to maturity. Again, the process through which He was perfected was suffering.

For both He who sanctifies and those who are being sanctified are all of one, for which reason He is not ashamed to call them brethren. (verse 11)

Jesus is *"He who sanctifies,"* and we are *"those who are being sanctified."* The *"one"* from whom Jesus and we proceed is the Father, from whom we receive our sanctification. Because we each go through the process of sanctification and maturity, we are given the right to our place in the family of God.

Quoting from Psalm 22, the passage continues,

He is not ashamed to call them brethren, saying: "I will declare Your name to My brethren; in the midst of the assembly I will sing praise to You." (Hebrews 2:11–12)

It is exciting to note that Jesus is going to sing in the midst of the church!

Picture #4: The Family

There is to be an unfolding revelation of God the Father to His children in the church through His Son Jesus. The revelation of God's fatherhood is what will bring the children to maturity even as they are perfected through suffering.

Though He was a Son, yet He learned obedience by the things which He suffered. (Hebrews 5:8)

The relationship between the Father and the Son is a study of the relationship of a father bringing a son into maturity. Thus, Jesus became the pattern and the pathway for us. Jesus was never disobedient. Yet He had to *learn* obedience. You and I have to learn it in the same way He did: by obeying! There is just no other way. We don't find out what obedience is by sitting and listening to sermons on obedience. These sermons may help us or motivate us, but obedience is learned by *doing*.

The key phrase in the obedience of Jesus was, *"Not My will, but Yours, be done"* (Luke 22:42). Every step of obedience in the Christian life is a step of self-denial. Jesus said if anyone desires to come after Him, he must deny himself. (See Matthew 16:24.) This is always painful because our ego never likes to be denied. The ego wants things, and following the Lord is a continual denial of ego.

Our Responsibility to Our Fellow Believers Is Love

While our vertical relationship to God can be characterized in this context as obedience, our horizontal responsibility to our brothers and sisters is a special kind of love. There are various Greek words that all tend to be translated as "love." Four of them are *eros* (sexual passion), *storgé* (natural family affection), *philadelphia* (brotherly love), and *agape* (divine love).

Love is not a spiritual gift, but the outworking of *character*. In 2 Peter we see seven progressive steps that bring us to this special kind of *agape* love:

> *But also for this very reason, giving all diligence, add to your faith virtue, to virtue knowledge, to knowledge self-control, to self-control perseverance, to perseverance godliness, to godliness brotherly kindness, and to brotherly kindness love* [*agape*].   (2 Peter 1:5–7)

The Scripture says, *"Add to your faith..."* So, we start with the basis of faith, and then we add the seven things to that in succession:

1. Virtue (excellence)
2. Knowledge (knowing God's will)
3. Self-control (temperance)
4. Perseverance (patience, endurance)
5. Godliness (holiness)

We have come a long way down the list, but we have not yet come to love. The attitude that love means merely giving somebody an embrace at a prayer meeting is not in line with Scripture. Love is something that has to be cultivated and achieved, and it is really high up the ladder. Then,

6. Brotherly kindness (goodwill toward men)
7. Love (*agape*)

The word *agape* means, in particular, "I love my enemies." When you can love your enemies, you have made it to the top.

Many religions have martyrs who will die for their faith—Judaism, Communism, and Islam, to name but a few.

60

Picture #4: The Family

But there is one difference about the genuine Christian martyr in that he loves his enemies. If he does not, he is no better than the Communist or Muslim martyr.

Most of us are not qualified to be martyrs; God could not give us that privilege. I am convinced that if you are going to be a real martyr, you have to train for it by laying down your life daily. A martyr does not become one by a sudden, dramatic accident, but as the result of a process.

I have learned that every time I minister fruitfully, it is due to self-denial. As long as I am pleasing myself, I am not ministering the life of Christ. The two are opposites. Christ's life flows only where self has been denied. Jesus said we are to take up our cross daily. Your cross is the place where your will and God's will *cross*—and you have to come to that place of surrender on a daily basis. A person can be very religious, yet never die to his own will.

> *The Father is the source of every family, heavenly or earthly.*

Many Christians have not even achieved "brotherly kindness." It is not always easy to love every one of our fellow Christians. Sometimes, it is easier to love nonbelievers than Christians because it doesn't matter to them whether you are baptized by immersion or sprinkling or if you raise your hands in prayer or not.

I recall an incident in my life when I was involved in some meetings with about thirty other leaders. We were to be paired together with a different leader each night at a different meeting. There was one brother with whom I totally disagreed about baptism. I said to myself, *I just hope I don't get*

61

put together with him! And, you guessed it—I was put together with him for three nights. He and I are now close friends.

In conclusion, let me relate a little incident from the days when some of the Scottish Christians up in the Highlands were being severely persecuted by the English Army. As a Scottish lassie was on her way to a secret meeting of believers, she was arrested by an English policeman who asked her where she was going. She did not want to lie, but she did not want to betray her fellow believers, either, so she lifted her heart to the Lord in prayer and asked Him for an answer. This is what she said to the policeman, "My Older Brother died, and I'm on my way to my Father's house to hear the will read." What a good answer! Jesus is the Elder Brother, God is our Father, and it is our Father's house. We are a family!

Again, the essential feature of this picture of family is our shared life-source. God our Father in heaven is the life-source of His entire family. We all share a common life. This is what binds us together—not denominations or doctrines or labels.

We need to accept one another as brothers and sisters because God has accepted us as His family. It is one thing to know that we are accepted by God, but quite another to know experientially the acceptance of our brethren. Some of us have never known the warm, loving embrace of an earthly father or brother. May these ones be destined to find it for the very first time in the family of God!

Chapter 7

Picture #5:
The Temple

Jesus Christ Himself [is] *the chief corner stone, in whom
the whole building, being joined together, grows into
a holy temple in the Lord.*
—Ephesians 2:20–21

e now come to the fifth picture, that of the building or *the temple.* Let's begin by reviewing Paul's statement in Ephesians in connection with the family.

*Now, therefore, you are no longer strangers and foreigners,
but fellow citizens with the saints and members of the household of God* [or members of God's family]....
(Ephesians 2:19)

Paul then moved from the picture of the family to the picture of the temple:

*...having been built on the foundation of the apostles and
prophets, Jesus Christ Himself being the chief corner stone,
in whom the whole building, being joined together, grows
into a holy temple in the Lord, in whom you also are being
built together for a dwelling place of God in the Spirit.*
(verses 20–22)

The Christians—the true believers—are the people in whom God dwells and moves. Because of this relationship, He is their God and they are His people.

> *...in whom the whole building, being fitted together, grows into a holy temple in the Lord, in whom [Jesus] you also are being built together for a dwelling place of God in the Spirit.* (verses 21–22)

Notice that all three persons of the Godhead are involved once again. The Father indwells those who are in the Son by the Spirit. The end purpose of the church here is to be a habitation, a dwelling place of God.

The end purpose of the church is to be a habitation, a dwelling place of God.

In Hebrew, the word for a house (*beit*), which includes the concept of a home or family, is directly connected with the word "to build." So there is a close connection, in Hebrew thought, between a family and a building. In fact, the word *house* was used in Hebrew not to describe a physical dwelling, but rather a family of people. Those two thoughts always go together. Notice the emphasis on building in this passage: "*built,*" "*building,*" "*temple,*" "*built,*" "*dwelling place.*" Five times, the thought is brought out in those verses.

The principle is this: God has always required His people to provide Him with a dwelling place. When God delivered the Israelites out of Egypt, brought them to Mt. Sinai, and gave them His first covenant, one of the first things He required of them was that they build Him a tabernacle. This tent was the dwelling place of His manifested presence—His Shekinah glory—and it traveled with Israel all the way through the wilderness.

After God brought the Israelites into the Promised Land, He gave them instructions to build a temple for Him in a certain city of His choice—Jerusalem. Solomon constructed the most glorious, costly, and elaborate edifice that has ever been built by humanity. Through Israel's idolatry and disobedience, however, this temple was eventually destroyed by the Babylonians under Nebuchadnezzar. But again, after God in His mercy granted Israel a restoration from Babylon, one of their first assignments was to build Him another temple.

It is very interesting to note that God did not leave the decision about the dwelling place to His people; He determined it Himself—the location, the types of materials, and the shape of the structure. However, the Bible also makes it clear that these buildings (the tabernacle and the two temples) were only patterns of something infinitely more valuable and important. This idea is brought out very clearly by the words of Stephen to the Jewish council:

> *However, the Most High* [the true God] *does not dwell in temples made with hands, as the prophet says: "Heaven is My throne, and earth is My footstool. What house will you build for Me? says the LORD, or what is the place of My rest? Has My hand not made all these things?"* (Acts 7:48–50)

The Material of the Temple

Any material building constructed by men, no matter how wonderful it may be, is not the final dwelling place of God. It is just a temporary place that He honors with His presence as long as His people meet His conditions. The final, eternal temple of God, the one that all others are just a preview and a pattern of, is made up of *people*. People are the most valuable creatures in the universe. The temple of God obviously has to be made of the most valuable material— not gold or silver or marble, but people. This truth is clearly brought out in various passages of the New Testament:

> *According to the grace of God which was given to me, as a wise master builder* [apostle] *I have laid the foundation, and another builds on it. But let each one take heed how he builds on it. For no other foundation can anyone lay than that which is laid, which is Jesus Christ. Now if anyone builds on this foundation with gold, silver, precious stones, wood, hay, straw....* (1 Corinthians 3:10–12)

There are two kinds of buildings you can erect: those that will stand the test and those that will not. You can build in great quantity with wood, hay, and stubble; there is no difficulty in obtaining those materials in large quantities, but they will not stand the test. Or you can build in much smaller quantities with much more precious materials, and they will stand the test.

> *...each one's work will become clear; for the Day will declare it, because it will be revealed by fire; and the fire will test each one's work, of what sort it is. If anyone's work which he has built on it endures, he will receive a reward. If anyone's work is burned, he will suffer loss; but he himself will be saved, yet so as through fire.* (verses 13–15)

This Scripture is talking about our contribution in the service of God's house; it is going to have to stand the test of fire.

Picture #5: The Temple

For we must all appear before the judgment seat of Christ, that each one may receive the things done in the body, according to what he has done, whether good or bad.

(2 Corinthians 5:10)

Every Christian is going to appear before the judgment seat of Christ to be judged for all the service that he or she has offered God in His house. This is not a judgment of salvation or condemnation, for there is no condemnation for those who are in Christ Jesus. (See Romans 8:1.) It will not be concerning the destiny of our souls, but it will be concerning the work that we have done in the house of God. Every man's work will be tried by fire. If it stands the test, he will receive a reward; if it is burned up, he will lose his reward, but his soul will still be saved.

The prize-giving has not yet come; it lies ahead. It behooves each one of us to ask what type of material we are putting into the building. Will it stand the test of fire? Paul said to the leaders in Corinth,

Do you not know that you are the temple of God and that the Spirit of God dwells in you? If anyone defiles the temple of God, God will destroy him. For the temple of God is holy, which temple you are.

(1 Corinthians 3:16–17)

It seems that the Corinthian believers were somewhat ignorant of what they really were intended to be. This, again, is one of the important reasons for looking in the mirror of God's Word: to see what we really are! Paul rebuked them, "Don't you know that you're God's temple? You'd better be careful how you live."

67

Keeping the Temple Pure

In connection with the temple, there is always a warning against defiling it—both the collective temple and the individual temple.

We have looked at the collective temple, which is all believers united together. Now let's look at the individual temple:

Or do you not know that your body is the temple of the Holy Spirit who is in you, whom you have from God, and you are not your own? For you were bought at a price; therefore glorify God in your body and in your spirit, which are God's.
(1 Corinthians 6:19–20)

Every believer has the privilege of providing his physical body to the Holy Spirit as a temple to dwell in. God, through Jesus Christ, redeemed your body so that it might be a temple for His Spirit. Notice again that we are warned to be careful that we do not defile or destroy the temple. Whether it is the collective temple or the individual temple, we are required to take care of it and to preserve it in purity, in health, and in holiness because it is the temple of the Holy Spirit. We are obligated to provide Him with a temple that honors Him and serves His purpose. I personally believe that the care of our physical bodies is much more important in the sight of God than most of us recognize it to be.

Do not be unequally yoked together with unbelievers. For what fellowship has righteousness with lawlessness? And what communion has light with darkness? And what accord has Christ with Belial [Satan]? Or what part has a believer with an unbeliever? And what agreement has the temple of God with idols? For you are the temple of the living God. As God has said: "I will dwell in them and walk among them ["walk in them" KJV]. I will be their God, and they shall be My people."   (2 Corinthians 6:14–16)

Notice again that it is the collective temple we are talking about here. This is the conviction upon which God becomes our God, that He is allowed to dwell in us and walk in us. I like the phrase *"walk in them"* from the King James Version. It indicates that God has a mobile temple that is not confined to one place. Wherever we are, God is; He goes where we go. As His body, we provide Him with an instrument; but as a temple, we provide Him with a dwelling place. In this sense, it is not really accurate to talk about going to church, as though there is a certain place where we meet God. Instead, where we come together, there is where the church is. And where the church is, God is. If we go to the seashore, the church goes to the seashore. If the church goes to the seashore, God goes to the seashore. He dwells in us and walks in us, and on that condition He is our God and we are His people.

Living Stones

Coming to [Jesus] as to a living stone, rejected indeed by men, but chosen by God and precious, you also, as living stones, are being built up a spiritual house, a holy priesthood.   (1 Peter 2:4–5)

In this spiritual house that God is building for His eternal dwelling place, you and I and all our fellow believers together are *"living stones"*! We are being built together to constitute the final, eternal house that God has destined from eternity, of which all His previous dwelling places in the Old Testament were but previews and patterns.

I have spent a number of years of my life in Jerusalem, where the only material permitted for building is stone. This has greatly helped to preserve the unique character and beauty of Jerusalem. All permitted buildings in Jerusalem are built out of stone from a quarry somewhere to the north.

We are "living stones" in God's eternal, spiritual house.

In the 1940s, I lived in a town north of Jerusalem, and I used to pass the place where they quarried the stones and then carried them into Jerusalem. I remember seeing a stone that had fallen off the truck on its way into the city and was just left by the roadside. Nobody picked it up; it was just left there. I thought to myself, *That stone lies there in its individual, egotistic self-will. No chisel will ever be applied to that stone. It'll stay just the way it is—but it will never get into the building.* Believers like that have been quarried out, but they have never been built in. They are not finding their places in God's purposes.

Note what 1 Kings has to say about the temple of Solomon:

> *And the temple, when it was being built, was built with stone finished at the quarry, so that no hammer or chisel or any iron tool was heard in the temple while it was being built.* (1 Kings 6:7)

That is remarkable! The dimensions for every stone were predetermined, and every stone was shaped and cut into its predetermined dimensions at the quarry. There was no last-minute hammering or chiseling in the actual structure of the temple.

God is doing the same for you and me. He quarries us out of this world by the gospel, and then He proceeds to shape us, so that when the final edifice rises, there will be no more hammering and chiseling. We have to be ready to be shaped now, a process that we all must undergo if we are going to take our part in that temple.

The Essential Feature of the Temple and God's Requirement

Let's look now at the twofold application of the temple. The essential feature of this picture of the church is that the temple is *God's dwelling place*. It is where God is going to reside forever. We always tend to think about getting to heaven, but the ultimate purpose of God is to get heaven to earth! The last picture in the Bible of God's people, found in Revelation 21:1–4, is of a beautiful dwelling place coming down out of heaven to earth. Study that passage about the New Jerusalem sometime; it is a glorious picture of God's dwelling coming to earth.

What is required of us? We are to be willing to be quarried out, shaped, and chiseled; we are to have our edges knocked off, to fit in with a predetermined dimension, and to be made ready before the final structure arises. This is a huge commitment on our part, but one that brings an eternal reward!

After reminding the believers that they are the *"temple of the living God"* (2 Corinthians 6:16), Paul made reference to several Old Testament passages, saying,

*Therefore "Come out from among them and be separate, says the Lord. Do not touch what is unclean, and I will receive you. I will be a **Father** to you, and you shall be My **sons and daughters**, says the LORD Almighty."*
(2 Corinthians 6:17–18, emphasis added)

Notice how close the picture of the family and the picture of the temple are, which we have previously seen in Ephesians 2:19–22. The temple and the family are united. God is the Father of His family, and He is the God who dwells in His temple.

Once again, the lesson is pressed home regarding God's requirement of holiness, for the next chapter begins with these words:

Therefore, having these promises, beloved, let us cleanse ourselves from all filthiness of the flesh and spirit, perfecting holiness in the fear of God. (2 Corinthians 7:1)

This is something that we have to do: cleanse ourselves from all filthiness of flesh and spirit. I believe *"filthiness of the flesh"* is immorality, drunkenness, and so on, and *"filthiness of the...spirit"* is essentially occult involvement. We are to perfect holiness in the fear of God. The message is one that emphasizes the need for purity and for care in our attitude toward the temple.

My personal attitude in this regard is that I desire never to be a cause of harm to a family or a church. I think they are the two most sacred things on earth. It is my sincere desire and prayer that I will never offend one or the other. If you touch the work of God, remember, you are going to have to answer to Him.

Chapter 8

Picture #6:
The Bride

*Christ also loved the church and gave Himself for her, that
He might sanctify and cleanse her with the washing of water
by the word, that He might present her to Himself a glorious
church, not having spot or wrinkle or any such thing, but
that she should be holy and without blemish.*
—Ephesians 5:25–27

We turn now to the sixth picture, the bride. Although
the word *bride* is not actually used in Ephesians,
the concept is specifically stated in other passages
of the Bible, and it is implied in this passage:

*Husbands, love your wives, just as Christ also loved the
church and gave Himself for her, that He might sanctify
and cleanse her with the washing of water by the word, that
He might present her to Himself a glorious church, not having spot or wrinkle or any such thing, but that she should be
holy and without blemish. So husbands ought to love their
own wives as their own bodies; he who loves his wife loves
himself. For no one ever hated his own flesh, but nourishes
and cherishes it, just as the Lord does the church. For we are
members of His body, of His flesh and of His bones. "For*

this reason a man shall leave his father and mother and be joined to his wife, and the two shall become one flesh." This is a great mystery, but I speak concerning Christ and the church. (Ephesians 5:25–32)

Paul began by speaking to believing husbands about their relationship to their wives. He said the relationship must be one of love, devotion, and care—all very sound and practical advice, and much needed today. Yet this is not the full meaning of the passage, because Paul then went on to say that the husband/wife relationship is patterned on the relationship of Christ to His church, and he added, *"This is a great* [or profound] *mystery."* It is, indeed. I am sure no human mind can ever fully fathom that mystery. But he said very clearly, *"I speak concerning Christ and the church."* Thus, we see with absolute clarity the two persons in this union: Christ is the Bridegroom and the church is His bride.

> *Human history began with a marriage and will end with a marriage.*

This relationship was very beautifully foreshadowed in the original creation of Adam and Eve as recorded in the opening chapters of Genesis. One of the remarkable features of the creation of Adam was that God had everything ready for him before he appeared on the scene. His entire environment was there: the vegetation, the animals, the weather, and the heavenly bodies—everything he would need.

This is a wonderful picture of God's provision for us in the new creation. Everything we need is already there when we arrive on the scene. There was just one thing missing for Adam: a mate. This was not a mistake on God's part.

God had a purpose in not immediately providing a mate for Adam, for He wanted Adam to understand something of the longing that He has for personal fellowship with human beings. So He allowed Adam to experience the lack of that fellowship, the lack of a mate. He then provided a mate, as recorded in Genesis:

> The LORD God said, "It is not good for the man to be alone. I will make a helper suitable for him."...So the LORD God caused the man to fall into a deep sleep; and while he was sleeping, he took one of the man's ribs and closed up the place with flesh. Then the LORD God made a woman from the rib he had taken out of the man, and he brought her to the man. The man said, "This is now bone of my bones and flesh of my flesh; she shall be called 'woman,' for she was taken out of man." (Genesis 2:18, 21–23 NIV)

The Bible puts tremendous emphasis on marriage. We need to fully appreciate how central a place marriage plays in Scripture. Human history began with a marriage—and the first matchmaker was God. God is still in the matchmaking business! One day, just as God presented Eve to Adam, He is going to present the church to Jesus at the marriage supper of the Lamb. (See Revelation 21:2–3, 9–11.) Let's look more closely at the circumstances of this spiritual marriage.

Making Ourselves Ready

Human history will come to a glorious climax with the marriage of the church, the bride, to Jesus Christ, the Bridegroom:

> And I heard, as it were, the voice of a great multitude and as the sound of many waters and as the sound of mighty

peals of thunder, saying, "Hallelujah! For the Lord our God, the Almighty, reigns. Let us rejoice and be glad and give the glory to Him [here is one primary cause for rejoicing], *for the marriage of the Lamb* [Jesus] *has come and His bride has made herself ready." And it was given to her to clothe herself in fine linen, bright and clean; for the fine linen is the righteous acts of the saints.*

(Revelation 19:6–8 NASB)

The marriage of the church to Jesus Christ will be a cause for rejoicing throughout the universe.

It is interesting to note that the bride was expected to provide or prepare her own clothing. In the Bible, "fine linen" is always a type of purity. In one place in Ezekiel, priests who were girded with wool were not permitted access to the presence of the Lord. (See Ezekiel 44:15–18.) There had to be absolute purity in the priesthood. In Deuteronomy 22:11, the Israelites were instructed not to wear garments of mixed material, such as wool and linen. So, here, *"fine linen"* speaks of absolute purity. And it says the fine linen is the *"righteous acts of the saints"* or *"the righteousness of saints"* (KJV).

There are two Greek words for righteousness: one is *dikaiosune* and the other is *dikaioma*. *Dikaiosune* is righteousness in the abstract; *dikaioma* is righteousness in action. When you and I believe in Jesus Christ, His righteousness, *dikaiosune*, is imputed to us—we are made righteous with His righteousness. When we live out our faith, we express that imputed righteousness in *dikaioma*, which is outworked righteousness or our acts of righteousness.

Interestingly, the word used here is *dikaioma*, or the plural, *dikaiomata*. The fine linen is the righteous acts of the saints. That is a very searching statement. *"His bride has made herself ready."* How? By her righteous acts.

In every culture that I have ever known, there is one rule about marriage. The bridegroom never prepares the bride; the bride always prepares herself. The responsibility is placed on her. The Scripture says that His bride has made herself ready by her outworked, righteous acts. The imputed righteousness of Christ will not avail for the bridal feast. It has to be the outworked righteousness.

Years ago, in Jerusalem, my wife and I had a missionary friend whom we knew well and who had become sick. She lay sick for a long while, and she thought she was going to die. One night, the Lord gave her a vivid dream. In this dream, she was working on a beautiful white dress. As she looked at the dress, she saw that much of it was not yet finished; there was a lot more work to do on it. When she woke up in the morning, she realized the Lord had shown her that she was not ready to go home because her work was not yet finished. I always think about this incident when I hear the verse, *"The marriage of the Lamb has come, and His wife has made herself ready."* Every one of us has wedding attire to complete, and we complete it by our acts of obedience. This is very important.

There is a parallel passage about outworked righteousness in Philippians:

> *Therefore, my beloved, as you have always obeyed, not as in my presence only, but now much more in my absence, work out your own salvation with fear and trembling; for it is God who works in you both to will and to do for His good pleasure.* (Philippians 2:12–13)

There is a balance there. God works in you, first *"to will,"* and then *"to do,"* God's pleasure. The Christian life is not about struggling to do something against our wills that we do not want to do. Rather, God works in us the will to do what He wants. Then He works in us the ability to do it.

God works *in* us only insofar as we work *out* what He works *in*. The measure of what God can work *in* is determined by the measure of what we work *out*. So there is a two-way process. God is working into us; but, by the way we live (our righteous acts), we are working out what God has worked in. This is the preparation of the bride. The fine linen is the righteous acts of the saints, so make sure you have the proper attire.

The Relationship between Bridegroom and Bride

I see three main elements in this picture of Christ as the Bridegroom and the church as the bride.

Mutual, Unreserved Commitment

First of all, there is *mutual, unreserved commitment* on both sides. Jesus gave Himself up for the church, holding nothing back. He poured out His entire lifeblood. That is what marriage is, too. Even on the human level, God intends it to be a total self-giving of two people, the one to the other. Neither is entitled to hold anything back. It is required of the church that she give herself to Jesus, the Bridegroom, just as fully and totally as He gave Himself up to redeem her on the cross.

Careful Preparation

The second step is *careful preparation*. We saw that the bride, the church, had made herself ready. She had prepared her attire, consisting of righteous acts. One single provision was not sufficient for everything, but her attire was continually being prepared. I like to think of life in the same way. As you and I walk in faith and obedience, fulfilling the will of God and keeping His commandments, we are preparing our attire—that fine linen that is bright and clean.

Union That Produces Fruit

The third feature I see in this picture is *union that produces fruit*. The purpose and consummation of marriage is the union of two people. *"The two,"* it says, *"shall become one flesh"* (Matthew 19:5). Out of that union comes forth fruit—new life. I believe that is the purpose of God in the relationship of Christ, the Bridegroom, to the church, the bride. I believe that out of that glorious union, not yet consummated, will come eternal fruit. The eternal purposes of God for all subsequent ages will be unfolded out of the union of Christ with His church.

The Essential Feature of the Bride

Let us look at two verses in 1 Corinthians that tell us the essential feature of the bride is to reveal Christ's glory.

> *But I want you to know that the head of every man is Christ, the head of woman is man, and the head of Christ is God.* (1 Corinthians 11:3)

In descending order, God the Father is the head of Christ, Christ is the head of the man or the husband, and the husband is the head of the woman or the wife. There is a divine order of headship that starts in heaven and moves down into every home. This involves responsibilities on both sides.

> *For a man indeed ought not to cover his head, since he is the image and glory of God; but woman is the glory of man.* (verse 7)

It was the male who was first created in the image and likeness of God to show forth God's likeness and glory to the rest of the creation. The wife was also made in the image of God, but her responsibility is to reflect her husband's glory. Likewise, as the bride of Christ, it is our responsibility to reflect His glory.

This is a very deep and practical teaching. I want to relate it to the marriage relationship because it is so close to that between Christ and His bride. Some women have the idea that because the Bible teaches the wife to be in submission to her husband, it implies inferiority. This is not so. Submission is not inferiority because Christ is in submission to the Father, but He is not inferior to the Father. In fact, He said, *"I and My Father are one"* (John 10:30). Submission is not inferiority but placement; it is being where you ought to be.

There are responsibilities between husband and wife. When I say that my wife is my glory, I am not really placing the responsibility so much on my wife as I am on myself. It is a very challenging responsibility. Somebody once asked a well-known preacher, "What kind of a Christian is Mr. Smith?" The preacher answered, "I can't tell you; I haven't met his wife!" That is a very wise answer. If you want to know what kind of Christian Mr. Smith is, look at Mrs. Smith. She is his glory. As such, she reveals what he is really like. This challenges the husband much more than it does the wife. If you want to know what kind of Christian I am, you have to look at my wife. If my wife is restful, secure, joyful, fruitful, and relaxed, she is my glory. But if she is insecure, frustrated, and bitter, it tells you a lot about me. She is not my glory. It is my business to protect her. Ephesians 5:23 says, "[Christ] *is the Savior of the body,"* which is the church.

The problems in marriages that we see today began when the first man failed to protect his wife. You have to get behind the surface of the account in Genesis, but it is there. God placed Adam in the garden to *"tend and keep it"* (Genesis 2:15). The Hebrew word for *"keep"* means to protect it. He failed by letting the snake in. He ought never to have let the snake in because it was one of the beasts of the field; it had no place in the garden. Then Eve failed because she was away from her husband and met the snake in her own strength and wisdom, which she was not expected to do. Both of them were out of divine order. Surely, this tells us that the remedy for our problems is divine order.

> *The bride of Christ, His church, is to reflect and manifest the glory of the Bridegroom.*

The wife reflects what her husband is, and children reflect what their parents are. As a visiting preacher, I have discovered that a married couple can conceal their real attitudes toward me, but their children rarely do. If I go into a home where the children show me love and respect, I know that is what their parents feel. But when the children are undisciplined and disrespectful, the parents may talk nice to me, but I question whether that is their real attitude. We are always revealing ourselves in those to whom we are related.

God is present everywhere, but His *glory* is where His presence is manifested—where it can been seen and experienced. Many of us know what it is to feel the glory of God in our bodies or in the atmosphere, or to see it on the faces of other Christians. And the purpose of God in the church is to manifest the glory of Christ, the Bridegroom, in the church, the bride. Jesus is not coming for a spiritually bent, haggard, worn out, old crone of a bride. Please do not misunderstand me. I am not in any way speaking disrespectfully of old age. I am just pointing out that the bride Christ is coming for is going to glorify Him.

That we who first trusted in Christ should be to the praise of His glory. (Ephesians 1:12)

We are to be the demonstration of His glory so that all the universe will praise His glory when they see it in us.

Let's return to our main Scripture in this chapter:

Husbands, love your wives, just as Christ also loved the church and gave Himself for her, that He might sanctify and cleanse her with the washing of water by the word....
(Ephesians 5:25–26)

I believe that this sanctifying and cleansing is what Christ is doing right now. The Greek word for *word* in this Scripture is *rhema*, which means the spoken word. One of the things that God does with a spoken teaching is to cleanse and sanctify the believers through the word that goes forth. Christ redeemed the church by His blood so that He might thereafter sanctify it by His word. Christ came by water and by blood. (See 1 John 6.) As the Redeemer, He came by blood, and as the Sanctifier, He came by water. He redeems the church by His blood; He sanctifies it by the water of His spoken word. It is only after the church has been sanctified that it will be what He intends it to be, which is described in the next verse:

...that He might present her to Himself a glorious church, not having spot or wrinkle or any such thing, but that she should be holy and without blemish. (verse 27)

This means that the church will be permeated with the manifest presence of God.

When you see a young woman who is really in love with her husband, her face just beams love at him. She is radiant. That is how God wants the church to be—a radiant church, without spot or wrinkle, unbelievably beautiful. Isn't it good that God can do it? And He *is* going to do it!

Our Requirement as the Bride

What is required in our relationship to Christ, the Bridegroom, as His bride? We can learn this by reading what Paul wrote to the church at Corinth, which was the product of his ministry:

For I am jealous for you with godly jealousy. For I have betrothed you to one husband, that I may present you as a chaste virgin to Christ. But I fear, lest somehow, as the serpent deceived Eve by his craftiness, so your minds may be corrupted from the simplicity that is in Christ. For if he who comes preaches another Jesus whom we have not preached, or if you receive a different spirit which you have not received, or a different gospel which you have not accepted; you may well put up with it!

(2 Corinthians 11:2–4)

Loyalty to Jesus

To understand this picture, it helps to be acquainted with the basic principles of marriage among the Jewish people, in which there were two main ceremonies. The first was betrothal, which is something like an engagement. The second, which usually followed about a year later, was the actual marriage ceremony, and was followed by the physical union between the man and his bride. In Hebrew custom, betrothal was a very sacred, binding covenant agreement between a man and a woman. Although they still lived apart and did not come together in physical relationship, the woman was bound to the man by that covenant. If, in the course of that time, she broke her engagement to marry someone else or had sexual relations with another man, she was treated as an adulteress and the covenant was officially nullified by something that was known as a divorce. That is how solemn the betrothal commitment was.

This practice is exemplified in the story of Joseph and Mary. They were betrothed, but not yet married, when Joseph discovered that Mary was pregnant. He did not yet know that this conception was by the Holy Spirit, in God's plan to bring His Son into the world, and the Scripture tells us that Joseph *"was minded to put her away secretly"* (Matthew 1:19), or divorce her.

> *Our loyalty to Christ will be tested during our "engagement" period here on earth.*

In a similar way, when we become Christians, we are engaged to Christ, but the marriage has not yet taken place—that is still in the future. In this period between engagement and marriage, our loyalty to Christ is being tested. Paul was saying, "I want you to be a chaste virgin when you marry the Bridegroom."

There are some very beautiful thoughts in that statement because if any group of people, by natural standards, did not qualify to be a chaste virgin, it was the Corinthian Christians. They were prostitutes, homosexuals, and drunkards. Yet the grace and blood of Jesus gave them the privilege of being redeemed and cleansed, and therefore, in God's sight, of being a chaste virgin. It was as if they had never sinned. (See Isaiah 1:18; Romans 4:3–8.)

Nevertheless, Paul said to be careful not to lose your virginity. Be careful that you do not get tricked into a wrong relationship that will make you unfit to be the bride. This is so highly relevant to our contemporary situation.

But I fear, lest somehow, as the serpent deceived Eve by his craftiness, so your minds may be corrupted from the simplicity that is in Christ. (2 Corinthians 11:3)

Paul was afraid for these Christians that the devil would get at their minds and corrupt them from the pure simplicity of faith in Jesus Christ and total commitment to Him. In the next verse, he described the way this could happen. Indeed, don't we see this happening all around us in the churches of America today?

For if he who comes preaches another Jesus whom we have not preached.... (verse 4)

What kind of "other Jesus" was he referring to? Perhaps Jesus as a great teacher or the greatest guru, just a little higher than Buddha or Socrates or Plato or Martin Luther King—but not as a redeeming Savior. Or maybe a Jesus who was not born of a virgin? Or who is not truly divine? Those would be examples of *"another Jesus"* and exactly what Paul was talking about.

Then Paul said, *"If you receive a different spirit..."* (verse 4). These were Spirit-baptized Christians he was addressing. Was it possible for them to receive a different spirit? Apparently. How? Through receiving a wrong picture of Jesus. In other words, they might open their minds to an error that would, in turn, open their spirits to a spirit of error.

Paul went on, *"If you receive...a different gospel..."* (verse 4). This could be a gospel that speaks only about the love of God and never about the judgment of God. Or a gospel that claims the Fatherhood of God even over the unconverted. But the Bible does not say that the unconverted are the children of God; it says they are the children of the devil. All these things are happening today because the devil is seeking to corrupt the bride from her loyalty to Jesus Christ.

At the close of this age, it is my firm conviction that there will be only two groups in Christendom—not two denominations, but two groups. One will be the bride and the other will be the harlot. What will the difference be? Water baptism? Speaking in tongues? I don't believe so. I believe the distinction will be loyalty to Jesus Christ. The bride will remain true; the harlot will be seduced from her loyalty to Jesus. We see both of them presented in the book of Revelation:

> *Then one of the seven angels who had the seven bowls came and talked with me, saying to me, "Come, I will show you the judgment of the great harlot who sits on many waters, with whom the kings of the earth committed fornication, and the inhabitants of the earth were made drunk with the wine of her fornication."* (Revelation 17:1–2)

> *Then one of the seven angels who had the seven bowls filled with the seven last plagues came to me and talked with me, saying, "Come, I will show you the bride, the Lamb's wife."* (Revelation 21:9)

In these verses, the harlot and the bride are set in opposition to one another. Not by a denomination or a doctrine, but by a relationship to Jesus Christ. Both are well advanced in formation in the church today. The bride is nearing completion, and the harlot is surely being manifest.

We must closely guard our relationships with Christ. Some people say you should always stay in your present church. I don't counsel one way or the other. Preachers really have no authority to tell individual believers that. Just ensure that you do not end up in the harlot church—because many churches have a lot more of the harlot than the bride in them.

So Christ was offered once to bear the sins of many. To those who eagerly wait for Him He will appear a second time, apart from sin, for salvation. (Hebrews 9:28)

The qualification for seeing Jesus appear for salvation is *"those who eagerly wait."* The key word is *expectancy.* He will come for those who are expecting Him as Savior. For the rest, He will come as Judge.

Holding Fast Our Confession

What, therefore, is required in our relationship to one another? *Exhortation* and *example.*

Let us hold fast the confession of our hope [or faith] without wavering, for He who promised is faithful.
(Hebrews 10:23)

One of the themes of the book of Hebrews is a continual exhortation to stand fast in faith and not go back to the Law. The Hebrew Christians were in great danger of doing that— of almost giving up their profession of faith in Jesus the Messiah and becoming enamored again with the Old Testament worship and sacrifices. The writer of Hebrews continually pointed out the superiority of Christ and the new covenant over the Law and the old covenant. The book is addressed to people who had made a profession of faith in Christ but were in danger of turning back.

In fact, there are five separate exhortations in Hebrews on the dangers of turning back. Here the message is for us to hold fast and not give up what we have professed.

> *And let us consider one another in order to stir up* [or *"pro-voke"* KJV] *love and good works....* (verse 24)

Part of our responsibility is not merely to hold fast ourselves, but also to encourage one another and consider how we can provoke one another to love and good works. The word *provoke* is deliberately paradoxical. Normally, we tend to provoke people to bad acts, such as anger and jealousy. But we are to consider how we can provoke one another to *good* acts, to the outworked righteous acts of obedience.

> *...not forsaking the assembling of ourselves together, as is the manner of some, but exhorting one another, and so much the more as you see the Day approaching.* (verse 25)

"The Day" is the day of Christ's return. The nearer we come to the day, the greater is our responsibility to meet together, challenge one another, provoke one another to do what is good, exhort one another, and watch over one another.

Here is where I believe the small group has a unique function. It is where we can best encourage and exhort one another. In a large gathering, the person who is really troubled or on the verge of backsliding can remain hidden. But in a small group of ten or twelve people, very little remains hidden for long. In a big group, the person who has some deep, inner, personal problem probably will never come out with it. But in a small group, as we lay bare our lives to one another and meet together to encourage and pray for one another, deeper issues emerge.

In my experience with small groups, religious Christians often come to a point where they are sorely tempted to turn back. New believers seem to have few problems, but those who are accustomed to being religious may have many. In my way of thinking, the cell group is not for a prayer meeting or a Bible study. In a Bible study, somebody can remain hidden. In a prayer meeting, people can pray beautiful prayers. But when it comes to opening up to one another, every one of us has to decide if it is really worth it. Do I really want people to know me *that* well? Would I prefer to keep my mask on?

> *We need to "provoke" one another to love and good works.*

This is something very much related to what we are looking at because the word that is used in Hebrews 10:25 means "your synagogue," the place where you gather together. It is not the word *ecclesia*, the church assembly. I believe it is really speaking about small group meetings where people can become honest with one another.

It concerns me that people can sit in a church for years and have deep personal problems that they never reveal to anybody. For instance, in my ministry of deliverance as a visiting preacher, I have discovered that there are homosexuals in many churches. You would be surprised how many evangelical Pentecostal churches have people with the problem of homosexuality. But it never is revealed because they are ashamed and they do not dare to come out into the open with it. I once received a four-page letter from a young man. The first three pages were devoted to getting me ready for what he wanted to tell me. The fourth page revealed that he was a homosexual. It took him all that time to get up the courage to make that statement. I wrote back and told him that there was hope, there was a way out. He wrote back and said, "You're the first person who has ever done anything but discourage me or reject me."

We need to have the kind of relationship with believers in which our problems can come out and be dealt with justly and mercifully. We should encourage one another, correct one another, but *not* reject one another. Someone once said, "Correct me, but don't reject me." This is what people are crying out for. I really believe that this passage in Hebrews is particularly relevant for the times and situations in which we find ourselves.

To conclude, let's look at a verse from the first chapter of Song of Solomon. This is the young lady speaking: *"Draw me away! We will run after you"* (verse 4). You will notice that she moves from singular to plural: *"Draw **me**,"* and *"**We** will run."* This is a picture of exhortation and example. When the Lord can draw you, the people who see you running will want to run with you. So there is the responsibility of example in our relationship to the Bridegroom. All through the Song of Solomon, we are reminded of this example. The bride is asked, *"What is your beloved more than another beloved?"* (Song of Solomon 5:9). "I'll tell you!" is the answer of the bride. This is how we need to provoke people to love and good works.

Chapter 9

Picture #7: The Army

Therefore take up the whole armor of God, that you may be able to withstand in the evil day, and having done all, to stand.
—Ephesians 6:13

o far, we have looked at six specific pictures of God's people in Ephesians: the assembly, the body, the workmanship, the family, the temple, and the bride. Now we are going to look at the seventh picture: the army. This last picture is as great a contrast as it could possibly be to the previous picture. What two representations could be less like one another than a bride and an army?

For this final picture, we will turn to the last chapter of Ephesians. As in the case of the picture of the bride (in which the word bride is not actually mentioned), the word army is not specifically used here, but the implication is absolutely beyond doubt.

Finally, my brethren, be strong in the Lord and in the power of His might. Put on the whole armor of God, that you may be able to stand against the wiles of the devil. For we do not wrestle against flesh and blood, but against principalities, against powers, against the rulers of the darkness of this age, against spiritual hosts of wickedness in the heavenly places. Therefore take up the whole armor of God, that you may be able to withstand in the evil day, and having done all, to stand. (Ephesians 6:10–13)

Here is fair warning that believers will most certainly face warfare. There will come what Paul called *"the evil day"*—the day of affliction, testing, and satanic pressures. Therefore, Paul said, *"Put on the whole armor."* What kind of person puts on armor? Obviously, the answer is a soldier. Indeed, the entire picture is very closely based on the battle gear of the Roman legionary in the time of Paul. The church is compared to a Roman legion, the most effective military unit of the ancient world—one that actually conquered most of the known world for the Roman Empire.

As God's army, believers are involved in a spiritual war. There has been a war between the forces of God and the forces of Satan throughout human history, but the coming of Jesus as Messiah, Savior, and Deliverer brought the conflict out into the open. At one point, the Pharisees were criticizing Jesus because of His ministry of casting out evil spirits. They accused Him of being in league with Beelzebub, which was one of the titles of Satan.

But Jesus knew their thoughts, and said to them, "Every kingdom divided against itself is brought to desolation, and every city or house divided against itself will not stand. If Satan casts out Satan, he is divided against himself. How then will his kingdom stand? And if I cast out demons by Beelzebub, by whom do your sons cast them out? Therefore they shall be your judges. But if I cast out demons by the

Spirit of God, surely the kingdom of God has come upon you." (Matthew 12:25–28)

Jesus said that Satan's kingdom is not divided, and it is in total opposition to the kingdom of God. In the last phrase, He spoke about His ministry of casting out evil spirits as the demonstration that the kingdom of God had come on the scene. So here we have what I call "the clash of kingdoms": the visible, manifested clash between God's kingdom—represented by Jesus and the church—and the kingdom of Satan and his demons.

Spiritual Weapons and Battlefield

We need to understand the weapons and battlefield of this spiritual conflict:

For though we walk in the flesh, we do not war according to the flesh, for the weapons of our warfare are not of the flesh, but divinely powerful for the destruction of fortresses. We are destroying speculations and every lofty thing raised up against the knowledge of God, and we are taking every thought captive to the obedience of Christ.
(2 Corinthians 10:3–5 NASB)

Paul said we are in a war *in the spiritual realm,* and therefore we must utilize spiritual weapons—not bombs, bullets, or tanks. These spiritual weapons are capable—through God's power—of destroying Satan's fortresses. Verse five clearly reveals the battlefield: *"Destroying speculations and every lofty thing raised up against the knowledge of God, and...taking every thought captive to the obedience of Christ."* Three key words, *"speculation," "knowledge,"* and *"thought,"* all relate to one particular realm: the mind.

The mind of humanity is the battlefield of this spiritual war.
Satan has deceived human beings through their minds, taking them captive by building fortresses of unbelief and prejudice. Our assignment as God's army is to make war with the spiritual weapons that God has committed to us. We are to release people from Satan's bondage by breaking down his strongholds in their minds and enabling them to bring their thoughts into captivity to the obedience of Christ. This is our military assignment as the army of God.

From Bride to Army

Let us consider the process by which the bride becomes the army, which is really exciting. We find the process or transformation described in Song of Solomon. Here the bridegroom is speaking to his bride—a picture of Christ speaking to His church:

> *You are as beautiful as Tirzah, my darling, as lovely as Jerusalem, as awesome as an army with banners.*
> (Song of Solomon 6:4 NASB)

This is a rather unexpected combination—the words *"beautiful," "darling,"* and *"lovely"* are followed by the picture of *"an army with banners."* A feminine or bridal description turns into a military one! And then, in the tenth verse of the same chapter, the chorus (or spectators) offers this description of the bride (the church):

> *Who is this that grows* [or *"appears"* NIV] *like the dawn, as beautiful as the full moon, as pure as the sun, as awesome as an army with banners?*　　　　(verse 10 NASB)

The chorus (the world) is amazed to see the church appearing as an army. Notice the beauty of the picture:

- "[Appears] *like the dawn*"—rising after a night of darkness.
- "*As beautiful as the full moon*"—the moon in its function of reflecting the sun as the church reflects or manifests Christ.
- "*As pure as the sun*"—with Christ's own purity and righteousness.
- "*Awesome as an army with banners*"—again, the bride becomes the army, startling both Satan and the world.

This is the order: First, Christ sees His bride as an army; then, she also appears to the world in this way. This is why it is important for us to see ourselves as Christ sees us by looking in the mirror of God's Word. When we begin to see ourselves in this way by faith, then the Holy Spirit transforms us into what we see.

The Essential Feature of the Army of God

God's purpose in presenting this picture of the church, or the essential feature of God's army, is to manifest God's victory. In dealing with this tremendous theme, we need to see, first of all, that the Lord is a military commander and a man of war.

The LORD is a man of war; the LORD is His name.
(Exodus 15:3)

Who is this King of glory? The LORD strong and mighty, the LORD mighty in battle. Lift up your heads, O you gates! Lift up, you everlasting doors! And the King of glory shall come in. Who is this King of glory? The LORD of hosts, He is the King of glory. (Psalm 24:8–10)

We are familiar with the phrase *"the LORD of hosts,"* but the wording obscures some of the meaning for us today because we are not familiar with Elizabethan English. The Hebrew word that is translated *"hosts"* is *tsaba*, which is the standard Hebrew word for an army. It is also used of the modern Israeli army. Therefore, God is the Lord of armies. He is also a God of battle and a *"man of war."* He is worthy and capable of being our Commander. It is good to know this. To have confidence in your commander is a very important element of military life. Morale always fails among troops when they lack confidence in their commander. But we can have our morale strengthened by the knowledge that the Lord knows His job. He is a God of battle—a man of war, the Lord of armies.

> *The essential feature of God's army is to manifest God's victory.*

Then we need to know that Christ has already won the victory. Paul said that God in Christ *"disarmed principalities and powers"* (Colossians 2:15)—Satan's entire kingdom with all its authorities and rulers. Christ stripped them of their armor and made a show of them openly, triumphing over them in the cross. The cross was the place where Christ once and for all sealed Satan's defeat. The enemy procured his own defeat by sending Christ to the cross. Since the time he realized what he had done, he has been busy trying to keep Christians ignorant of what the cross accomplished because it accomplished his total defeat. (See, for example, Hebrews 2:14–15.)

Christ does not want to defeat Satan alone, however. He wants us to share in His victory and its fruits. Here we have a glorious statement:

Picture #7: The Army

Now thanks be to God who always leads us in triumph in Christ, and through us diffuses the fragrance of His knowledge in every place. (2 Corinthians 2:14)

Consider the two adverbial phrases in the above sentence: *"always"* and *"in every place."* Just think about this. It leaves out no time and no place. God *always* leads us in triumph in Christ *in every place.*

The word *triumph* is a very distinct, official word in the context of the Roman Empire. If a Roman general had been particularly successful in overseas wars and had added territories to the Roman Empire or defeated dangerous enemies, the senate would vote him a triumph when he came back to Rome. This was the highest honor that could be afforded to a Roman general. The triumph consisted basically of this: The general was placed in a chariot drawn by two white horses. He was led through the streets of Rome while all the people of Rome stood on the sides of the street and applauded him.

Behind the chariot, they would parade all the general's emblems of his conquests. For instance, if he had been in a land where there were wild animals that were not familiar in Rome, they would bring specimens of these animals—maybe tigers or elephants—and parade them behind the chariot. After the animals would come all the kings and generals whom that general had defeated and taken captive. They would be led in chains in humiliation. Finally, there would follow rank after rank of prisoners who had been captured in the war. And these would be the emblems and the demonstration to the people of Rome of what the general had achieved by his victory.

When Paul spoke about Christ triumphing, that was the picture he had in mind. Christ is in the chariot, and behind Him, on display, are all the forces of evil that He has defeated. The principalities and powers of Satan and all the things that oppose God and us are being led in captivity behind the chariot.

Paul said, "Thanks be to God who always leads us in triumph in Christ." Where are we in the scene? Some Christians would picture themselves being led in chains behind the chariot, but that is the place for the enemies. No, we are in the chariot. Do you know how to get there? I can tell you this great secret in one simple word: by faith—you just have to believe. You can't work for it; you can't pray for it; you must just believe it. Thanks be to God, who always causes us to share in Christ's triumph. Wherever we go, we are part of the spectacle, and the whole universe lines up and applauds what He has done.

God's Requirements of His Army

Now let us see what is required in our relationship to the Commander in Chief. We looked at this verse at the beginning of the chapter, but we will go on from there.

Finally, my brethren, be strong in the Lord and in the power of His might. Put on the whole armor of God....Take up the whole armor of God. (Ephesians 6:10–11, 13)

Putting on the Whole Armor

It is our responsibility as soldiers in Christ's army to put on our armor. Paul warned us very clearly that we are in a conflict. God has provided the armor, and Paul listed six items of armor in the following verses:

Stand therefore, having girded your waist with truth, having put on the breastplate of righteousness, and having shod your feet with the preparation of the gospel of peace; above all, taking the shield of faith with which you will be able to quench all the fiery darts of the wicked one. And take the helmet of salvation, and the sword of the Spirit, which is the word of God; praying always with all prayer and supplication in the Spirit. (verses 14–18)

In one of his great hymns, Charles Wesley talked about the weapon of *"all prayer."* So we have six pieces of armor, plus the weapon of all prayer. Of these seven items, only two are weapons of offense; all the rest are weapons of defense. But the sword of the Spirit, which is the Word of God, and the weapon of all prayer are weapons of attack.

> *Through faith, we share in Christ's triumph and are victorious in Him.*

If you look closely at this picture, you will find that you are completely protected from the crown of your head to the soles of your feet except for one place: your back. There is nothing to protect the back except your fellow soldiers. This shows that we cannot afford to turn our backs and that we had better have somebody behind us who can protect us.

Teaching and Leading a Disciplined Life

Then we need to address our character as soldiers, as Paul emphasized in 2 Timothy:

And the things that you have heard from me among many witnesses, commit these to faithful men who will be able to teach others also. (2 Timothy 2:2)

The basic principle of discipleship is teaching others what you have been taught. The Navigators missionary organization will point out to you that there are four spiritual generations mentioned in this verse: Paul, who taught Timothy, who was to teach faithful men, who were to teach other faithful men. This is the way of perpetuating the truth in the ministry. Teach men, who will teach men, who will teach men...

Mathematically, the implications are almost incredible. I am not a mathematician, and you would have to use a calculator, but consider this: If one man wins one man and teaches him for one year, at the end of that year, you have two men who are able to teach. Suppose each of them wins another man and teaches him for another year. Now you have four men who are able to teach. At the end of five years you will have sixteen men. But at the end of about thirty years, there is nobody left to win! The whole world has been included.

That is geometric progression. On the other hand, if you were to win a thousand people to Christ every day, that would be 365,000 people a year. This number seems staggering. However, after twenty years, the other process (of one man winning and teaching another man for a year) would have completely left behind this process of simply winning people and leaving them there. Mathematically, it works. The problem with most of us is that it means starting very small. We would rather reach out for something bigger and more dramatic. This method is smaller but more effective.

In this connection, Paul went on to say something very significant to Timothy:

Picture #7: The Army

You therefore must endure hardship as a good soldier of Jesus Christ. No one engaged in warfare entangles himself with the affairs of this life, that he may please him who enlisted him as a soldier. (2 Timothy 2:3–4)

Military discipline demands that you be prepared to endure hardship. Comfort and luxury are not primary considerations. One mark of a seasoned soldier is that he will always make himself as comfortable as possible anywhere, whether it is in a commandeered house or in the bottom of a trench. A good soldier does not depend on circumstances and can settle down wherever he is. He is detached from the normal way of life of the people around him.

So this is a complete picture of discipleship in the army of the Lord—teaching others and leading a disciplined life.

Loyalty to Our Fellow Soldiers

What is involved or required in our relationships to one another? *Loyalty.* First Chronicles 12 lists representatives from all the tribes of Israel who came to Hebron under their leaders, in military order, to make David king.

Now these are the numbers of the divisions equipped for war, who came to David at Hebron, to turn the kingdom of Saul to him, according to the word of the LORD. (1 Chronicles 12:23 NASB)

I believe that this is a picture of the way God is going to unite His people. The tribes will gather together under their leaders, the "tribes" being the various parts of the body of Christ that are going to be represented under their leadership with just one purpose: to make Jesus King.

101

Then there is a list of how many Israelites came from every tribe, with the captain specified.

Of Zebulun, there were 50,000 who went out in the army, who could draw up in battle formation with all kinds of weapons of war and helped David with an undivided heart. (1 Chronicles 12:33 NASB)

These were men who could keep their places in the ranks, side by side, with an undivided heart. They were loyal and committed to one another. In a battle, you need to know that the man at your right hand will still be there on your right hand regardless of the weather and regardless of the danger. You have to be able to rely on that man.

> *God's true soldiers are those who can keep rank with an undivided heart.*

This picture is what the Lord is instilling in us regarding our need for committed loyalty to one another. God's true soldiers are those who can keep rank with an undivided heart. The Hebrew means "a heart and a heart." This kind of person is not one who is sweet to your face but criticizes you behind your back! You cannot go into battle with a man like that; he is more dangerous to you than the enemy.

God is saying that we need to be loyal to one another. This does not mean that you have to agree with everything somebody else does. It does mean that you will not betray him or stab him in the back, but will rather stand by him and protect him from harm.

Picture #7: The Army

All these, being men of war, who could draw up in battle formation, came to Hebron with a perfect heart.

(verse 38 NASB)

Keeping battle formation and having a unified heart go together. If your heart is divided, you will not keep rank. You must be a person that the Commander and your fellow soldiers can count on to be in your place.

You must be a loyal member of the army of God.

Chapter 10

The Seven Pictures and Their Application

hat an amazing revelation the apostle Paul had of the church! I pointed out earlier that the church is the demonstration of God's manifold, or many-sided, wisdom:

> *To the intent that now the manifold wisdom of God might be made known by the church to the principalities and powers in the heavenly places....* (Ephesians 3:10)

Each of the seven aspects of God's people that we have been studying presents a different aspect of God's wisdom. We need to be on our guard against focusing on any one aspect to the exclusion of the others. It is dangerous to become one-track in our approach and see only one facet of God's people. We must grow into a complete understanding and practice of all these pictures or we will miss out on a great deal of what God has for us!

Let's review the seven pictures of the church and their references from Ephesians:

1. 1:22   The assembly
2. 1:23   The body
3. 2:10   The workmanship

The Seven Pictures and Their Application

4. 2:18–19   The family
5. 2:20–22   The temple
6. 5:25–32   The bride
7. 6:10–13   The army

Now, let's go through each picture, in turn, and underline the two main lessons that we learned from each—the essential, distinctive nature of the picture and the particular responsibility that is placed on us as we represent each picture individually and corporately.

The Assembly

• *The essential feature* is being God's governmental authority. The church is God's representative body on earth through which, by spiritual power and authority, He rules the nations and brings His purposes to pass.

• *What is required of us?* On a personal level, respect for order. We are not fit to govern if we do not have respect for due order. We cannot govern the universe until we govern ourselves. This means order in our conduct and in our relationships one to another. Here is an area where we have a lot of work to do. Corporately, we must recognize the office (or gifting) that each person holds in the assembly. God has given certain offices in the assembly: apostles, prophets, shepherds, teachers, miracles, gifts of healing, tongues, and so on. We have to recognize the office or *charisma* with which each person functions.

The Body

• *The essential feature* is being the agent of Christ's will. The function of the body is to do the will of the One for whom the body was prepared. As the body of Christ, our function is to do the will of Christ. He is the Head and we are the parts of the body. Jesus depends on us as the members of His body to carry out His redemptive purposes in the earth. He is not going to preach the gospel anymore; we are going to preach the gospel. He is not the personification of active ministry; we are. We are His hands and His feet.

• *What is required of us?* Individually, we have to recognize and appreciate our differences, and corporately, we must acknowledge our interdependence, as parts of the body. We cannot say to one another, "I don't need you." We are to be different and diverse, but interdependent. The body becomes effective only when we recognize this truth. Remember, there is no such thing as an effective, fruitful "lone ranger" Christian!

> *Each picture of the church reflects God's wisdom.*

The Workmanship

• *The essential feature* is that we are to be the revelation to the universe of God's creative genius! We are His creative masterpiece. To the principalities and powers in the heavenlies, the church is set as a picture of the manifold (many-sided) wisdom of God. It represents God's creative genius at its highest point.

• *What is required of us to be part of this masterpiece?* For each of us as individuals, this requires yieldedness or pliability; and corporately, it requires "merge-ability." If we are a word in a poem, we must be the right word in the right place, and be rightly related to all the other words. If we are a member of an orchestra, we must play according to the score. We must fit in with God's design, allowing Him to make us and place us where He wants.

The Family

• *The essential feature* is that God the Father is the life-source of all of us, and that we are together, not in an institution or an organization, but in a family. Jesus is our Elder Brother, and we are all members of the same family, showing the nature of God as Father.

• *What is required of us?* Individually, it requires obedience to the commands of our Father. Jesus learned obedience through suffering and is the "pattern Son" for all Christians. Corporately, we are commanded to love one another. Jesus calls us His brothers because God calls us His sons; and if God calls our fellow believers His sons, we have to call them our brothers. This is not always easy. As the saying goes, you can choose your friends, but you cannot choose your family. As a family, we have to accept one another. Romans 15:7 says, *"Accept one another, just as Christ also accepted us to the glory of God"* (NASB). How can we glorify God apart from being a true spiritual family?

The Temple

• *The essential feature* is being a dwelling place for God. Paul said, *"We are the temple of the living God"* (2 Corinthians 6:16 NASB). Rather than Moses' tabernacle or Solomon's temple, *we* have become God's dwelling place—both collectively, as a body of believers, and individually; each of us individually is a "living stone" in a living temple.

• *What is required of us?* As living stones, we are to be shaped and fitted, submitting to the discipline of God and to the ministries that God has placed in the church. When we have allowed ourselves to be chiseled and hammered into shape, then, corporately, we must be willing to take our places in the temple where we belong, with one stone on either side, two stones beneath us, and in most cases, two stones above us, too! This is required if we are going to be part of the temple.

The Bride

• *The essential feature* is to show the glory of Christ. Human history begins and ends with a marriage. Jesus demonstrated His unreserved commitment to us by totally giving of Himself. The church is to be the bride of Christ, to whom He is going to be united eternally at the marriage supper of the Lamb. As Jesus gave Himself without reservation to the church, now He asks the church to give herself without reservation to Him.

• *What is required of us?* Individually, as the bride, each of us must make careful preparation to put our wedding garments in order. *"The righteous acts of the saints"* (Revelation 19:8) are the fine linen that we are going to appear in. Do you want to have an incomplete wedding gown at the marriage supper? Corporately, we should exhort one another by example. This is part of our responsibility to "hold fast" and to encourage one another to love and good works.

The Army

• *The essential feature* is being a demonstration of God's invincible power to manifest His victory! We are pitted in relentless warfare against the spiritual kingdom of Satan and equipped with spiritual weapons that enable us to cast down Satan's strongholds in the main battleground: the mind. We liberate the enemy's captives and win this world for our Lord and Savior, Jesus Christ.

• *What is required of us?* First, on a personal level, military discipline is required. God is waiting for us to rule ourselves, particularly in our conduct and relationships. How is it with you today? How is your personal conduct? Your family? Your financial picture? Your mind? Then, corporately, we are to be loyal to one another, totally committed to one another. As soldiers in battle, we are required to be ready to defend our fellow soldiers, regardless of the danger.

A True Reflection of His True Church

Even though you may intensely desire to reflect the complete image of what the church can be, all these applications may seem overwhelming. Remember the key: While we look into the mirror of God's Word, we see our real condition. Yet, as we look, the Holy Spirit transforms us into what God wants to make us. As we fall in love with Him, He will transform us into a true reflection of His true church.

> *As we fall in love with God, He will transform us into a true reflection of His true church.*

And we, who with unveiled faces all reflect the Lord's glory, are being transformed into his likeness with ever-increasing glory, which comes from the Lord, who is the Spirit.

(2 Corinthians 3:18 NIV)

Part 3:

The Structure of the Church

Chapter 11

The Universal Church

n part one, we considered God's vision for the church. In part two, we considered the sevenfold nature of the church and the applications and implications for us as believers. We now move to the structure of the church. Structure is important because it is the practical outworking of the identity of the church that we have been discovering.

In defining the word *church,* I pointed out that the word *ecclesia* was not invented by the writers of the New Testament, but was simply given special meaning related to the original word. The church is an assembly, a group of people called out for a special task. We should note that, in the Bible, the word *church* never refers to a meeting place; it always refers to the *people* who meet there. It is never applied to an actual, material building made of stone or brick or timber. The church in the New Testament is an assembly formed by calling people out from the world on the basis of their personal relationship to Jesus Christ.

The universal church is made up of all true Christians worldwide. It is the totality of all who believe in Jesus Christ. Another word that is often used to describe the global or corporate church is *catholic.* Many people—particularly Roman

Catholics—are not aware of the fact that the word *catholic* is derived from a Greek word meaning "universal." So whether you say *universal* or *catholic*, you are saying the same thing.

It is interesting that the word *church* is used in only two places in the Gospels, each time by Jesus Himself. In Matthew 16:18, Jesus spoke of the universal church, and in Matthew 18:17, He spoke of the local church. In this chapter, we will begin to examine the important distinctions between the two as we consider the universal church.

The Revelation of Jesus' Identity

When Jesus came into the region of Caesarea Philippi, He asked His disciples, saying, "Who do men say that I, the Son of Man, am?" So they said, "Some say John the Baptist, some Elijah, and others Jeremiah or one of the prophets." He said to them, "But who do you say that I am?" Simon Peter answered and said, "You are the Christ, the Son of the living God." Jesus answered and said to him, "Blessed are you, Simon Bar-Jonah, for flesh and blood has not revealed this to you, but My Father who is in heaven. And I also say to you that you are Peter, and on this rock I will build My church, and the gates of Hades shall not prevail against it."   (Matthew 16:13–18)

Again, this is the first use of the word *church* in the New Testament, and the situation in which it is presented is significant and definitive. For the first time, Jesus challenged His disciples (who had been with Him for some time) to acknowledge His true identity, asking them, "What do other people say about Me? What does the world at large say?" They gave Him a number of answers: John the Baptist risen from the dead, Elijah, Jeremiah, or one of the prophets.

Then Jesus came straight to the point and said, *"But who do you say that I am?"* The impetuous Simon Peter gave a bold and definite answer: *"You are the Christ, the Son of the living God."* Jesus responded with a special blessing on Simon Peter: *"Blessed are you, Simon Bar-Jonah, for flesh and blood has not revealed this to you, but My Father who is in heaven."* The identity of Jesus is not revealed to the natural senses, understanding, or reasoning. The people Jesus had lived with in Nazareth for thirty years still did not know who He was. They saw Him as the carpenter's son. Likewise, the people who met Him in the synagogue did not know who He was. The true revelation of His identity could come only supernaturally through a revelation granted by God the Father.

> *The universal church is made up of all true Christians worldwide.*

Then Jesus went on to make a statement in relation to Peter: *"You are Peter, and on this rock I will build My church."* Some people contend that Peter is *the* rock on which the church is built, but this belief is not in line with the original language. The name for Peter in Greek is *petros*, meaning a stone or a pebble. The word that is translated *"rock"* in this passage is *petra*, meaning a great, towering cliff. It is the name given to a place east of the Jordan River because of its tremendous rock formation—a place that many tourists still visit. This is proof of the meaning of the word. *Petros* and *petra* are not the same, although they are obviously related in sound and meaning.

So what Jesus actually said to Peter was, *"You are Peter [petros, a little stone], and on this rock [petra, a massive rock] I will build My church."* Peter obviously was not the rock!

What was the rock? It was the revelation and the confession that Peter made, guided by the Holy Spirit. Through this exchange, Peter entered in to a new relationship with Jesus. Notice here that the Father—by the Spirit—revealed the Son. This is very exciting to me! You cannot get into the church of Jesus Christ and bypass a single member of the Godhead. Entrance into the church involves relationship with each member of the Trinity. They are all intimately concerned with who gets into the church. And only on the basis of this revelation does one have access to the church.

Receiving the Revelation

Peter went through four distinct stages in receiving the revelation of the identity of Jesus.

1. *Confrontation:* There was a direct, person-to-person confrontation between Jesus and Peter. There was no one in between them—no mediator or priest.

2. *Revelation:* Peter received a revelation that was not a product of his own reasoning, understanding, or senses. The Holy Spirit granted it to him supernaturally.

3. *Acknowledgment:* Peter acknowledged the revelation, which is important. It is one thing to receive a revelation; it is another thing to acknowledge it.

4. *Public Confession:* Peter made a public confession of what he acknowledged. He said out loud, in public, *"You are the Christ* [Messiah], *the Son of the living God."* Jesus said, *"On this rock* [this acknowledgment or confession] *I will build My church."*

No one can enter the true church of Jesus Christ by any other route. There has to be a direct encounter with

Jesus and a revelation of who He is by the Father, through the Holy Spirit. There must be an inward acknowledgment of that revelation in the heart and an outward, public confession of that acknowledgment. This single entrance into the true church of Jesus Christ is guarded jealously by Father, Son, and Holy Spirit. You cannot dishonor, ignore, or slight any member of the Godhead and enter into the church.

Again, the entrance must conclude with a public confession. There is no such thing as a secret Christian; it is impossible. Jesus said,

Therefore whoever confesses Me before men, him I will also confess before My Father who is in heaven. But whoever denies Me before men, him I will also deny before My Father who is in heaven. (Matthew 10:32–33)

When God deals with you by the Holy Spirit, you must either confess or deny. The refusal to confess is, in fact, a denial. There is no neutrality. Jesus said in Matthew 12:30, *"He who is not with Me is against Me."*

In Matthew 11, we can see how jealously this revelation of Father and Son is guarded:

At that time Jesus answered and said, "I thank You, Father, Lord of heaven and earth, that You have hidden these things from the wise and prudent and have revealed them to babes. Even so, Father, for so it seemed good in Your sight. All things have been delivered to Me by My Father, and no one knows the Son except the Father. Nor does anyone know the Father except the Son, and the one to whom the Son wills to reveal Him." (verses 25–27)

The Son reveals the Father and the Father reveals the Son, in each case by the Holy Spirit.

Therefore, entrance into the true church of Jesus Christ depends upon this revelation of the identity of Jesus. Those who have entered into this relationship with Christ are necessarily members of His church. In actual fact, we do not have the option of *not* being members of the church. The only option that we have is our relation to Jesus Christ. If we desire to be related to Jesus Christ as our personal Lord and Savior, we must be members of His church. It is impossible to be truly related to Him by the Holy Spirit without belonging to His universal church. If you decide you do not want to be a member of His church, you must renounce your relationship to Him. You cannot have it both ways.

Let me point out something else important from Matthew 16:18, where Jesus (in the original Greek) put tremendous emphasis upon two words: *"I will build **My church**."* The church that we are talking about is the church that Jesus calls *"My church."* It is *His* church. He has the unique, sovereign right to do in it and with it and through it what He wills. He doesn't need to ask anybody's permission. This is the church that we are dealing with.

Entrance through the Door

Now we turn to a Scripture passage that clearly outlines the specific way of entry into the true church of Jesus Christ, the universal church. The church is symbolically presented in a parable as the sheepfold. Jesus is presented as the Shepherd and the church as the sheepfold (as it is many times in the New Testament), the place of gathering together the sheep, who are the true disciples of Jesus Christ.

[Jesus said,] *"Most assuredly, I say to you, he who does not enter the sheepfold by the door, but climbs up some other way, the same is a thief and a robber. But he who enters by the door is the shepherd of the sheep. To him the doorkeeper opens, and the sheep hear his voice; and he calls his own sheep by name and leads them out. And when he brings out his own sheep, he goes before them; and the sheep follow him, for they know his voice. Yet they will by no means follow a stranger, but will flee from him, for they do not know the voice of strangers." Jesus used this illustration, but they did not understand the things which He spoke to them. Then Jesus said to them again, "Most assuredly, I say to you, I am the door of the sheep. All who ever came before Me are thieves and robbers, but the sheep did not hear them. I am the door. If anyone enters by Me, he will be saved, and will go in and out and find pasture."* (John 10:1–9)

That last verse is particularly emphatic: *"I am the door."* The word *the* is specific, definitive, and exclusive. It means, "I am the door and there is no other door." Then Jesus said that if anybody comes in to the sheepfold in some other way, other than by the Door, he is a thief and a robber. He is talking about the assembly of God's people on earth, of course, for no thieves and robbers are admitted to heaven. Jesus did not say it would be impossible to get in some other way, but He said anybody who gets in some other way would advertise his real nature. He would be nothing else but a thief and a robber.

Consider the background of this parable and how all three persons of the Godhead are again involved. The Father is the Owner of the whole estate, including the sheepfold, the sheep, and everything else. The Holy Spirit is the

Doorkeeper or Porter. Jesus is two things: first, the Door and second, the Shepherd. He clearly said each of those two things about Himself. How can Jesus be both a door and a shepherd? My answer is that Jesus crucified is the Door, and Jesus resurrected from the dead is the Shepherd. In other words, there is no way into the sheepfold but by *"Jesus Christ and Him crucified"* (1 Corinthians 2:2) on the cross for our sin. Jesus rose from the dead to be the Shepherd of all who would come to Him through the cross.

Hebrews emphasizes the fact that through His resurrection, Jesus is the Shepherd:

> *Now may the God of peace who brought up our Lord Jesus from the dead, that great Shepherd of the sheep, through the blood of the everlasting covenant, make you complete in every good work to do His will, working in you what is well pleasing in His sight, through Jesus Christ, to whom be glory forever and ever.* (Hebrews 13:20–21)

The Great Shepherd is the one who was raised from the dead by the Father. Through the blood of the covenant, shed upon the cross, we can be made perfect to do His will. Again, *Jesus crucified* is the Door, the only way of access to God, while *Jesus risen from the dead* is the Shepherd who takes care of the souls of those who trust in His work on the cross.

If the Holy Spirit does not recognize you, your motives, and your inner faith, He will not open the door. If the Holy Spirit does not open the door to you because you fail to meet God's conditions, you have only one other alternative, and that is to climb up some other way. If you do that, you are a thief and a robber. In regard to this, Jesus made a tremendously significant statement: *"All who ever came before Me are thieves and robbers, but the sheep did not hear them"* (John 10:8). That statement refers to all who ever claimed in any previous age of human history to show man the way to God. It would include all the Oriental cults and philosophies, such as Buddhism and Hinduism, the Greek philosophies, such as Platonism, and many others.

The New Testament is an uncompromising message. Any person, before or after Jesus, who claims to direct any human soul to God by any other way than that of the cross is a deceiver, a thief, and a robber. If he claims to participate in the blessings of Christianity, he is laying claim to something that is not legally his. There are cults and groups today that talk about peace and joy and love, but they do not come by the way of Jesus Christ and Him crucified. The peace, joy, and love they talk about are not legitimately theirs. They are thieves and robbers.

> *The only way to become a member of the true church is through Jesus Christ.*

A thief does not advertise his intentions or identity; he operates in secret. This is the truth about those who profess to be able to give you true joy, peace, and salvation but do not emphasize the necessity of Jesus Christ crucified on the cross for our sins. Jesus said of Himself, *"I am the way, the truth, and the life. No one comes to the Father except through Me"* (John 14:6). If these words are not true, Jesus was either deceived or a deceiver. But I believe they are true, and they portray that the only way of access into the company of God's people on earth is by Jesus Christ. Father, Son, and Holy Spirit will bear testimony to this and will refuse acknowledgment to anybody who comes by any other way.

The modern world particularly dislikes the fact that it is being forced into a place of total commitment. As a matter of fact, some church members dislike it. They do not accept this uncompromising demand by almighty God—Father, Son, and Holy Spirit—that you must make a definite, personal, public commitment on the basis of revelation.

Modern intellectual man also does not like to acknowledge that he is unable to work out eternal truths by his own reason, that he cannot understand spiritual realities by his own senses but must receive them as a revelation from God. The average intellectual does not want to have to depend on God for the knowledge of the truth.

Christ Is the Foundation

For no other foundation can anyone lay than that which is laid, which is Jesus Christ.   (1 Corinthians 3:11)

The entire building, the universal church, has one unique, supreme foundation, and it is already laid. We are not invited to lay it; we accept the fact that it has already been laid. Christ is the only foundation. Speaking of Jesus as the unique foundation, Peter pictured the church built as living stones upon Him:

You also, as living stones, are being built up a spiritual house, a holy priesthood, to offer up spiritual sacrifices acceptable to God through Jesus Christ. Therefore it is also contained in the Scripture, "Behold, I lay in Zion a chief cornerstone, elect, precious, and he who believes on Him will by no means be put to shame."   (1 Peter 2:5–6)

Peter was actually quoting Isaiah 28:16:

Therefore thus says the Lord GOD: "Behold, I lay in Zion a stone for a foundation, a tried stone, a precious cornerstone, a sure foundation."

Peter clearly showed us that this sure foundation is none other than Jesus Christ. In Psalm 62:1–2 and again in verses 6–7, David also established this truth with incontrovertible clarity:

Truly my soul silently waits for God; from Him comes my salvation. He only is my rock and my salvation; He is my defense; I shall not be greatly moved.   (Psalm 62:1–2)

There is salvation in none other than God, and God only is the Rock on which salvation is built. David repeated these words a few verses later:

He only is my rock and my salvation; He is my defense; I shall not be moved. In God is my salvation and my glory; the rock of my strength, and my refuge, is in God.

(verses 6–7)

David very clearly and definitely linked together the two things—the rock (the foundation) and salvation. He plainly stated that each alike is found alone in God. If we build on another rock, we claim there is salvation in another than Jesus Christ. This is against the Scriptures. He *only* is my rock and my salvation. He is the only foundation of the universal church, and no man can lay another!

Note how the universal aspects of the church apply to the picture of the church as the temple, which we studied in Part Two:

Now, therefore, you are no longer strangers and foreigners, but fellow citizens with the saints and members of the household of God, having been built on the foundation of the apostles and prophets, Jesus Christ Himself being the chief cornerstone, in whom the whole building, being fitted together, grows into a holy temple in the Lord.

(Ephesians 2:19–21)

The church is like a building that is being constructed, with each particular believer as a stone in that building. The foundation of the church is Jesus Christ, upon whom believers are built into a holy temple. Thus, the end purpose of the church is to be a habitation or dwelling place for God.

Christ the Head

We can also see much application in the universal church to the body of Christ:

[God] *gave Him to be head over all things to the church.*

(Ephesians 1:22)

This statement is very definite. Christ is not the head over *some* things; He is the head over *all* things. Everything in the entire church is at His disposal and under His control. Nobody else can contest His authority. It is given to Him uniquely.

If we look at the end-time prophecies given in Daniel 7 and Revelation 12–13 of the political systems of the last days, various types of beasts emerge. One interesting feature about them all is that they have many heads. In a certain sense, they are monsters. One thing that will never have many heads is the church of Jesus Christ. It will never become a monster. I venture to say that the decisive spiritual issue that we have yet to confront is who the Head of the church is. As we will see in future chapters, the struggle at the close of human history will revolve around this very issue. The universal church has precisely one Head and that Head is Jesus Christ. It has one foundation and that foundation is Jesus Christ. We can give it neither another head nor another foundation! So the church as a whole is the body, of which Jesus Christ is the Head.

The Church's Headquarters

Along with the fact that the church is God's personal representative under Jesus' headship, Hebrews reveals another important fact about the universal church:

> *But you have come to Mount Zion and to the city of the living God, the heavenly Jerusalem, to an innumerable company of angels, to the general assembly and church of the firstborn who are registered in heaven.*
> (Hebrews 12:22–23)

The church is enrolled or registered in heaven. The condition for being enrolled in heaven is being born again through faith in Jesus. Thus, the church has one head, Jesus, and one headquarters, heaven.

I have seen the tremendous problems and frustrations that come from trying to run the church from some earthly center. I was a missionary in East Africa with a mission that was run from Toronto, Canada. The process of our seeking to act on a situation seemed endless: calling a committee, making a decision, writing to Toronto, waiting for the mission board to meet, and then waiting for them to write back with their decision! By the time this process was concluded, the opportunity had passed. Action was effectively ruled out. The church will never be a match for the devil until we realize we have one headquarters in heaven. Every believer, servant, minister, or missionary has the right of direct access to headquarters. Only a church run directly from headquarters will defeat the enemy.

I was preaching for a short time in the church of a full-gospel preacher. About once a day, he would say to me, "I'll have to go phone headquarters." Every time he phoned headquarters, he came back more frustrated and confused than the time before! This experience caused me to stop and ask myself, *Where is my headquarters?* I remember at that time coming to a very firm decision. My headquarters are in heaven, and that is where I have to go. When I go there, I am not frustrated and confused.

The church of Jesus Christ is one body, and one Spirit controls it.

There is a contrast here between the Judaic church order, with its center in the earthly Jerusalem, and the New Testament church, with its center in the heavenly Jerusalem. Let us look at this contrast.

> *For this Hagar* [the concubine of Abraham through whom Ishmael was born] *is Mount Sinai in Arabia* [the place where the Law was given], *and corresponds to Jerusalem which now is, and is in bondage with her children; but Jerusalem above is free, which is the mother of us all.* (Galatians 4:25–26)

Every true church of Jesus Christ has one mother church: the Jerusalem above, which is free. Its headquarters is not on

Mt. Sinai, where the Law was given. The universal church is headquartered in heaven. Like produces like. A free church produces free churches unbound by legalism, human rules, titles, or traditions. The implications of this are staggering!

Further, we see another key fact in Ephesians 4:4: *"There is one body and one Spirit."* The church of Jesus Christ is one body, and one Spirit controls it. That Spirit is the Holy Spirit. If there were many different spirits in control, the result would be chaos. For example, if I decided to go through a doorway, but there were other spirits in me that refused to accept this decision, I would be incapable of effective action. This is, of course, the condition of a person who is truly demon-possessed. He loses the ability to do what he wants to because there are other spirits at work besides his own spirit. But in the true church of Jesus Christ, there is only one Spirit in control, and the Holy Spirit has one body to operate through—the church.

> *For as we have many members in one body, but all the members do not have the same function, so we, being many, are one body in Christ, and individually members of one another.* (Romans 12:4–5)

> *For as the body is one and has many members, but all the members of that one body, being many, are one body; so also is Christ....But now God has set the members, each one of them, in the body just as He pleased.* (1 Corinthians 12:12, 18)

In these Scriptures, we see both unity and plurality under divine control. There is one body, but in that one body there are many members. Each believer is a member somewhere in that vast body.

The choice of what member I will be and where I will function is not mine, but God's. Later in 1 Corinthians 12, we read, *"And God has appointed these in the church"* (verse 28). To be set as a member in the body corresponds to being set in your place in the church. And Paul pointed out that each member depends on the other. In the universal church, no member is independent of the others.

Representatives of Jesus

Let us now consider the role of the universal church as the personal representative and agent of Jesus. In sending forth His first group of disciples, Jesus said, *"He who receives you receives Me"* (Matthew 10:40). In other words, "You are My representatives. There is no other way that I can come to people except through you. If you go, then I'll go with you. And if they receive you, then they'll receive Me."

At the end of Matthew's gospel, Jesus presented the same thought in another way:

All authority has been given to Me in heaven and on earth. Go therefore, and make disciples of all the nations, baptizing them in the name of the Father and of the Son and of the Holy Spirit, teaching them to observe all things that I have commanded you; and lo, I am with you always, even to the end of the age. (Matthew 28:18–20)

Jesus was saying, "The authority has been given to Me, but to make it effective, *you* have to go!" Until we use the authority that is committed to us through Jesus Christ, the world will not know He has that authority! The only way the world can understand the authority now vested in Jesus is when the church goes out in obedience to His command and exercises and demonstrates that authority. This is the only way that Jesus can effect His will. It is through us.

In John 20:21, we see another of Jesus' breathtaking statements to His disciples: *"Peace to you! As the Father has sent Me, I also send you."* In other words, "I'm sending you in exactly the same way that the Father sent Me." Jesus came as the personal, authorized, visible representative of the Father. He said, *"He who has seen Me has seen the Father"* (John 14:9). If we are sent in the same way, we have an obligation to say to the world, "If you've seen us, you've seen Christ."

Jesus effects His will and authority through the universal church.

Jesus said that the Father gave Him the words to speak. (See John 17:8.) In the same way, the church's obligation is to say to the world, "Jesus gave us the words to speak." Jesus said, "The Father who dwells in Me does the works that I do." (See John 14:10.). What must we say to the world? "It is Christ in us who is doing the works that we do."

This is what is implied in the statement of John 20:21, *"As the Father has sent Me, I also send you."* The universal church is the visible, authorized, personal, unique representative of Jesus Christ. If the church fails to do the job, there is no other means by which it can be done!

Attestations of Membership

There are two official, public attestations of membership in the universal church, two baptisms that signify a person as being accepted as a member of the body. The first is baptism in water, the second is the baptism in the Holy Spirit. Baptism in water is an acknowledgment by a human leader and fellow believers, but the baptism in the Holy Spirit is a supernatural seal placed upon the person by the Head of the body, Jesus Christ, attesting that he is a member of the body.

> *Baptism in water and baptism in the Holy Spirit bring believers into unity.*

Now, each of these baptisms has one supreme purpose, which is to make effective the unity of the body. Let's look in Galatians 3 regarding water baptism and then in 1 Corinthians 12 regarding the baptism in the Spirit.

For you are all sons of God through faith in Christ Jesus. [We are made children of God by the simple, basic fact of faith in Jesus Christ.] *For as many of you as were baptized into Christ have put on Christ. There is neither Jew nor Greek, there is neither slave nor free, there is neither male nor female; for you are all one in Christ Jesus.*
(Galatians 3:26–28)

This is the meaning of water baptism. We lose our separate national, racial, and social identities. We become one in the body. The baptism in the Holy Spirit has the same purpose:

For [in] *one Spirit* [which is the correct translation—not "by" one Spirit] *we were all baptized into one body; whether Jews or Greeks, whether slaves or free; and have all been made to drink into one Spirit.* (1 Corinthians 12:13)

Baptism in water and baptism in the Holy Spirit alike have this supreme purpose—to help us to understand and to make vivid and effective our membership in one body and our relationship to each other. We are no longer to think about each other in terms of race, class, or social background. *"There is neither Greek* [Gentile] *nor Jew, circumcised nor uncircumcised, barbarian, Scythian, slave nor free, but Christ is all and in all"* (Colossians 3:11). In Jesus Christ, we experience a new unity in His body.

This is the universal church.

Chapter 12

The Local Church

e now turn to the church as it functions in any given locality: the local church. For many years, I was a fanatic about membership in the local church, but I did not really know what the local church was! It came as a kind of revelation to me how clear, definite, and simple the local church is. It was not a revelation that came to me by a vision, but was rather a sudden understanding of simple statements made in Scripture, which I had known and preached for years but had never been able to apply properly.

The Authority of the Local Church

I mentioned in the last chapter that the word *church* is used only twice in the Gospels. Each time it is used by Jesus, and each time it occurs in Matthew's gospel. We saw in Matthew 16 that Jesus said, *"On this rock I will build My church"* (verse 18), referring to the universal church. In Matthew 18, He again used the word *church*, but the context makes it clear that He was speaking about a local church or a church in a given locality. He was speaking of the circumstances in which a believer has an obligation to tell his complaint to the church. It stands to reason that you and I will never be able to bring our complaint or problem before the universal church because it is scattered in every continent. Also, some members have already passed out of time into eternity. The first complete gathering of the *total* universal church, as I see it, will take place when the Lord Jesus Christ descends from heaven and we all meet the Lord in the air. (See 1 Thessalonians 4:13–18.) This first actual meeting of the total universal church will be under the direction of none other than Jesus Himself.

In the meanwhile, we find the church functioning in its local capacity. Jesus said,

> *Moreover if your brother sins against you, go and tell him his fault between you and him alone. If he hears you, you have gained your brother. But if he will not hear you, take with you one or two more, that "by the mouth of two or three witnesses every word may be established." And if he refuses to hear them, tell it to the church. But if he refuses even to hear the church, let him be to you like a heathen and a tax collector. Assuredly, I say to you, whatever you bind on earth will be bound in heaven, and whatever you loose on earth will be loosed in heaven. Again I say to you that if two of you agree on earth concerning anything that they ask, it will be done for them by My Father in heaven. For where two or three are gathered together in My name, I am there in the midst of them.*
>
> (Matthew 18:15–20)

Jesus said that the first step in settling a dispute between you and another believer is go to the person alone. (In my experience, few Christians ever follow this procedure.) If you do not get satisfaction when you go to him alone, take one or two more people as witnesses of your discussion. If he still will not listen to you, the only alternative left is to take it to the local church. The dispute must be submitted to the local church, and its decision is final.

Notice the tremendous authority vested in the local church—it is absolutely stunning! People often view the local church as a nice option or helpful resource, but in God's view it is like the Supreme Court of the United States! The local church is the final court of appeal in all vital matters: disputes between believers, matters of doctrine, and matters of moral conduct. In God's view, the local church is of extreme importance. This is why it is essential that we understand the church, that we take our correct place in it, and that we submit ourselves to it.

> *The authority vested in the local church is stunning; it is the final court of appeal in all vital matters.*

The Scripture says that, when the local church comes together and arrives at a decision on a case, anybody who will not listen to the decision and abide by it is to be treated as a heathen (Gentile) and a tax collector—both of whom were generally shunned by the Jewish community in Jesus' day. The idea here is that the person has forfeited his right to be considered and treated as a Christian until he repents and submits himself to that authority. How does he forfeit that right? By refusing to accept the decision and come under the discipline of the local church.

To me, this is terrifying because I know of no local church that is qualified to exercise that measure of authority. Yet, if I were ever put in such a position, I would do everything that

I could think of to avoid resisting and refusing the decision of a local church. We are dealing with things that are very serious and very important!

The local church not only resolves disputes between believers, but also judges matters of doctrine. In the fifteenth chapter of Acts, we find a tremendous discussion among the Jewish believers as to what was to be required of Gentiles who professed faith in Jesus Christ. Paul and Barnabas had won many Gentiles to the Lord and had baptized them, but they had not required them to become adherents of the law of Moses. In Jerusalem, the orthodox Jewish believers in Christ strenuously objected. It was a major dispute whose outcome affects all of us who are Gentile Christians.

Paul and Barnabas went up to Jerusalem to settle this matter with all the apostles and the elders. Their conclusion was put before the whole church at Jerusalem and ratified by the whole church, which must have numbered some thirty thousand believing Jews at that time. A Jewish friend once said to me, "If you've got two Jews, you've got an argument. If you've got three, you've got a revolution!" I marvel at the grace of God that thirty thousand Jews could come to absolute unanimity on this vital point of doctrine: *"Then it pleased the apostles and elders, with the whole church"* (Acts 15:22).

Notice that the leadership at this point did not act independently of the whole church. They had prepared the way, but theirs was not the final decision, nor was theirs the final authority. The narrative continues:

Then it pleased the apostles and elders, with the whole church, to send chosen men of their own company to Antioch with Paul and Barnabas, namely, Judas who was also named Barsabas, and Silas, leading men among the brethren. They wrote this letter by them: The apostles, the elders, and the brethren, To the brethren who are of the Gentiles in Antioch, Syria, and Cilicia: Greetings. Since we have heard that some who went out from us have troubled you with words, unsettling your souls, saying, "You must be circumcised and keep the law"—to whom we gave no such commandment—it seemed good to us, being assembled with one accord, to send chosen men to you with our beloved Barnabas and Paul, men who have risked their lives for the name of our Lord Jesus Christ. We have therefore sent Judas and Silas, who will also report the same things by word of mouth. For it seemed good to the Holy Spirit, and to us, to lay upon you no greater burden than these necessary things.... (Acts 15:22–28)

The final decision was the decision of the Holy Spirit made manifest in the body of Christ. It is to the body of Christ that the mind of Christ is given! In 1 Corinthians 2:16, Paul said, *"We have the mind of Christ."* Never change it and say, *"I* have the mind of Christ." Again, it is the *collective* body that has the mind of Christ through the Holy Spirit. This doctrinal decision of such vital and far-reaching importance was arrived at in total unity by the entire body, the local church. Look once more at the beautiful words of Acts 15:28: *"It seemed good to the Holy Spirit, and to us* [being assembled with one accord], *to lay upon you no greater burden."*

In God's view, the local church is not only the place of harmony and the court of final appeal, but it is also the judge of moral conduct. Let's look at an example of this.

The Local Church

Paul, called to be an apostle of Jesus Christ through the will of God, and Sosthenes our brother, To the church of God which is at Corinth. (1 Corinthians 1:1–2)

Notice that Paul was writing to the entire assembly of believers in Corinth. Now see what he said:

It is actually reported that there is sexual immorality among you, and such sexual immorality as is not even named among the Gentiles; that a man has his father's wife! And you are puffed up, and have not rather mourned, that he who has done this deed might be taken away from among you. For I indeed, as absent in the body but present in spirit, have already judged (as though I were present) him who has so done this deed. In the name of our Lord Jesus Christ, when you are gathered together [the whole church], *along with my spirit, with the power of our Lord Jesus Christ, deliver such a one to Satan for the destruction of the flesh, that his spirit may be saved in the day of the Lord Jesus.* (1 Corinthians 5:1–5)

In this assembly, there was a case of extreme immorality—incest. A man was cohabiting with his father's wife. Paul said that the Gentiles did not even have a name for that kind of thing. He added, "Here you are boasting about your spiritual gifts and your speaking in tongues and prophesying, while there is this awful immorality in your midst that you have not even dealt with. Shame on you! It's your responsibility as a church to deal with this immorality." The whole church bears the responsibility and the authority for moral and ethical standards. These things cannot be passed to a committee or presbytery or some group that meets off in a corner. They should not be hushed up or swept under the rug. The New Testament is a very frank, outspoken book. It calls a spade, a spade.

Paul was saying, "I'm not impressed by your spirituality. You're tolerating immorality, even incest. Deal with it as a church. Come together, and in the authority of my presence and the authority of the Lord Jesus Christ, dismiss this person from your fellowship. He is no longer eligible for fellowship in the body of Christ. Hand him over to Satan—not for the destruction of his soul, but for the destruction of his flesh, that through the judgment of God, in time, he may be spared from the judgment of God in eternity." This was a terrible thing.

> *Today's church must be awakened to its responsibilities and privileges.*

> *For what have I to do with judging those also who are outside? Do you not judge those who are inside? But those who are outside God judges. Therefore "put away from yourselves the evil person."* (1 Corinthians 5:12–13)

Here Paul said that we have nothing to do with judging unbelievers. They are outside our jurisdiction. However, believers are to judge believers. It is the collective responsibility of the church to exercise judgment on the conduct of their fellow believers. Some people know only one Scripture about judgment: *"Judge not, that you be not judged"* (Matthew 7:1). But there are many other Scriptures in the New Testament about judgment. The church must maintain ethical and moral purity by exercising judgment and discipline upon its members.

Notice what Paul said in 1 Corinthians 6, which is exactly in line with what Jesus said in Matthew 18 about the church as the final court of appeal:

Dare any of you, having a matter against another, go to law before the unrighteous, and not before the saints?

(1 Corinthians 6:1)

Paul said that it is wrong for a *believer* to go to court against a *fellow believer*. Believers have no right whatever to settle this type of dispute in a secular court of law. The question must be settled in the church. (It also does not say that it is wrong for a believer to go to court against an unbeliever.) Paul continued,

Do you not know that the saints [believers] *will judge the world? And if the world will be judged by you, are you unworthy to judge the smallest matters?* (verse 2)

The church today is asleep, totally unaware of its responsibilities, its privileges, and its authority. It must be awakened to them.

Awake, awake! Put on your strength, O Zion; Put on your beautiful garments, O Jerusalem, the holy city! For the uncircumcised and the unclean shall no longer come to you. Shake yourself from the dust, arise; sit down, O Jerusalem! Loose yourself from the bonds of your neck, O captive daughter of Zion! (Isaiah 52:1–2)

It is time that the church of Jesus Christ arose and shook itself! It needs to be shaken! It is better to shake yourself than to let God shake you because, when God shakes you, you cannot stop at will. The whole church of Jesus Christ needs a bulldozer. It needs an earthquake. It needs a divine revolution, and I want to tell you, it is on the way! It is time to have God's view of the church, not man's view. I loved the young people of the Jesus Movement in the 1960s and 1970s whose motto was, "Tell it like it is!" Oh, how I want to see it, and tell it, like it is!

The Nucleus of the Local Church

The unfolding and growth of a local church takes place in phases, and the first phase is the basic cell. Just as a human body physiologically grows out of a cell, so the body of Christ in a particular locality grows out of a cell. I suggest that, in order to form a picture of the nucleus or initial cell of a local church, we look again at Matthew 18:20.

> *For where two or three are gathered together in My name, I am there in the midst of them.* (Matthew 18:20)

Actually, I prefer the more literal translation: "Where two or three *have been led together* into My name, there am I in the midst of them." The phrase "have been led together" immediately poses a very important practical question: By whom are we led? The answer is clear. You can find it in Romans 8:14: *"For as many as are* [regularly] *led by the Spirit of God, these are sons* [the children] *of God."*

In order to live as a child of God, I must be led regularly by the Spirit of God in all that I do. This is what identifies the child of God in his daily living. So, when the Scripture speaks about children of God being led together, it is clear that the One who leads them together is the Holy Spirit. In everything that we consider in connection with the local church, let's remember that the Holy Spirit is the directive force. Jesus is the Head over the church, but He exercises His authority within the church by means of the Holy Spirit. We must confess that Jesus Christ is Lord, but in 2 Corinthians 3:17 it says, *"Now the Lord is the Spirit [the Holy Spirit]; and where the Spirit of the Lord is [the Holy Spirit], there is liberty."* The lordship of Jesus Christ over the church is effective only insofar as we allow the Holy Spirit to be Lord in the church.

Therefore, when we come to the forming of the nucleus of the local church, it is the Holy Spirit who must bring the people together. If not, then they are not living as Christians. This is the basic requirement: two or three who have been led together into Jesus' name, not in Jesus' name. The phrase "into My name" suggests a focal point around which the people gather. What is it? The name of Jesus. The Holy Spirit will never bring believers together on any other basis. In other words, He will never bring people together on the basis of a doctrine or church membership. There is only one authorized focal point for the true local church, and that is the name of Jesus Christ.

> *Jesus Christ is the center and the meeting place of every true local church.*

When we are led together and gathered together into the name of Jesus Christ, we are in fact meeting around the invisible person of Jesus Christ! He is the center and the meeting place of every true local church. It gathers around Him—not around a human leader or doctrine, not around an experience, but around a Person.

There is a vivid parallel to this truth in Deuteronomy. Before Israel was allowed to enter the Promised Land, God made it clear that He would accept their worship and their sacrifice in only one place. He would both choose that place and put His name in that place. God said,

However, you may slaughter and eat meat within all your gates, whatever your heart desires, according to the blessing of the LORD your God which He has given you; the unclean and the clean may eat of it, of the gazelle and the deer alike. Only you shall not eat the blood; you shall pour it on the earth like water. You may not eat within your gates the tithe of your grain or your new wine or your oil, of the firstborn of your herd or your flock, or any of your offerings which you vow, of your freewill offerings, or of the heave offering of your hand. But you must eat them before the LORD your God in the place which the LORD your God chooses, you and your son and your daughter, your male servant and your female servant, and the Levite who is within your gates; and you shall rejoice before the LORD your God in all to which you put your hands. (Deuteronomy 12:15–18)

There was only one place that God chose and allowed for meeting with Him. Anything that was offered in worship and sacrifice to God could be eaten only in that place. We see further details in the sixteenth chapter. You may recall that it was assumed that every male Jew would go up to Jerusalem to the temple every year for the Passover. There were no exceptions.

Therefore you shall sacrifice the Passover to the LORD your God, from the flock and the herd, in the place where the LORD chooses to put His name. (Deuteronomy 16:2)

You may not sacrifice the Passover within any of your gates which the LORD your God gives you; but at the place where the LORD your God chooses to make His name abide, there you shall sacrifice the Passover at twilight....You shall rejoice before the LORD your God, you and your son and your daughter, your male servant and your female servant, the Levite who is within your gates, the stranger and the fatherless and the widow who are among you, at the place where the LORD your God chooses to make His name abide.
(Deuteronomy 16:5–6, 11)

The historical unfolding of God's purposes shows clearly that the place He chose was Jerusalem and the building was the temple built by Solomon. God said He would place His name there. It was the only authorized place that any Israelite, any person in covenant relationship with God under the old covenant, was entitled to offer his worship and his sacrifices.

That temple was destroyed, and today a Moslem mosque sits on or near the original temple site. This is why the Jews are so concerned about this particular area of Jerusalem. They can never reestablish their form of worship until they have that place. There is no other place where they are entitled to offer their sacrifices, according to the old covenant.

For believers in Jesus Christ, the Old Testament temple has been replaced by the body of Jesus Christ. Jesus made this clear in John's gospel, where He contrasted the temple of His day, built on that same sacred site, with His own person.

So the Jews answered and said to Him, "What sign do You show to us, since You do these things?" Jesus answered and said to them, "Destroy this temple, and in three days I will raise it up." Then the Jews said, "It has taken forty-six years to build this temple [the temple of Herod], and will You raise it up in three days?" But He was speaking of the temple of His body. (John 2:18–21)

Jesus spoke of the transition from the temple built on the sacred site to the temple that is His body. The authorized meeting place now is the name of Jesus Christ. I believe God is just as definite and specific about this requirement in the new covenant as He was about the corresponding requirement in the old covenant. We have no authority to meet on any other basis than as we are led together by the Holy Spirit into the name of Jesus. I believe that such gatherings are the basic cell groups or fellowship groups out of which the local church is built.

The Harmony of the Local Church

In Matthew 18, Jesus spoke about two agreeing or harmonizing in prayer:

Assuredly, I say to you, whatever you [who harmonize and agree and have been brought together by the Holy Spirit into My name] *bind on earth will be bound in heaven, and whatever you loose on earth will be loosed in heaven.* (verse 18)

This authority is not committed to any nondescript group of believers who happen to drop in for an evening of fellowship. It is two or three (or more) growing out of those who have been led together by the Spirit of God, whose focal point of meeting is the name and the person of the Lord Jesus Christ. These have been brought into a relationship of spiritual harmony. Where two or three can harmonize and

144

are of one accord, *whatever* they decree or pray, bind or loose, is as effective and authoritative as if almighty God Himself had done it. This is the great secret of being led together by the Holy Spirit into a relationship of harmony.

Therefore, one of the key words to understanding Christianity is the word *harmony*. The gospel is intended to produce harmony in the home, in the larger company of believers, in the community, and, indeed, wherever it is accepted. Wherever there is no harmony, the gospel really has not done its work.

The basic evidence that the gospel is at work is harmony between God and man and harmony between one believer and another. In these little cells of harmony, there is limitless divine authority and power. Out of these cells will unfold the whole body.

> *Wherever there is no harmony, the gospel really has not done its work.*

It is extremely important to understand that, in order to have a healthy body, you must have healthy cells. So it is with home cell groups in a church. If the small, individual groups and the personal relationships within those groups are not right, we can never have a healthy local church or right relationships within the larger body.

This is one of the great basic problems of modern Christianity: Often, we are not right in the small, daily personal relationships. For example, if husband and wife—as believers in Jesus Christ and baptized in the Holy Spirit—cannot live in peace, what hope is there for unity in a larger gathering? For many years, we have been busy trying to build large congregations without observing that they cannot be healthy until the individual, intimate, personal relationships are healthy.

Again, the basic requirement in this smallest group can be summed up in the word *harmony*—inward personal harmony. Most of us are not even in harmony with ourselves, let alone with anybody else. We need to ask ourselves, "Am I in harmony with my wife, my family, and my closest relatives, or is there discord and frustration?" Compare this concept of relational harmony with that of musical harmony: Musicians only have to be a little bit off-key to spoil the whole sound!

> *Again I say to you that if two of you agree on earth concerning anything that they ask, it will be done for them by My Father in heaven.* (Matthew 18:19)

One day, God led me to examine the root of the Greek word used for *"agree"* in this verse. It is *sumphonos,* the same word from which we get the word *symphony.* The term means to be in harmony or in one accord. It is not mere intellectual agreement; it is spiritual. Wherever two people come together in spiritual harmony, anything they ask will happen. It is not easy to be and to live in spiritual harmony, but it certainly is powerful when we achieve it!

The world appreciates harmony. It is the basic, exportable product of the gospel, and it starts with two or three who have been led together into the name of Jesus. I am absolutely convinced that there is no permanent solution for the problems of the church unless it solves the problems in our homes; this is absolutely scriptural.

The Local Church

The Local Church Defined

We fail to appreciate that Jesus actually planted the gospel in homes in His earthly ministry. He would normally go to the synagogue, the recognized institutional meeting place that corresponds to the "church." In the synagogue, He would give people as much as they would accept. Sometimes, they threw Him out; sometimes, they listened to the end. Where did He go from there? He went into a house. For instance, in Capernaum, He went to the house of Peter's mother-in-law. This is where He went with the people who were willing to go deeper with Him. We read in Matthew 10 that, when He sent out His first twelve disciples, He said, *"Whatever city or town you enter, inquire who in it is worthy, and stay there till you go out"* (verse 11). Where was the gospel to be planted? Not in the synagogue, but in some worthy home in each city. The small group, such as the family, is really the basic nucleus out of which the local church is to be built up.

One City, One Church

I now enter a territory that I acknowledge is very idealistic. Nevertheless, I suggest to you that it contains God's viewpoint of the local church in a city. Let me offer you my admittedly radical definition of the complete local church. If you accept this definition, it involves a revolution because it is not compatible with present-day Christian practice, as a whole. Simply stated, it is this: *The local church is that part of the universal church resident in any given locality.* There is no further qualification required. You never have to "join" the local church because it is not your decision to make. If you are in the universal church, then automatically, without further qualification, you are also a member of the local church in the city where you live. Again, you do not have an option.

In regard to the universal church, the only option you have is your personal relationship to Jesus Christ, and if you are in a relationship with Jesus Christ, then you are a member of the universal church. The matter is settled.

We have looked at two instances of the word *church* in the Gospels, both of which are found in Matthew. In this light, let's look at some interesting statistics about the use of the word *ecclesia*, or church, in the entire New Testament. Here are the different ways in which the word *church* is used, in both singular and plural forms:

Church (singular) in a city	35 times
Church (singular) in a house	4 times
Churches (plural) in a province	36 times
Church universal	20 times
Church local, but not exactly defined	16 times
Churches (plural) in a city	0 times
Church (singular) in a province	0 times
Old Testament church in the wilderness	1 time
Assembly (of the city of Ephesus)	3 times
TOTAL:	115 times

What is significant is the use of the singular and the plural. The New Testament never speaks at any time in nearly forty occurrences of church*es* (plural) in a city. In one small locality, there is never more than one church. On the other hand, the New Testament never speaks of a singular church in a province. A church can never grow to a kind of vast organization that embraces people living in many different areas.

In other words, there are only two defining areas of a local church: One is a house and the other is a city. The important thing is that, whatever we view as one unit of the local church within an area, there is only one church. There never can be two churches overlapping, much less competing, in the same area. This is the vital conclusion. It is totally unscriptural to speak of two churches overlapping or occupying the same area. It is completely ruled out by the usage of the New Testament, without one single exception. The present pattern in a city is that there are many local churches, each with one leader. However, God's original order is different—one local church in a city with many leaders. This is the practical and revolutionary conclusion.

Man's View versus God's View

Man looks over the church in a city and sees the Baptists, the Catholics, the Presbyterians, and the Pentecostals. He sees all the many churches, each with their single leaders. I submit to you that God does not view the scene in this way at all. He looks down and does not see the different denominations and nondenominational factions. He sees only His people in a city. Actually, He views it as different flocks (or congregations) comprising *the* church in a city.

Thus, we promote unity in ways that God does not accept. We try to unify all the Baptists or all the Presbyterians or all the Methodists in a city or a region. God does not acknowledge that effort, fine as it is, as His best. His church in a city is comprised of men and women from all these denominations, and no one denomination is the complete church, if you can accept that.

As an example, let's consider the city of Charlotte, North Carolina. Looked at from a human point of view, there are over thirty Presbyterian churches, numerous Baptist,

Catholic, and Episcopal churches, plus many others. Yet, as far as God is concerned, looking down at the city from heaven, He sees one church. He sees *the church* in Charlotte, not the Baptists, Episcopalians, Presbyterians, and Catholics. The only qualification to join the church is a specific relationship to Jesus Christ. Thus, every person within the area who is in relationship with Jesus Christ is automatically a member of the church in Charlotte. You are not offered the choice; it is not your decision. The only decision you have to make is your relationship to Jesus Christ.

A Biblical Pattern

Let me now offer an elementary, idealistic pattern. Obviously, only the Holy Spirit can put together the specific application in a region, consistent with the needs and culture of that area.

Imagine a city divided up into four main subareas, with each subarea subdivided into four smaller areas. Altogether, you have sixteen subareas.

Now, the Spirit of God begins to move, and people are born again all over the place. Let's say there is a real revival in the northwest section, which spreads to the northeast section. This goes on until the whole city has become influenced by this move of God. So we have groups of twos and threes and fours and fives, and then big house groups growing up all around the area.

Out of these new believers, who are initially just disciples, the Holy Spirit will begin to bring forth natural local leadership. It never takes long. In any group, there will always be some who will begin to display a greater sense of responsibility, who will mature more rapidly, and who will emerge as leaders. For example, if Sister Jane has a terrible fever in the middle of the night, she phones Brother Bob almost automatically, indicating that she is really treating him as an elder. Soon, in every subsection of that city, two local leaders have emerged. They are operating within their groups in each case, but they have the capacity for leadership.

Now, let's suppose that these local groups all meet for prayer on the same night, say Tuesday night. People cannot hop from group to group; they must make a commitment. They become knitted together in fellowship and harmony to do business with almighty God. The prayer groups are now meeting all over the city on Tuesday night, and leadership has emerged. But the real key to making this work is fellowship among the local leaders. Without this fellowship, there cannot really be any effective fellowship among the local believers. When the local leaders come into regular fellowship with one another, then the barrier to the fellowship of the believers is taken away. It all depends on the local leaders coming into fellowship.

In our picture of the four main sections of the city, the local leaders now say, "We'll meet on Monday night to have a leaders' meeting. We'll discuss our problems, level with one another, and be open. It will not be just a talking session, but we'll really come to grips with our own personal problems and the problems of our flocks. We'll share one another's needs in prayer, exchange revelations, and check everything we're doing with the opinion of our fellow leaders."

Now, in every one of the four sections of that city, you have eight men meeting regularly every week on a Monday night as a fellowship of leaders. You would have eight leaders meeting every Monday, then going back every Tuesday ready to meet the spiritual needs of their own groups. Again, they exchange their problems, their needs, their revelations, and their ideas on doctrine. No man acts on his own. It is the collective mind of the group that is the final arbiter of decisions and doctrines: *"We have the mind of Christ"* (1 Corinthians 2:16, emphasis added).

Now we can go just one step further. On the first Monday of every month, these four groups of local leaders meet in one big leaders' group. Now you have thirty-two leaders meeting. Every other Monday in the month, they meet eight at a time. Every Tuesday, they are leading their own groups, but there is no division whatever in the body of Christ. They are all in fellowship, they all acknowledge one another, and there is no barrier between this group meeting and having fellowship with that group. (Today, members of one church are almost forbidden to fellowship with members of another church. God has not given any man the authority to make that kind of decree. I believe it is bringing division to the body of Christ.)

> *Local churches that work together in Christ will impact their city for God.*

This group of thirty-two is now in a position to act collectively on behalf of the whole city. If the city needs an evangelistic impact, they can corporately invite an evangelist. If the city needs a teaching seminar, they can invite teachers to hold a seminar. Jesus said both *"I am the good shepherd"* (John 10:11) and *"I am the door of the sheep"* (John 10:7). In a very vital sense, the shepherds are the door to the congregation. When the church is functioning properly, mobile teaching ministries such as mine will not come to an area unless they come through the door of the shepherd leaders. I love to enter by the door! But there are many "wolves in sheep's clothing" (see verse 12) who are actually thieves and robbers, and who are creating endless problems in many cities. The only solution is for the collective leadership of the city to close the door to these ministries. The thirty-two respected men can get together and say, "Now don't go to those meetings. That man is preaching false doctrine, and he's living with another man's wife, so it cannot be right." Then there would be real authority.

The wolves will continue to come in and spoil the flock until the leaders get together. In several cities in America, and in other nations, this exact model of brotherhood and corporate leadership is emerging.

I was in a gathering once in the city of Seattle with about thirty-five other mobile ministries. We were invited by the charismatic presbytery of the city. However, it was very expensive to invite all these ministries to Seattle, so meetings were held each night around the city to help offset the cost of the leadership conference. According to the testimony of local ministers, those meetings, and the corporate gathering of these mobile ministries, made a greater impact on the city of Seattle than any evangelistic campaign ever held in that city.

As I was meditating on what had happened at this conference, the Lord asked me this question: "Now tell me this: Whom did I have more trouble with—the city of Nineveh or the prophet Jonah?" And I said, "Lord, when You got Jonah straightened out, You had no problems with Nineveh." And He said, "It's exactly the same today. If I can get the leadership straightened out, I'll have no problems with the cities."

This, I believe, is the divine pattern. The local church begins as a place of harmony. It becomes the final court of appeal. God's order is the unity of the church (a single church) and a plurality of leadership in it. Corporate city leadership is established that unites and protects the church. Yet man has turned this order upside down and introduced a plurality of churches with singular leadership. I stand as a witness that we are being faced with a choice and a decision: Will the church adopt God's view or man's view of its life and structure? I see evidence that some brave souls in countless cities are taking up the challenge. Will you?

The book of Joel pictures latter-day restoration, and judgment on those who reject restoration. Let's look at its picture of judgment:

Multitudes, multitudes in the valley of decision! For the day of the LORD is near in the valley of decision. (Joel 3:14)

The valley of decision is the place God brings people that they never can get out of until they have made a decision. It is the place where you either have to say yes or no—there is no third answer. That is where the church is coming on this matter. The church has to decide if it wants to follow its own ways and practices or if it wishes to submit to the clearly defined and stated pattern of God in Scripture. We cannot have it both ways. I am a witness that the time has come to make a choice. I feel a certain sense of divine sanction on that statement. You are confronted with a decision. The time of going to church to sit in a pew and go through sweet religious exercises is closing. Now is the time for action and reality.

The Local Church

The Stability and Growth of the Local Church

How does the local church stay on track in its nature and purpose? To answer this question, we will look at a passage in Colossians:

Let no one cheat you of your reward, taking delight in false humility and worship of angels, intruding into those things which he has not seen, vainly puffed up by his fleshly mind.... (Colossians 2:18)

Hold On to a Relationship with Christ

The above Scripture speaks of getting off-center from one's faith by paying attention to inconsequential "revelations," such as special forms of humility (e.g., neglecting the body or wearing shabby clothes). This type of humility is an expression of the will, not the spirit. Nor should we engage in the worship of angels.

The more reliable translations use wording similar to "the things that he has seen," which speaks of someone passing off a special vision as being from the Lord. Do not be cheated by people with their "super revelations," introducing something "new" that is actually unimportant and will draw you away from the person of Jesus Christ. The Scripture says that such a person is "vainly puffed up by his fleshly mind." This type of person appears to be super-spiritual but is in fact very carnal. He can succeed in getting you sidetracked, however, only if you are not holding on to the Head.

If you lose your vital personal relationship with the Head, you will be cheated and deceived. The real insurance against being led astray is to maintain your direct relationship with Jesus Christ. As long as you do that, people will not be able to cheat or deceive you. The people who go into error and get sidetracked are those who have failed to maintain their primary relationship with Jesus, which is the condition of being in the church!

Continuing in Colossians 2, we read,

> *...and not holding fast to the Head, from whom all the body, nourished and knit together by joints and ligaments* [*"bands"* KJV], *grows with the increase that is from God.*
> (verse 19)

Notice that the growth *of* the body comes *from* the body. The same concept is stated in Ephesians 4:16: *"The whole body...causes growth of the body for the edifying* [building up] *of itself in love."* It is the body that makes itself grow, not some super-preacher. When all the members are functioning correctly, the body grows naturally. Many people look to a preacher or a gimmick—some method or new revelation—to make the body grow. But the Word clearly teaches that the body increases with its own natural growth when it is functioning right.

Joints and Ligaments

In Colossians 2:19, notice that the body receives two things: (1) it is *nourished* from right relationship with the Head, and (2) it is *knit together* in unity and strength by the joints and ligaments. So two things hold this body together: joints and ligaments. Now, what is meant by these terms? This is basic anatomy and reflects the state of knowledge at the time of the early church. I suggest to you that the joints are personal relationships, first to Christ, and second to our fellow believers. Ligaments are universal attitudes that we have toward other believers, even if we are not in a direct personal relationship with them.

The Local Church

Consider how absolutely vital the joints are in the body. When I was a medical orderly in the British army, the sergeant drilled a few things into my head about anatomy. I learned that, in your arm, you have three main bones, one from the shoulder to the elbow and two others from the elbow to the wrist. Now, I could have all three of these bones in perfect health and still have a useless arm. Why? Unless the elbow is functioning, the bones can't function correctly, either. This scenario is true time and again in the church. Each individual member may be perfectly whole and healthy, but the body isn't able to function because the relationship between those members is wrong. Many members in the church are not functioning because the joint that relates them to the member next to them is out of order. When one member is wrongly related to the next member, it can paralyze the whole body.

> *When one member is wrongly related to the next member, it can paralyze the whole body.*

Recall the order from Colossians 2:18–19: First of all, we hold fast to the Head, who is Christ. Second, we must be "jointed," or correctly related, to our fellow believers, always with special attention to those who are closest to us. It is so easy to love people at a distance, but when we really get to know them, it is not nearly as easy!

In our congregation in London, for example, there was a woman who would pray like an angel for the poor Africans. But one day, an African man joined our prayer meeting and knelt next to this woman. Believe me, she did not enjoy it!

She loved black Africans from a distance, but not next door. There are many Christians who have similar problems in real relationships. It is the person next to me that I have to be rightly related to first and foremost.

The Ligaments

Let's look at the other connection mentioned, the ligaments. The Scripture tells us that there are two bonds that hold together the body of Christ. We read in Colossians 3:14,

> *But above all these things put on love, which is the bond of perfection.*

The word for *"bond"* here is the same one that is translated as *"ligaments"* in Colossians 2:19. Love is the bond that holds the complete, mature body together in unity. The other bond is mentioned in Ephesians. (You will find that much in Ephesians 4 is closely parallel to Colossians 2 and 3).

> *Bearing with one another in love, endeavoring to keep the unity of the Spirit in the bond of peace.*
> (Ephesians 4:2–3)

The two great bonds, the overall attitudes, that keep the body united and functioning are love and peace. How many Protestants really feel love and peace toward Roman Catholics? There are many more today who do so than there used to be, but I can remember standing at Speakers Corner in London, years ago, and listening to the open-air preachers. There were the Catholics tearing the Protestants down and the Protestants tearing the Catholics down. They did not have time to condemn anybody or anything else. Their attitudes reflected a total lack of love and peace.

I should point out here that all these joints and bonds are invisible; you cannot see them with the eye. This is a real problem for many Christians. There is a parallel in the Old Testament where Israel was constantly tempted to represent or replace the invisible God by some kind of visible image. God strictly forbade idolatry, yet there is something in carnal man that wants to make things visible. He wants to have something that he can put his finger on and say, "This is my god. This is where it stands, and this is the label on it."

This tendency did not end with the Old Testament. In the New Testament era, God brought into being (through Jesus Christ and the Holy Spirit) a body that is held together by invisible bonds and joints. But all through the centuries, Christians have not been able to stop short at the invisible and say, "That's it." They have always sought to replace the invisible relationships and the invisible spiritual structure with some kind of human, visible, labeled organization and structure. This is very obvious in church history.

> *The two great bonds that keep the body of Christ united are love and peace.*

Years ago, while I was living in London, I had some contact with a particular denomination. To be a part of that group, you had to enroll in a certain organization, sign your name, make certain pledges, and then take a certain position that was designated by a military rank and uniform. You might think, "That's wonderful! That makes them one." But you could not be more wrong. Within that organization—and this is no more true of that particular group than any other—there were all sorts of strife, jealousy, resentment, and refusals to acknowledge the ministry or the authority of someone else. When one member or another of that group came to me for deliverance, I often discovered that the root problem was an absolute hatred of other leaders in the organization. All the outward structure of signing the pledge, putting on the uniform, and going to the appointed place at the appointed time did not produce the real thing—inward unity, love, and right relationship. The true picture of the local church had become lost in all the activity.

People get so wrapped up in the external that they fail to see that the internal is missing. It is common to have people in the same church all believing the right doctrine, paying their tithes, and attending the same building, but politely hating one another. You might say, "How could that be? How could they as Christians actually hate one another?" The answer is that they have been deceived by their idols. The visible structure that has replaced the invisible one deludes them. For that matter, how could people under the old covenant, who had seen all the glorious demonstrations of God's power, carve things out of tree trunks and set them up in the corners of their houses as their gods? But they did.

I once read about a man whose village was invaded during the Vietnam War. An American soldier saw him carry a piece of wood out of the hut. He left behind his furniture, his clothing, even some members of his family, but the one thing he had to protect was this piece of wood. So the soldier asked, "What's that?" He said, "It's my god; I'm saving it." Isn't that tragic? Imagine having a god that needs *you* to save *it!* Yet millions of people all over the world think like that. One guarantee with God is that He does not need defending or saving, and one thing about the true church is that it does not need defending. It just needs to walk in the truth!

How have people become so deceived? They have not yet realized that what makes Christians one—unified members of the same body—is primarily invisible. Am I rightly related to Jesus Christ? Am I rightly related to my fellow believers? Am I rightly related to my wife, children, and parents? This is where it begins.

Again, I emphasize this truth because of years of experience in ministering to people: The most common reason why people need deliverance is resentment, or in many cases, hatred, either for a wife, husband, or parents. People who consider themselves good Christians may actually be filled with venomous resentment. They become this deceived by replacing the invisible with the visible. They cling to something they can see instead of the eternal. They are like that poor man in Southeast Asia carrying out his god in his arms, not realizing that the things that were of *real* value were being left behind.

The Central Purpose of the Local Church

In closing this chapter, let's consider the central purpose of the local church. It might surprise you to know that the supreme objective of the local church is *fellowship*. Most people would not even think of this. Yet I have come to see that the New Testament makes it primary. Fellowship is the sole universal purpose of the local church—not to preach the gospel, build churches or hospitals, or send out missionaries. All those are secondary. They are the *results* of true fellowship. If we do not have the fellowship, we will never have the results God intended.

Called into Fellowship

God is faithful, by whom you were called into the fellowship of His Son, Jesus Christ our Lord. (1 Corinthians 1:9)

You will recall that the church is a group of people who are called out. This is the "negative" aspect of our being called: We are called out of the world. What, then, are we called *into*? Once the church is "led together" into the name of Jesus, what do they do? The answer is that they share Jesus Christ together. Paul put it in this way: *"You were called into the fellowship of* [God's] *Son, Jesus Christ our Lord"—fellowship* being the end purpose.

The word for *"fellowship"* in Greek is another distinctive New Testament word like *ecclesia*. It, also, is taken from secular language but given a special application. The word comes from a root word that means "to have things in common" or "to share things together." It could be translated, "The sharing together of Christ." This is the supreme purpose and objective of the local church.

Let's look at a similar statement made by the apostle John:

That which was from the beginning, which we have heard, which we have seen with our eyes, which we have looked upon, and our hands have handled, concerning the Word of life; the life was manifested, and we have seen, and bear witness, and declare to you that eternal life which was with the Father and was manifested to us; that which we have seen and heard we declare to you, that you also may have fellowship with us; and truly our fellowship is with the Father and with His Son Jesus Christ. (1 John 1:1–3)

This Scripture tells us why we were given the New Testament record of Jesus. John, one of the gospel writers and a close witness of Jesus' life and ministry, said, "We're telling you what we saw and what we heard. We didn't just get it from a distance; we didn't just have it in theory. We touched Him. We watched Him in action—the Lord Jesus Christ, the Word of Life. He was made manifest; He was made flesh and dwelt among us. We saw, heard, and observed everything, and we declare it unto you firsthand."

The primary objective of the local church is fellowship, which, in turn, produces true outward ministry.

And why was this firsthand account written? Why, indeed, was the New Testament record given? *"That which we have seen and heard declare we to you, that you also may have fellowship with us"* (verse 3). It was given to bring us into the fellowship of the apostles! What is that fellowship? The second half of that verse says, *"And truly our fellowship is with the Father, and with His Son Jesus Christ."*

The purpose of the writing of the New Testament was to bring those who hear and believe the Word into the fellowship of the Godhead: a fellowship between the Father, the Son, and all who believe, through the Spirit!

Let us look at two more related Scriptures:

Having many things to write to you, I did not wish to do so with paper and ink; but I hope to come to you and speak face to face, that our joy may be full. (2 John 12)

And these things we write to you that your joy may be full. (1 John 1:4)

What brings fullness of joy more than face-to-face fellowship? Fellowship is meeting one another, meeting God, and meeting Jesus Christ. This is the purpose for which God has called us out of the world and into the church.

Let's look at one final verse as a principle:

That which is born of the flesh is flesh, and that which is born of the Spirit is spirit. (John 3:6)

Flesh gives birth to flesh, and Spirit gives birth to Spirit. Always! I believe the secret is this: *Only in the place of fellowship does spiritual birth take place.* This is why fellowship is primary. Until we come together into that place of fellowship around Jesus Christ in the Spirit, anything we do is flesh. Out of that fellowship are born the spiritual purposes of God: the witnessing, the preaching, the hospital visitations, and the missionaries. They are products of fellowship; they are born by the Spirit out of fellowship.

Where we do not have true fellowship, all we have are programs and activities that are flesh begotten by flesh. Anything born of the flesh can never be anything but flesh! Again, spiritual birth takes place only in the place of fellowship. We see this truth in the life of the early church in Acts.

When the Day of Pentecost had fully come, they were all with one accord in one place. (Acts 2:1)

The church as we know it came into being (or was birthed) in the place of fellowship: *"They were all with one accord in one place."* We also note that there were five prophets and teachers in the church of Antioch, having fellowship together, ministering to the Lord, and fasting.

Now in the church that was at Antioch there were certain prophets and teachers: Barnabas, Simeon who was called Niger, Lucius of Cyrene, Manaen who had been brought up with Herod the tetrarch, and Saul. As they ministered to the Lord and fasted, the Holy Spirit said, "Now separate to Me Barnabas and Saul for the work to which I have called them." (Acts 13:1–2)

The first official missionary journey described in Scripture was birthed in the fellowship of those who were waiting and ministering to the Lord in Antioch. We will come back to this Scripture later as we explore different aspects of the ministry of the church.

The key to remember now is this: No fellowship, no spiritual birth. You can be as active as you please with witnessing, preaching, and missionary endeavors, but there is no Spirit without fellowship. Fellowship is the place of spiritual birth. As we fellowship around the person of Jesus Christ, the true purposes of God are begotten by the Holy Spirit.

Chapter 13

Apostolic Teams and Elders: The Two Legs of the Body

arly in this book, I mentioned the saying, "We can't see the forest for the trees!" In other words, you can lose the vision of the whole in your preoccupation with its individual parts. I have sometimes felt that way in my many years of studying the church. At one point, I determined to back out of the forest and study the forest as a forest and not as a group of trees. I set my mind to really look at the church as a whole. In this endeavor, I discovered a truth about the church that has revolutionized both my approach to it and my understanding of it.

Let me begin with these words of Jesus:

Whoever comes to Me, and hears My sayings and does them, I will show you whom he is like: He is like a man building a house, who dug deep and laid the foundation on the rock. And when the flood arose, the stream beat vehemently against that house, and could not shake it, for it was founded on the rock. (Luke 6:47–48)

The only secure house is one built on a solid foundation. For those of us familiar with the land of Israel, this image is very vivid. The house I had constructed in Jerusalem was actually built on top of another house that had been constructed over one hundred years earlier. Because the first house was founded on bedrock, I was able to add three additional stories above the two existing ones.

Therefore, in Luke 6, Jesus was talking about something that was very familiar to His hearers: You must get down to the bedrock when you build. It is the same with us. If we are going to build the real church, we will have to work very hard to get down to the biblical bedrock. We must remove layers of assumptions, traditions, and erroneous teaching to lay a pure foundation. That is what I hope this book will help to accomplish.

Two Main Leadership Elements

I would like to suggest that there are two basic forms of leadership in the church. The first is mobile—apostolic teams. The second is local—presbyteries, or groups of elders, acting in plurality. I like the word *presbyteries,* which is simply a transliteration of the Greek word *presbuteros,* which means an elder. Elders are not well known in the West, but they are the backbone of cultures in the Middle East and Africa. Likewise, the government of elders was nothing new in the New Testament. It was familiar to God's people from many centuries back. As a matter of fact, I think elders really are the permanent form of government that starts in Genesis and goes through to Revelation.

The phrase *apostolic team* is only recently being used in the church. Yet apostolic teams are as foundational in the New Testament as presbyteries are. In fact, apostolic teams emerged first and presbyteries second. It is interesting that the New Testament gives more attention to the work of apostolic teams than to that of presbyteries. In all four Gospels, the central focus is an apostolic team led by Jesus, but the word *church* occurs only twice. (See Matthew 16:18; 18:17.) The book of Acts is concerned primarily with the ministries of Peter, Philip, and Paul, who were either evangelists or members of apostolic teams. Very little is said in the book of Acts about what elders do. There is a good deal said about elders in the New Testament epistles, but there is still a far stronger emphasis on apostolic teams.

It is in the restoration of these two units of leadership—one mobile and one residential—that the church will find both real power and real order. However, these main leadership elements of the church are very little understood. Therefore, we begin this section of the structure of the church with a look at the forest—the big picture. If we get the big picture right, we will get the details right, as well.

Plural

The first feature of both apostolic teams and presbyteries is that each is generally *plural*. You would have to search a long way through the New Testament to find an apostle functioning on his own. Apostles usually moved in teams, and much larger teams than we are prepared to adjust to. I believe presbyteries invariably are plural. In fact, the very word *presbytery* demands the plural, for it is a collective noun.

Sovereign

The second feature is that each is *sovereign* in its own sphere, but not independent. I hope you can understand that you can be sovereign but not independent. Actually, every member of the body of Christ is sovereign. He is responsible for his own life, and there are areas in which no one else can dictate to him. At the same time, none of us is independent from the other members of the body.

Interdependent

This leads us to the third statement: Each is *interdependent*. As an example, let us note, first of all, that apostles appoint elders. Acts 14:14 says, *"But when the apostles Barnabas and Paul heard this..."* Barnabas and Paul were apostles, and verse 23 says this about these same men:

> *So when they had appointed elders in every church, and prayed with fasting, they commended them to the Lord in whom they had believed.*

So, it was apostles who appointed elders. There is no record in the New Testament of elders being appointed by anybody but apostles. Paul wrote to Titus,

> *For this reason I left you in Crete, that you should set in order the things that are lacking, and appoint elders in every city as I commanded you.* (Titus 1:5)

Until elders are appointed, something is lacking. I do not believe a church is a church without elders. In fact, the appointment of elders is the decisive transition from mere disciples to a church, as we saw in Acts 14. Titus was appointing elders in Crete as Paul's delegated representative, so again, the appointment of elders was an apostolic responsibility. The pattern is clear that apostles ordain elders.

The other side of this relationship is that elders send out apostles:

> *Now in the church that was at Antioch there were certain prophets and teachers: Barnabas, Simeon who was called*

Niger, Lucius of Cyrene, Manaen who had been brought up with Herod the tetrarch, and Saul. As they ministered to the Lord and fasted, the Holy Spirit said, "Now separate to Me Barnabas and Saul for the work to which I have called them." Then, having fasted and prayed, and laid hands on them, they sent them away. (Acts 13:1–3)

These men were the senior leadership of that particular church and seemed to be functioning as elders. As such, it was their task, by the direction of the Holy Spirit, to send out Saul (Paul) and Barnabas. From that point onward, Paul and Barnabas are called *apostles*. Interestingly, Paul was never an apostle until he had been sent out from the church at Antioch. When we come to the definition of an apostle, I will return to this point.

The reciprocal authority of apostles and elders is what I call "the reproductive cycle," which I discuss in more detail in chapter 15: Apostles appointing elders, and elders sending out apostles, with neither group independent of the other. I believe God ordained it this way, and I believe God always ordains relationships like this in the body. He never wants anybody to be completely independent.

Dependent on God's Grace

Apostolic teams and presbyteries are both *dependent on God's grace*. People are continually looking for a system that will keep them from having to depend on God's grace, but even the best system will break down without the grace of God. Therefore, when problems arise, do not always blame the system; examine whether or not people are in the grace of God. Even making our Christian marriages work depends on God's grace. Once more, God ordained it that way because He never wants us to be independent of Him.

Directed by the Holy Spirit

Next, each can function effectively only when *directed by the Holy Spirit*. Not only grace, but also the Holy Spirit, is necessary for presbyteries and apostolic teams to work correctly. This point really goes together with grace because it is the Holy Spirit who is the Spirit of grace. In Acts 13:2, we read,

> *As they ministered to the Lord and fasted, the Holy Spirit said, "Now separate to Me Barnabas and Saul for the work to which I have called them."* (Acts 13:2)

Notice something very significant: As they ministered to the Lord, the Holy Spirit said, "Separate to *Me*." We very seldom think of the Holy Spirit as "the Lord." Jesus is Lord *over* the church, but the Holy Spirit is Lord *in* the church. So it all depends on the Holy Spirit.

In regard to Paul's second missionary journey, we read,

> *Now when they had gone through Phrygia and the region of Galatia, they were forbidden by the Holy Spirit to preach the word in Asia. After they had come to Mysia, they tried to go into Bithynia, but the Spirit did not permit them. So passing by Mysia, they came down to Troas. And a vision appeared to Paul in the night. A man of Macedonia stood and pleaded with him, saying, "Come over to Macedonia and help us." Now after he had seen the vision, immediately we sought to go into Macedonia, concluding that the Lord had called us to preach the gospel to them.* (Acts 16:6–10)

The apostles' direction always came from the Holy Spirit, even when the direction was what *not* to do! Note, also, that a vision was given to Paul, which obviously came to him by the Holy Spirit. It was a historic moment in church history when the gospel moved from Asia to Europe for the very first time! The Holy Spirit showed Paul where the kingdom should advance next, and it ultimately went all the way through Europe and to the West.

The principle of being led by the Holy Spirit is found in one of the key Scriptures in my life, Romans 8:14:

For as many as are led by the Spirit of God, these are sons of God.

The Greek word for *"sons"* speaks of a mature child, not an infant. You become an infant by being born again, but you become a mature son by being led by the Holy Spirit. Many people who are born of the Holy Spirit are not led by the Holy Spirit, and they never reach maturity. In the Greek, the word *"led"* is in the continuous present tense: "For as many as are continually, regularly being led by the Holy Spirit, these are the sons of God." It is not enough to have a nodding acquaintance with the Holy Spirit on Sunday morning in church. We have to have a twenty-four-hour-a-day relationship with the Holy Spirit to function as sons of God.

> *The apostle thinks of extension, the elder of preservation.*

My layman's view of church history is that we have spent nineteen centuries trying to find a safe system so that we do not have to depend on the Holy Spirit. However, we are not to be led by principles or concepts. We are to be led by the Holy Spirit. You might say, "Doesn't God have principles and concepts?" Certainly, He does. But when we encounter a situation, we are not smart enough to know which principle and which concept to apply. We have to depend on the Holy Spirit, which is painful for the old nature. A law or system is like a map telling you the way ahead. The old nature says, "Give me the map. I'll make it. I'm smart." Then, sometime later, on a dark, rainy night, when you can't read your map, a gentle voice says in your ear, "May I help you?" That is the Holy Spirit, who has come to take you beyond where the map alone can lead.

Interact with Prophets

Finally, apostolic teams and presbyteries *interact with prophets*. We have previously noted that the functioning presbytery in Acts 13:1 was composed of both prophets and teachers. In Ephesians, we read,

> *Now, therefore, you are no longer strangers and foreigners, but fellow citizens with the saints and members of the household of God, having been built on the foundation of the apostles and prophets.* (Ephesians 2:19–20)

These are not Old Testament prophets because apostles are mentioned first. Paul recognized that it takes both apostles and prophets to bring a church into being. Prophets are involved foundationally within the church, and thus interact with both apostolic teams and presbyteries. We will look at the ministry gift of prophet in a later chapter.

The Main Tasks and Arenas of the Leadership Groups

There are some important distinctions in the ministry tasks and arenas of apostolic teams and presbyteries. First of all, presbyteries function within a given locality. If a man is an elder in Corinth and he moves to Rome, he does not automatically become an elder in Rome. The church in Rome does not have to recognize him. But if a man is an apostle, he is an apostle anywhere. The same is true of the other mobile ministries—prophets, evangelists, and teachers. Apostolic teams are available to the whole body and have the world as their parish. Indeed, the main function of the apostle is to extend the borders of the kingdom of God.

The main task of presbyteries is order and conservation through government, as seen in 1 Timothy 5:17:

> *Let the elders who rule well be counted worthy of double honor, especially those who labor in the word and doctrine.*

Elders rule, govern, and give leadership. Apostolic teams give input to presbyteries, but, again, their main thrust is to extend the borders of God's kingdom. The elder lives to bring his people into maturity, peace, and order. The apostle lives to plow up a new field for the gospel. There is a completely different passion in each. The apostle thinks of extension, the elder of preservation.

In capturing the picture of the apostolic heart, let me set several Scriptures side by side.

> *The former account I made, O Theophilus, of all that Jesus began both to do and teach, until the day in which He was taken up* [into heaven], *after He through the Holy Spirit had given commandments to the apostles whom He had chosen.* (Acts 1:1–2)

Notice to whom Christ gave the commandments. He did not give the commandments to the whole church. He gave them to the appropriate people—the apostles. Now let's look at the commandments, and you will see the nature of the apostolic ministry.

> *And Jesus came and spoke to them, saying, "All authority has been given to Me in heaven and on earth. **Go therefore and make disciples of all the nations."***
> (Matthew 28:18–19, emphasis added)

The apostolic ministry is a "going" ministry. *Go into all the nations.* Jesus said, *"I am with you always, even to the end of the age"* (verse 20). On what condition is Christ with us? That we *go!* If we sit, He has made no commitment to be with us. Furthermore, the words *"to the end of the age"* mean that He does not have another program—there is no Plan B! The parallel passage in Mark 16 brings out the same message:

> *Go into all the world and preach the gospel to every creature. He who believes and is baptized will be saved; but he who does not believe will be condemned. And these signs will follow those who believe....* (Mark 16:15–17)

You have probably heard the complaint, "Lord, the signs don't follow!" The answer is that they are promised only to those who go! You may also have heard the saying that it is difficult to follow a parked car. A large part of the body of Christ is a parked car, parked on the church parking lot with no vision beyond it.

The apostle's heart yearns for the regions beyond!

> *And so I have made it my aim to preach the gospel, not where Christ was named, lest I should build on another man's foundation.* (Romans 15:20)

According to the grace of God which was given to me, as a wise master builder I have laid the foundation, and another builds on it. (1 Corinthians 3:10)

Notice in the above Scriptures that Paul laid the foundation where Christ had not been named before. The elders then laid the foundation within those committed to their care in their own cities, and therein lies the difference.

The Order of Authority in the Local Church

In 1 Corinthians 12:28, we are given a specific order of authority in the local church:

And God has appointed these in the church: first apostles, second prophets, third teachers, after that miracles, then gifts of healings....

There are many churches that never see miracles or gifts of healings, and one reason is that they do not have apostles. Apostles, prophets, teachers—these are given in order of authority, and that authority is vested on those three primarily because they handle the Word of God. Those involved in miracles and healings may not have much to do with the ministry of the Word. In fact, some people with the gift of miracles would do better to stay out of teaching.

> *Apostles are subject to the authority of the local church.*

The apostles are the senior leaders in the church. However, they should not normally override the sovereignty of local presbyteries. Even though they are the senior members, this does not mean that they can walk into any local church and order people around. That is contrary to the spirit and the ethic of the New Testament. In fact, New Testament apostles pleaded much more often than they commanded.

Notice, also, that when apostles were sent forth from churches, they returned after having completed their task and reported back to the churches that sent them out. They were subject to the authority of those local churches. They were not lords over the churches, but they were their sent-forth representatives. After Paul and Barnabas completed their first missionary trip, which is recorded in Acts 13 and 14, we read,

> *From there they sailed to Antioch, where they had been commended to the grace of God for the work which they had completed.* (Acts 14:26)

How had they been commended to the grace of God? By the laying on of the hands of the leading brethren of the church of Antioch. Notice that the apostles were commended to God for a work or task. They fulfilled the task for which they were commended to God, and then they returned to the local church to report what they had done.

> *Now when they had come and gathered the church together, they reported all that God had done with them, and that He had opened the door of faith to the Gentiles.* (verse 27)

This is a very different picture of the apostolic ministry than what some people would have us believe in today. The apostle is not an autocrat or dictator. He does not lay hands on people and tell them do this and that. Instead, he is the product, the offspring, of the moving of the Spirit in a local church. He is sent forth from the local church with the laying on of the hands of the leaders. He goes forth to fulfill a task, and he returns to the church that sent him with a report of what he has done. He is subject to the discipline of the body of Christ represented by the local church that sent him out. This is a vitally important principle. It is unscriptural for people to go around on their own without being sent by anybody— without being authorized by anybody, without anybody to whom they are accountable—and declare that they are apostles and have authority. It is totally contrary to the spirit and letter of Scripture. It is clear to me that this situation has to be changed, and I see that there is a pattern for doing it in the New Testament.

> *The church is primarily mobile and secondarily residential.*

Note, even in apostolic authority, the principle of interdependence within Christ's body. The local church sends forth an apostle who exercises general authority within the church, yet the apostle is accountable for his actions to those who know him best. He travels widely yet has a spiritual home base committed to caring for him. His is an "ascension gift," given directly by Christ to His church, yet he is exhorted to walk in humility and servanthood. He functions with great authority, yet always in plurality, so that he is modified and molded by his brothers. Such a man can be trusted!

The Correct Balance

We can summarize the differences between presbyteries and apostolic teams as local versus mobile, conservation versus extension, and governing versus going.

Apostolic Teams and Elders

Most of the discipling processes described in the New Testament actually took place in the context of apostolic teams, such as those of Jesus and Paul. This is a critical observation because teaching and training detached from this context will not necessarily produce the same results as the New Testament church had. The church was first manifested in a mobile form—only later in a residential form. This is a revolutionary concept, but, again, I think we need a revolution in the church! We always think of the church as a group of people who meet in a building and live in houses, but the first public manifestation of the church through Jesus was the mobile apostolic team. We must get back to thinking of the church as primarily mobile and secondarily residential, and that is going to be a major revolution.

In the contemporary church, the usual emphasis is about 95 percent on conservation and 5 percent on outreach. So, even if every planned activity in the contemporary church were to be totally successful, the overall result would be certain failure. Does that shock you? I hope it does! I, for one, would not want to be committed to a program that is certain to fail. We should consider a fifty-fifty emphasis on outreach and conservation, balancing the Great Commission with tending to our own cities and families.

Let me share a picture that I believe the Lord gave me. Apostolic teams and presbyteries are the two legs on which the body of Christ moves. If one leg is shorter than the other, the body cannot function successfully. There are also many other parts of the body, but none can take the place of the legs. These two legs should be of equal length, bearing equal weight.

Chapter 14

Apostles and Elders, Not Bureaucracy

e are looking at the two legs on which the body of Christ moves—apostolic teams and presbyteries. Coming to an understanding of this truth has cost me much prayerful study, but has resulted in a much clearer picture of the "forest" of the church. Seeing the larger picture of its structure has been a great blessing to me. I believe that the restoration of these two legs of the body has almost incalculable possibilities for the church.

However, in this chapter, I must seek to bring some balance regarding authority in the church. Some of what I say proceeds from my experience—some of which was painful—in trying to apply these principles. However, as I look back from my eighties at these experiences, I thank God I got back on track after some false steps!

In fact, what you will read now was the result of my evaluation of a particular movement that I became involved with. Ultimately, that movement became perverted, and I disassociated myself from it. But I learned some lessons that I will share here in the hope that we might, as the church, learn from our mistakes.

Apostles and Elders, Not Bureaucracy

The essence of what I want to emphasize is this: We must balance the true biblical teaching of authority with all the safeguards that the Bible places around human authority. The only unlimited authority is that of God Himself; every other authority has God-given limits placed upon it.

Safeguards on Authority

Genesis 1 clearly brings forth the truth that man was created to rule:

> *Then God said, "Let Us make man in Our image, according to Our likeness; let them have dominion over the fish of the sea, over the birds of the air, and over the cattle, over all the earth and over every creeping thing that creeps on the earth...." Then God blessed them, and God said to them, "Be fruitful and multiply; fill the earth and subdue it; have dominion over the fish of the sea, over the birds of the air, and over every living thing that moves on the earth."*
>
> (Genesis 1:26, 28)

Modern translations use the word *"rule"* instead of *"have dominion."* Man has an innate urge to rule. The problem is that fallen man usually does not rule in the right way. His carnal nature causes him to rule either from wrong motives or by illegitimate means, or both. The result is usually expressed in manipulation or domination. Wherever you encounter these things, you have met the devil! God never manipulates and He never dominates.

The Safeguard of Plurality

Probably because of this tendency in humanity to abuse authority, the New Testament places certain safeguards on authority, including apostolic teams and presbyteries. The first, as we have already seen, is *plurality*. No one person can say, "I'm it. You have to obey me." This does not set aside the position of being a leader among leaders, which is obviously demonstrated in the New Testament. Yet this position depends primarily on respect and recognition and should not be legislated or institutionalized, which is what has happened in Christendom. The position of leadership has been so institutionalized that even where there is no one qualified to fill it, we still place someone in the position!

In a presbytery, the responsibility for decisions and policy should be *corporate*. I have always believed in this principle but have sometimes let people get away without abiding by it, and the result was disaster. This is a situation where manipulation can easily move in. A man who knows how to manipulate his peers can also manipulate his overseer, and the end result is confusion. I emphasize to every presbytery, "You are responsible, collectively, for every decision and every policy. You cannot hide behind somebody else. You have to take your share of the responsibility." It is dangerous to undermine this principle.

Every authority has God-given limits placed upon it.

In an apostolic team, the recognized leader may have a greater measure of personal authority. Obviously, Paul led his apostolic team, in the same way that a football captain leads his team. Someone must give leadership to a team. However, it is still a team. Also, apostolic teams were not permanent. They functioned for a while, and then some left and some joined. One of our big problems is trying to make everything in this world permanent, when very little in this world is lasting. Only when we get into the next world will everything be permanent.

The Safeguard of Interdependence

The second safeguard is the *interdependence* between apostolic teams and presbyteries. Each needs the other. An apostle cannot swagger into a church and say, "Now listen, I'm an apostle, and you fellows do what I tell you." The eldership has a right to stand up and say, "We are responsible to God and to man for what happens in this place. If you convince us, we'll do it. But don't bypass us and go to the sheep." In Revelation 2:2, Jesus praised the church that tested those who said they were apostles and found them to be liars. That is the responsibility of the local eldership.

However, as I stated earlier, historically, the church has tended to overemphasize conservation at the expense of outreach, giving preeminence to the ministry of the shepherds who functioned in the role of pastor (also called overseer or bishop). Those traditions that emphasize communion or the Eucharist have held special sway over the people since, among certain groups, the practice may even be deemed necessary for salvation. The functions of apostle and prophet have basically been excluded.

I must say that the issue is not apostolic succession but apostolic ministry. I am suspicious of an apostolic authority that does not produce an apostolic ministry. Your history is important, but I want to know what you can produce today! The same thing happened to Israel in the Old Testament when the priests allocated excessive authority to themselves. As the only ones who were allowed to offer sacrifices, the priests held tremendous authority, and sometimes God had to raise up prophets to rebuke and challenge the priests. For example, read Malachi 1:6–10; 2:1–3. You could not be much more plainspoken than those verses! I am sure that there have been whole generations of priests in the history of the Christian church who have been just as guilty.

One thing we have to beware is that the people who do the organizing are usually the people with the pastoral ministries. I thank God for them, but I think they often unconsciously tend to organize in favor of themselves. So the person with an evangelistic ministry really gets the thin end of the deal.

In my long history, I have had the opportunity to watch some powerful men, such as A. A. Allen, T. L. Osborn, Gordon Lindsey, and others. Almost without exception, they were squeezed out of their denominations. Perhaps, at times, their attitudes were wrong, but the truth of the matter is that it is hard for the pastoral ministry to make a place for an evangelistic or apostolic ministry. Everybody gets conformed to a rather narrow mold, and it is considered dangerous to get outside the mold. But the moment you make a little box and tell the Holy Spirit where to operate, you can be absolutely sure of one thing: He will operate somewhere else! Nobody tells the Holy Spirit where to operate.

God's Invisible Government

As we consider the structure of the church and safeguards on human authority, I must now lay a most significant foundation, which I touched on earlier. It is what I call "invisible government." Jesus is Head over the church *in the heavenlies.* As Paul taught,

Apostles and Elders, Not Bureaucracy

[God] worked in Christ when He raised Him from the dead and seated Him at His right hand in the heavenly places, far above all principality and power and might and dominion, and every name that is named, not only in this age but also in that which is to come. And He put all things under His feet, and gave Him to be head over all things to the church, which is His body, the fullness of Him who fills all in all.

(Ephesians 1:20–22)

It is very clear from this passage that Christ is *the* head over all things to the church. If I wanted to find out where my own headquarters are, all I would have to do is locate my head! Likewise, the church's headquarters are where its head (Christ) is: *"in the heavenly places."* Indeed, Jesus governs His church from heaven through the Holy Spirit. We have no real earthly headquarters!

> *No earthly system can take the place of the Holy Spirit.*

We see this invisible government in Paul's apostolic ministry:

Paul, an apostle of Jesus Christ, by the commandment of God our Savior and the Lord Jesus Christ, our hope....

(1 Timothy 1:1)

Notice where Paul's apostleship originated: with God the Father—and it came via Jesus Christ the Son. All governmental authority comes *from* the Father and *through* the Son, to whom God has committed all authority in heaven and on earth. There is no other source of authority in the universe. To get that authority into the church, one other Person is needed: the Holy Spirit.

As they ministered to the Lord and fasted, the Holy Spirit said, "Now separate to Me Barnabas and Saul for the work to which I have called them." (Acts 13:2)

Who was the executive administrator of the Godhead? The Holy Spirit. As I said earlier, Jesus is Lord *over* the church, while the Holy Spirit is Lord *in* the church. Again, Paul was not called an apostle until the church had recognized his calling and sent him out. In the eternal counsel of God, he was an apostle before time began. God the Father decided it and directed it through Jesus, and the Holy Spirit administered it on earth. However, it was only when the *church* embraced it and acted on it that his apostleship was officially recognized. That is a pattern for all the administration of the church. It all comes from God the Father through Jesus Christ, who is the Head over all things for the church, and the Holy Spirit administers it all. For God's direction to be effective, His leaders on earth must respond, accept, and endorse.

Now the Lord is the Spirit; and where the Spirit of the Lord is, there is liberty. (2 Corinthians 3:17)

No system can take the place of the Holy Spirit. Most Christian groups need to give much higher priority to seeking the counsel and direction of the Holy Spirit. I often observe the attitude in believers that it is very "risky" to be led by the Holy Spirit. That attitude is an insult to Him. Instead, I say it is much more risky *not* to be led by the Holy Spirit! The Holy Spirit, the author of Scripture, says, in effect, "If you want to be a son of God, you have to be led by Me. There's no option." (See Romans 8:14.)

To suggest that the Holy Spirit is arbitrary and unreasonable is to paint a very unflattering portrait of God's Spirit.

Apostles and Elders, Not Bureaucracy

The problem is that we have not given nearly enough time or attention to seeking the true *leading* of the Holy Spirit.

The issue of Christ's invisible government in the earth by the Holy Spirit has profound implications for those of us who truly want to understand the church. Do we really comprehend that we have no real earthly headquarters, no permanent assignments, and a Commander who lives in the heavenlies? How many in leadership live in this light? It is so easy to substitute a denominational headquarters or human leader or church tradition, as fine as these may be. Remember, I am talking about a revolution in our thinking! Only the Holy Spirit, the Lord *in* the church, can produce this mind-set.

Heavenly Authority over Apostolic Teams and Presbyteries

On the earthly level, there is no human authority over apostolic teams and presbyteries. You may search the New Testament for such a layer of authority, but you will not find it. Jesus governs them directly from heaven through the Holy Spirit. Historically, man has almost invariably set other individuals or groups over apostolic teams and presbyteries and thus frustrated the government of Jesus. There is no bureaucracy that can meet the needs of this earth. We are living in a changing world full of crises and revolutions and wars, where people are open to the gospel at specific moments in a unique way, and then their hearts are closed again. Only the Spirit of God has the "computer" that tells us where to be at what time!

The kind of man who flourishes in a bureaucracy is usually not the kind of man who ought to be leading an apostolic team. Conversely, you may have a man in a bureaucracy doing a job that frustrates him who ought to be leading an apostolic team. You may also have a man who is flourishing in a bureaucracy in a position of authority he ought not to have. Is this situation common in the church today? I believe it is.

In fact, I learned from studying the life of Abraham the great danger of doing more than God asks. Remember that God commanded Abraham to leave his family, but he took Lot along. (See Genesis 12:1–5.) Lot was the father of the Moabites and the Amonites, who are still part of the prob-

> *We need to give high priority to seeking the Holy Spirit's counsel and direction.*

lem for Israel and the Middle East today. Also, remember how Abraham waited twelve years for a son by Sarah, so he decided to have a son by Hagar. (See Genesis 16:16–17:1.) The result was Ishmael and his descendents, a four-thousand-year continuing problem for Israel. If there ever was a warning in the Scriptures, it is not to do more than what God has asked. Such is the case with not building extra layers of bureaucracy in the church.

In looking at this issue, we see a precedent in the Old Testament as Israel found it difficult to live under God's invisible government and asked for a human king:

> *Then all the elders of Israel gathered together and came to Samuel at Ramah, and said to him, "Look, you are old, and your sons do not walk in your ways. Now make for us a king to judge us like all the nations." But the thing displeased Samuel when they said, "Give us a king to judge us." So Samuel prayed to the LORD. And the LORD said to Samuel,*

Apostles and Elders, Not Bureaucracy

"Heed the voice of the people in all that they say to you; for they have not rejected you, but they have rejected Me, that I should not reign over them." (1 Samuel 8:4–7)

You see, when we do not accept the invisible government of God and ask for a human substitute, we are rejecting God Himself!

According to all the works which they have done since the day that I brought them up out of Egypt, even to this day; with which they have forsaken Me and served other gods; so they are doing to you also. Now therefore, heed their voice. (1 Samuel 8: 8–9)

If you are a leader of God's people, sooner or later, you will discover that they will treat you the way they treat God. But God said, *"Heed their voice."* That is wisdom. Do not fight people when they want the wrong thing. Let them have it. Generally speaking, that is the only way they will learn.

[God said,] *"However, you shall solemnly forewarn them, and show them the behavior of the king who will reign over them." So Samuel told all the words of the LORD to the people who asked him for a king. And he said, "This will be the behavior of the king who will reign over you: He will take your sons and appoint them for his own chariots and to be his horsemen, and some will run before his chariots. He will appoint captains over his thousands and captains over his fifties, will set some to plow his ground and reap his harvest, and some to make his weapons of war and equipment for his chariots. He will take your daughters to be perfumers, cooks, and bakers. And he will take the best of your fields, your vineyards, and your olive groves, and give them to his servants. He will take a tenth of your grain and your vintage, and give it to his officers and servants. And he will take your male servants, your female servants, your finest young men, and your donkeys, and put them to his work. He will take a tenth of your sheep. And you will be his servants. And you will cry out in that day because of your king whom you have chosen for yourselves, and the LORD will not hear you in that day."* (1 Samuel 8:9–18)

Samuel was painting an accurate picture of human government. So much energy and finance is wasted in the intricacies and bureaucracy of human government. There is scriptural precedent in the New Testament for a temporary church council, but not a permanent body. Likewise, councils were called in church history to meet specific critical situations, but they were dissolved when the need had been met. Our modern pattern of committees, councils, and denominations existing to perpetuate themselves is a real problem.

> *People often treat God's leaders the way they treat God Himself.*

Of course, there is both room and need for committees, councils, and such things in God's work, but these must never be allowed to usurp the clearest representation of God's government on earth, the apostolic teams and presbyteries. Generally speaking, however, this is exactly what happens.

God's Government Working on Earth

Let us consider further the relationships between apostles and presbyteries in the outworking of God's government on earth, as well as God's built-in safeguards against excessive authority. This is absolutely crucial to understand: *Apostles were often directed to specific sections of humanity, yet they never claimed authority over single churches.* I knew a man in Africa whom I regarded as an apostle to East Africa, on the basis of his fruit in ministry. In a historical example, just before World War I, two men, James Saltzer and William Burton, went out from England to the Belgian Congo. In the next forty years, they established more than one thousand self-governing local churches. All the signs spoken of in the New Testament occurred in their ministry. They were apostles to the Belgian Congo. I think apostles are sent more to a section of humanity than to a geographical area, as we see in Paul's confrontation with Peter:

> *But from those who seemed to be something; whatever they were, it makes no difference to me; God shows personal favoritism to no man; for those who seemed to be something added nothing to me. But on the contrary, when they saw that the gospel for the uncircumcised had been committed to me, as the gospel for the circumcised was to Peter (for He who worked effectively in Peter for the apostleship to the circumcised also worked effectively in me toward the Gentiles)....* (Galatians 2:6–8)

In essence, they split up the ancient world according to the burdens God had given them. The apostles, however, did not claim exclusive authority over *specific* churches. To illustrate, let's consider Paul's relationship to the churches of Galatia and Corinth.

> *My little children, for whom I labor in birth again until Christ is formed in you.* (Galatians 4:19)

I do not write these things to shame you, but as my beloved children I warn you. For though you might have ten thousand instructors in Christ, yet you do not have many fathers; for in Christ Jesus I have begotten you through the gospel. (1 Corinthians 4:14–15)

Paul was the spiritual father of the churches of Galatia and Corinth. There is no question about that. How did he relate to them? He was provoked with both groups for allowing the Judaizers to sow the false teaching that a Gentile had to first become a Jew before he could be saved. Yet Paul did not say, "Why didn't you get my permission before you invited those preachers?" No, he said, "You ought to have known better than to believe them." Paul did not invoke his own authority. He never, apparently, claimed exclusive right over any church, even if he was the parent of that church. Instead, he appealed to them.

Brethren, I urge you to become like me, for I became like you. You have not injured me at all. You know that because of physical infirmity I preached the gospel to you at the first. And my trial which was in my flesh you did not despise or reject, but you received me as an angel of God, even as Christ Jesus. What then was the blessing you enjoyed? For I bear you witness that, if possible, you would have plucked out your own eyes and given them to me. Have I therefore become your enemy because I tell you the truth? [The Judaizers] zealously court you, but for no good; yes, they want to exclude you, that you may be zealous for them. (Galatians 4:12–17)

How do we respond when people under our authority stray? My personal reaction is not to impose my views on them. You can produce conformity for a while by imposing on people, but the end result is less than effective. Something in me in those situations says to give them advice, but then let them alone and allow them to find out for themselves.

> But it is good to be zealous in a good thing always, and not only when I am present with you. My little children, for whom I labor in birth again until Christ is formed in you, I would like to be present with you now and to change my tone; for I have doubts about you. [This is his basic response:] Tell me, you who desire to be under the law, do you not hear the law? (verses 18–21)

He was saying, "Can't you see for yourself what the Bible really says?" The ultimate appeal is to Scripture and their own understanding, maturity, and good sense.

We see that Paul's approach to the same problems in Corinth was identical:

> And I, brethren, could not speak to you as to spiritual people but as to carnal, as to babes in Christ. I fed you with milk and not with solid food; for until now you were not able to receive it, and even now you are still not able; for you are still carnal. For where there are envy, strife, and divisions among you, are you not carnal and behaving like mere men? For when one says, "I am of Paul," and another, "I am of Apollos," are you not carnal? (1 Corinthians 3:1–4)

Did he want all of them to say, "I am of Paul"? Absolutely not. Paul was just as upset with that as with the ones who said, "I am of Apollos"!

> Who then is Paul, and who is Apollos, but ministers through whom you believed, as the Lord gave to each one? I planted,

Apollos watered, but God gave the increase. So then neither he who plants is anything, nor he who waters, but God who gives the increase. Now he who plants and he who waters are one, and each one will receive his own reward according to his own labor. For we are God's fellow workers; you are God's field, you are God's building. According to the grace of God which was given to me, as a wise master builder I have laid the foundation, and another builds on it. But let each one take heed how he builds on it. For no other foundation can anyone lay than that which is laid, which is Jesus Christ. Now if anyone builds on this foundation with gold, silver, precious stones, wood, hay, straw, each one's work will become clear. (1 Corinthians 3:5–13)

Did Paul say, "Nobody else should build without my authorization"? No. He just said to take heed *how* they built. Then he warned that if they built with wood, hay, and straw, it would all be burned up. He did not say, "You should not build," but simply pointed out what would happen if they built in that way.

In the long run, the truth is the most powerful instrument we have. I am gripped by the statement of Paul in 2 Corinthians 13:8: *"For we can do nothing against the truth, but for the truth."* I am totally convinced of that. Do not even fight the truth. Try not to be stubborn. When confronted with the truth, bow to it. It may not always suit me, but I will bow to anybody who tells me the truth. Paul's approach was simply to tell the truth and let the chips fall where they may.

For it has been declared to me concerning you, my brethren, by those of Chloe's household, that there are contentions among you. Now I say this, that each of you says, "I am of

Apostles and Elders, Not Bureaucracy

*Paul," or "I am of Apollos," or "I am of Cephas," or "I am
of Christ." Is Christ divided? Was Paul crucified for you?
Or were you baptized in the name of Paul?*
(1 Corinthians 1:11–13)

Paul did not want them to be "his people," and that is
wise. The more people you have, the more of their problems
you have. Why make problems for yourself? I also note that
Peter wrote independently to the Galatians, just as Paul did.
(See 1 Peter 1:1.) There is no record that they checked with
one another. As the Holy Spirit led, both men ministered to
the Galatians. Again, the point is made: *Apostles were directed
to specific sections of humanity without taking authority over specific
churches.* I recognize how controversial this statement will be
to some who operate with apostolic networks or fellowships
of churches. I am not criticizing anyone's philosophy or approach. May I emphasize, however, that we must come as
servants to those to whom we minister, not as lords.

The Big Picture

The Bible paints a rather simple picture of Christ's body
moving forward on two legs: both apostolic teams and presbyteries. We need a scriptural balance between these two
ministries so that the body can function, not as a bureaucracy but as a living church. Jointly, they are under the direct, invisible government of Christ in the heavenlies and
made effective by the Holy Spirit on earth. Until apostolic
teams become functional, the church should consider itself
in a process of ongoing development.

May Christ indeed build His church!

Chapter 15

Reproduction, Not Succession

he picture of the local church that I have been paint-ing for you is indeed very organic. In fact, it bears little relationship to the artificial picture of many churches that are presented to us today. The high value upon loyalty and relationships is so much more typical of the Mid-dle East than the West. Having lived in both spheres, I would say that it is much harder to see the organic, relational life of the New Testament in Western nations. Yet, the pattern is there in Scripture. After over eighty years of life, I have come to the inescapable conclusion that we can never improve on God's patterns!

The "Reproductive Cycle": Apostles and Elders

One of God's patterns, which I briefly mentioned in chapter 13, is what I call "the reproductive cycle." This is ex-tremely interesting, as God always creates living things with the ability to reproduce. His commandment to Adam and Eve in Genesis 1:28 was clear: *"Be fruitful and multiply."* This is true in the natural; it is true also in the spiritual. God has ordained a method of self-reproducing for the two key ministries of the apostle and the elder. As within the rest of creation, these ministries in the church reproduce in a most "naturally-supernatural" way.

The apostolic ministry emerges first in a region, which makes sense because it is a ministry which *extends* the kingdom of God into new regions. The apostles ordain elders to *conserve* the fruit of their work, and from these groups of elders new *apostles* ultimately emerge. This is a cycle that can continue endlessly. It is far superior to seminaries and Bible schools because it depends on three things: intimate association, interdependence, and long-term relationships. It is not superficial training; everything is forged in the heat of ongoing mission work and church life. It is not untested or artificial.

We may see this pattern established as we look again at the first four verses of Acts 13:

> *Now in the church that was at Antioch there were certain prophets and teachers* [Barnabas, Simeon, Lucius, Manaen and Saul]....*As they ministered to the Lord and fasted, the Holy Spirit said, "Now separate to Me Barnabas and Saul for the work to which I have called them." Then, having fasted and prayed, and laid hands on them, they sent them away. So, being sent out by the Holy Spirit, they went down to Seleucia, and from there they sailed to Cyprus.* (Acts 13:1–4)

Before the Holy Spirit revealed the will of God, Paul and Barnabas were prophets and teachers. After the Holy Spirit spoke, the other leaders in the church laid hands on them and sent them forth as the representatives of the church at Antioch. There are six main purposes indicated in the New Testament for the laying on of hands:

1. To minister healing to the sick.
2. To help those seeking the baptism in the Holy Spirit.
3. To impart spiritual gifts.
4. To send out apostles.
5. To ordain elders.
6. To appoint deacons.

The laying on of hands is not just a formality. Spiritual authority and power is always released when the right people lay hands on others as they are led by the Holy Spirit.

The subsequent chapter discloses to us what Paul and Barnabas became after being commissioned in this way.

> *But the multitude of the city was divided: part sided with the Jews, and part with the apostles....But when the apostles Barnabas and Paul heard this, they tore their clothes and ran in among the multitude.* (Acts 14:4, 14)

These prophets and teachers had become apostles through being sent forth by local leadership.

We see the concept of apostolic teams in other places in the New Testament. For example, in Galatians, Paul wrote,

> *Then after fourteen years I went up again to Jerusalem with Barnabas, and also took Titus with me.* (Galatians 2:1)

Here we have Paul, Barnabas, and Titus. In Jerusalem, they had a confrontation with yet another apostolic team mentioned in Galatians 2:9: James, Peter, and John. The two teams met, settled their differences, gave each other the right hand of fellowship, and then parted. Notice that there was an overall framework of fellowship that embraced the whole body of Christ, yet specific teams were given specific tasks. Peter, James, and John were the apostles of the Jews, while Paul, Barnabas, and Titus were the apostles of the Gentiles. There are certain burdens and emphases within apostolic teams. They may have different graces that make them suitable for specific assignments.

Further on in Acts, we see the next apostolic team:

Now Barnabas was determined to take with them John called Mark. But Paul insisted that they should not take with them the one who had departed from them in Pamphylia, and had not gone with them to the work. Then the contention became so sharp that they parted from one another. And so Barnabas took Mark and sailed to Cyprus; but Paul chose Silas and departed, being commended by the brethren to the grace of God. And he went through Syria and Cilicia, strengthening the churches. (Acts 15:37–41)

Since John Mark had left the previous apostolic journey, Paul did not want him to come on the next one. As a result, a new pair of apostles went forth, Barnabas and John Mark. Paul departed on his second missionary tour with still another apostle, Silas. The same pattern occurs throughout Scripture: team ministry. We never see apostles operating independently.

But Paul chose Silas and departed, being commended by the brethren [in the church at Antioch] *to the grace of God.*   (Acts 15:40)

I believe we can infer that Paul and Silas were commissioned through the laying on of hands, as Paul and Barnabas were the first time, as the official apostolic representatives of the church at Antioch. Now we will see how the journey proceeded:

Then he [Paul] came to Derbe and Lystra. And behold, a certain disciple was there, named Timothy, the son of a certain Jewish woman who believed, but his father was Greek. He was well spoken of by the brethren who were at Lystra and Iconium. Paul wanted to have him go on with him.

(Acts 16:1–3)

Three cities are mentioned here: Derbe, Lystra, and Iconium. Since Lystra is the city mentioned twice, it must be the city in which Timothy's mother, a believing member of the local church, raised him. Timothy had graduated from the local church at Lystra with his first degree: the good report of the local brethren. No one ever has a right to step out in ministry who does not start with a good report from his local assembly. The first requirement is that you prove yourself on your home territory. If you cannot do it there, you cannot do it, period.

Since Timothy had this initial degree, Paul decided to draft him for service. Paul never would have taken the risk of including an untested man in his team. But Timothy had been tested where it counts—in the local church. He had been known and observed from childhood, under far closer observation than ever happens in a university. As a former university professor, I know a little about academia. When you are facing the challenge and uncertainty of reaching into the unknown, choose a man trained in close relationships at home and church over the man trained in a classroom.

So we have Paul, Silas, and Timothy on this journey. What does Timothy become through joining the party of

Reproduction, Not Succession

Paul and Silas? The answer is found in the book of 1 Thessalonians, which alludes to events from this very journey. Notice first who wrote the letter: *"Paul, Silvanus, and Timothy, To the church of the Thessalonians"* (verse 1). Then notice how they describe themselves:

> *Nor did we seek glory from men, either from you or from others, when we might have made demands as **apostles of Christ.*** (1 Thessalonians 2:6, emphasis added)

They were apostles. How did Timothy become an apostle? He was sent forth, duly commissioned by the elders of the church in Lystra. This commissioning is further described in Paul's epistle to Timothy:

> *This charge I commit to you, son Timothy, according to the prophecies previously made concerning you, that by them you may wage the good warfare.* (1 Timothy 1:18)

Prophecies had been given forth indicating the general nature of the ministry and the warfare for which God had ordained Timothy. We see this in greater detail in chapter four·

> *Do not neglect the gift [charisma] that is in you, which was given to you by prophecy with the laying on of the hands of the eldership [presbytery].* (1 Timothy 4:14)

Compare Acts 16:1–3 with these verses from 1 Timothy. I offer you my explanation of these Scriptures. My interpretation could easily be challenged, but I believe that the *charisma* referred to was the apostolic ministry imparted by prophecy with the laying on of the hands of the elders in his home church. Timothy became an apostle when he was sent out by the direction of the Holy Spirit by the elders. Some people think the gift referred to was the baptism of the Holy Spirit, but that is unlikely. That is a part of God's appointed program for every believer: Repent, be baptized, receive the Holy Spirit. This was some other *charisma* or spiritual gift. All of the five main ministry gifts—apostles, prophets, evangelist, shepherds, and teachers—are *charismata*, and so I believe the gift that Paul was speaking of here was the apostolic ministry received by Timothy through prophecy and the laying on of hands.

So we see the scriptural pattern: Paul and Silas came to Lystra and fellowshipped with the brethren. A young man of outstanding Christian character and a knowledge of Scripture, Timothy, was pinpointed through prophecy to join Paul's team. The elders acknowledged it, and the elders and the apostles together laid hands on Timothy, commissioning him as their apostolic representative together with the senior apostles Paul and Silas. The scriptural example is that the beginner works with those who are more experienced. Gradually, he comes to a place where he can work on his own.

> *Elders commission apostles, who then ordain other elders.*

In due course, Paul and Timothy came to the city of Ephesus. There Paul left Timothy behind as his representative, to finish off what needed to be done for the church there. Let's look at what Paul said about this:

> *As I urged you when I went into Macedonia; remain in Ephesus.* (1 Timothy 1:3)

Reproduction, Not Succession

Paul went on to Macedonia, leaving Timothy in Ephesus to continue the apostolic ministry there. He was Paul's coworker. Having proved himself in his initial ministry with Paul, Timothy was now considered competent to minister on his own, under general direction from Paul. Now what did he have to do in Ephesus? In chapter 3, we see one of Timothy's main responsibilities. Paul wrote,

> *This is a faithful saying: If a man desires the position of a bishop* [elder, pastor], *he desires a good work. A bishop then must be....* (verses 1–2)

After reminding Timothy of the qualifications for a bishop, Paul gave these further instructions:

> *Let the elders who rule well be counted worthy of double honor, especially those who labor in the word and doctrine. For the Scripture says, "You shall not muzzle an ox while it treads out the grain," and, "The laborer is worthy of his wages." Do not receive an accusation against an elder except from two or three witnesses. Those* [elders] *who are sinning rebuke in the presence of all, that the rest also may fear. I charge you before God and the Lord Jesus Christ and the elect angels that you observe these things without prejudice, doing nothing with partiality. Do not lay hands on anyone hastily.* (1 Timothy 5:17–22)

Timothy's responsibility in Ephesus was to lay hands on and ordain the elders in Ephesus. *We now have a complete reproductive cycle*: Prophets and teachers bring forth, by a spiritual birth, the apostolic ministry. The apostles go forth and come to the city of Lystra. Together with the elders, they bring forth an apostolic ministry, which goes to the city of Ephesus. The apostolic ministry appoints elders, and out of these elders, there is again the possibility for apostolic ministry to come forth.

You see that the two key ministries really are the apostles and elders. In the New Testament, much more is said about apostles and elders than about all the other ministries put together. But how do they emerge? From prophets and teachers. There is such interdependence in the body of Christ!

Apostolic Succession?

Notice that the Bible in no way endorses the principle of apostolic succession. This principle is that an apostle (or a bishop) must be ordained by someone who was ordained by someone else who was an apostle. Paul and Barnabas were at Antioch, which was not a long way from Jerusalem. There is no doubt that, in Jerusalem at that time, there were several apostles who had been personally ordained by the Lord while He was on earth. If the Lord felt that it was so essential that an apostle should ordain another apostle, He easily could have arranged for one or more of those apostles to come from Jerusalem to Antioch to lay hands on Paul and Barnabas. In actual fact, He did not do that.

Only New Testament believers will produce New Testament churches.

The principle of apostolic succession is actually set aside in the New Testament. In its place is the principle of spiritual birth born out of fellowship in the local church. Indeed, elders send out apostles, and apostles appoint elders. Apostles are answerable to the churches and elderships that send them forth, yet they will be the ones to establish further groups of elders!

We have already seen that Paul was ordained an apostle through the laying on of hands of his fellow ministers in the church at Antioch. Yet notice how Paul described his own apostolic ministry:

> *Paul, an apostle (not from men nor through man, but through Jesus Christ and God the Father who raised Him from the dead).* (Galatians 1:1)

> *Paul, an apostle of Jesus Christ, by the commandment of God our Savior and the Lord Jesus Christ, our hope.* (1 Timothy 1:1)

Again, there is the interrelationship between the divine and the human.

I am painting the ideal, perfect picture as a Bible teacher. I am fully aware that the ideal is hard to achieve. Years ago, I realized that even when we had the blueprint of the New Testament church, we often did not have the building materials available to build it: true New Testament believers! Only New Testament building materials can ever produce New Testament churches. However, I continue to trust God to move the body of Christ toward the true picture of the church in Scripture. I refuse to give up! Now in my eighties, I have seen the church in a process of sanctification and purification for over sixty years. I have seen a change in the fabric of the body of Christ that is truly exciting. There have been successive waves of restored truth in recent decades: authority, faith, deliverance, missions, and love, among many others. I long to see the church truly live as the church, with a lifestyle appropriate to her nature.

Part 4:

The Leadership of the Church

Chapter 16

Mobile Ministry: Apostles

In Part One of this book, we considered the nature of the church as God's portion and special people. In Part Two, we examined the seven pictures of the church offered by Paul in Ephesians. Then, in Part Three, we considered the overall structure of the church, both universal and local. I felt it was important to first address *who* and *what* the church is. Before we consider methods, patterns, and leadership principles that build the church, we must be sure exactly what it is we are building. We must build wisely on the right foundation, as Paul cautioned in 1 Corinthians 3.

We will now move into a study of the main ministries or leadership of the church. There will necessarily be some overlap of the functions of apostolic teams and elders that we covered earlier, but here they will be discussed mainly in the context of the nature of their specific callings and the day-to-day life of the church.

I have found it convenient in studying leadership ministries to divide them into two groups; first, the mobile ministries, and second, the resident ministries. We will begin with the mobile ministries.

The Mobile Ministries

You may have been surprised to find that most of the main ministries of the church are mobile. The church was never meant to settle down into the staid institution that it has often become. The church's early ministries were constantly bringing the gospel into geographic and spiritual vacuums. This was partly because of the emphasis on, and support of, mobile ministries. There are certain ministers who will never know the kind of settled, residential existence that most of us enjoy, for God has made them mobile at heart. It takes commitment and strength to stay put, and it takes another kind of commitment and strength to maintain a vision that extends beyond the horizon.

The church would never have become a world influence without the mobile ministries because they are not tied down to any particular locality but can function anywhere within the universal church. They are available to all sections of the church in all places. Again, the main list of these ministries is given in Ephesians:

> And [Jesus] *Himself gave some to be apostles, some prophets, some evangelists, and some pastors* [literally, shepherds] *and teachers.* (Ephesians 4:11)

Of the five ministries listed here, only pastors are essentially residential, so the remaining are the chief mobile ministries: apostles, prophets, evangelists, and teachers. In this chapter, we will consider the subject of apostles.

For ten years during my education as a youth in private school, churchgoing was compulsory once every weekday and twice on Sundays, which made eight times a week. I will never blot out of my memory the stained glass pictures of various Bible figures, among them Jesus in the carpenter shop and the twelve apostles. Not one of them appeared to be below fifty years of age. They had scraggly beards, long white hair, and wrinkled faces. You got the impression that leadership in the church is for people who are nearing the end of life. This is a complete misrepresentation. A careful study of the New Testament will show that all the apostles whom Jesus called in His earthly ministry were young men, not even middle-aged.

My picture of God was more or less the same. I pictured Him as a rather grumpy old man with a long white beard sitting in an office at the end of a long corridor. The last thing you ever wanted to do was tiptoe down that corridor, knock on the door, and get into that office, because you were headed for trouble if you did!

It has taken years for me to undo some of the religious impressions that were created in my boyhood. I believe that you, too, will have to do a lot of adjusting to get a clear, scriptural picture of an apostle. Generally speaking, the word *apostle* has traditional religious associations that make us think in terms of a dim, disagreeable old figure somewhere in the remote past whom it would be better not to meet. Certainly, I would say that 90 percent of professing Christians imagine that apostles belonged only to a period nineteen centuries ago. They would not consider the possibility of meeting an apostle in contemporary times. I hope that this impression will be corrected by what I have to say.

What Is an Apostle?

Let's consider the meaning of this word *apostle*, beginning with its origin in the original language of the New Testament.

The Greek word is *apostolos*, which has a very specific meaning: "one sent forth." Many people never realize that some very familiar passages in the Bible contain the word *apostle*. For example, Jesus said,

> *Most assuredly, I say to you, a servant is not greater than his master; nor is **he who is sent** [apostolos] greater than **he who sent** [apostolos] **him**.*
> (John 13:16, emphasis added)

"He who is sent" is the apostle. This Scripture underscores that fact that the root meaning of *apostle* is "one who is sent forth." In various Bible versions, *apostolos* is sometimes translated as "messenger." I will point out in due course that using this term is rather unfortunate and slightly misleading. The meaning of *apostolos* closely corresponds to a more familiar word in modern Christianity, which is the word *missionary*. *Missionary* comes from a Latin verb, and it means "one who is sent." Since *apostolos* means "one who is sent forth," the meanings are obviously very close. In considering the nature of apostles, you would do well to think more in terms of missionaries, though not all apostles are missionaries, nor are all missionaries apostles.

> *The church would not have become a world influence without mobile ministries.*

It is interesting to see the number of places where the word *apostle* occurs in the New Testament. We have no hesitation about using the word *evangelist*, yet that word occurs only three times in the New Testament. Only one man, Philip, is actually called an evangelist. Yet, when we look at the word *apostle*, there are twenty-eight people who are specified as having that ministry. Many Christians would not even consider giving that title to any living minister.

When I began my international preaching ministry, people used to ask me, "What do you do?" I would respond, "I travel and preach." So they would say, "You're an evangelist." I would say, "No, definitely not!" "Well, you must be. You travel and preach." The attitude was that the only kind of person who travels and preaches is an evangelist. If you do not travel and preach, then you must be a pastor! Those were the only two options, and of course, this is not scriptural.

Who Were the New Testament Apostles?

There are about fourteen people actually named as apostles before the day of Pentecost, and another fourteen named after the day of Pentecost.

The First and Perfect Apostle

The first person to be called an apostle was the Lord Jesus Christ Himself, which is appropriate. I understand Jesus to be the perfect pattern of every one of the main ministries. He is the perfect Apostle, the perfect Prophet, the perfect Evangelist, the perfect Shepherd, and the perfect Teacher. Hebrews not only names Christ as an apostle, but it also sheds light on the meaning of the word:

> *Therefore, holy brethren, partakers of the heavenly calling, consider the Apostle and High Priest of our confession* [or statement of faith], *Christ Jesus.* (Hebrews 3:1)

Jesus is called the Apostle and the High Priest of our confession. These are opposite sides of His total ministry. As the Apostle, He was the One who was sent forth by God to do a special task in the world that no one else could do. As the High Priest, He has returned to the presence of God to represent those who have accepted the ministry He had on earth. As the Apostle, He was sent forth from God to redeem us. As the High Priest, He returned to God to intercede on our behalf. What a beautiful picture of Christ's work!

We have further statements in John's gospel about Jesus being sent forth, beginning in John 10:36. Here Jesus was speaking to the Jewish people who challenged His claim to represent God:

> *...do you say of Him* [Jesus] *whom the Father sanctified and* **sent into the world***....* (emphasis added)

The Father sanctified Jesus and sent Him into the world. The verb *"sent"* in the Greek is *apostello*, from which the word *apostle* is derived. Having set Jesus apart, the Father sent Him into the world to become our Apostle—the Sent Forth One.

The Disciples as Apostles

In John 20:21, a similar thought is applied to the first disciples:

> *So Jesus said to* [His disciples] *again, "Peace to you! As the Father has sent Me, I also send you."*

In *"the Father has sent Me,"* the word *apostello* is used. Jesus was saying, "My Father has sent Me forth as an Apostle. Now I'm sending you in the same way that My Father sent Me." The apostleship was transferred.

Let's consider further these first twelve disciples who became apostles. We will look at the background of their appointment and the details of its wording:

But when [Jesus] saw the multitudes, He was moved with compassion for them, because they were weary and scattered, like sheep having no shepherd. Then He said to His disciples, "The harvest truly is plentiful, but the laborers are few. Therefore pray the Lord of the harvest to send out laborers into His harvest." (Matthew 9:36–38)

The need was for people to be sent forth into the harvest as laborers, which is precisely what Jesus did next:

And when He had called His twelve disciples to Him, He gave them power over unclean spirits, to cast them out, and to heal all kinds of sickness and all kinds of disease. Now the names of the twelve apostles are these....These twelve Jesus sent out. (Matthew 10:1–2, 5)

Again, we see the noun *apostolos* translated as *"apostles."* We also see the verb *apostello*, which is translated as *"sent forth."* Notice that, in verse one, they were called disciples, but after that, they were called apostles. They were promoted from disciples to apostles in the act of being sent forth.

Incidentally, Jesus' first apostolic team could have numbered at least thirty persons, including women.

Now it came to pass, afterward, that [Jesus] went through every city and village, preaching [evangelizing] and bringing the glad tidings of the kingdom of God. And the twelve [disciples] were with Him, and certain women who had been healed of evil spirits and infirmities—Mary called Magdalene, out of whom had come seven demons, and Joanna the wife of Chuza, Herod's steward, and Susanna, and many others [the Greek here is feminine:

"many other women"] *who provided for Him from their substance.* (Luke 8:1–3)

When people saw Jesus' team come in to a village, they saw the church in microcosm: people of both sexes from different socioeconomic backgrounds.

> *Jesus' disciples were promoted to apostles in the act of being sent forth.*

Likewise, missionary groups and organizations should be as diverse as possible so that, when their teams arrive in various nations, the people there will see the true church. I myself was part of an apostolic team outreach to Zambia with associates of different backgrounds and races, including my African daughter, Jesika. What a difference it makes not come to Africa with a lot white faces! It has a totally different impact on the people. Otherwise, they tend to think that Christianity is a Western or white man's religion. But when they see the church in this microcosm, they really respond.

Now, the number of those first apostles was twelve. However, we are all aware that Judas became the traitor. The Scripture says that he fell from his apostleship. (See Acts 1:25.) While waiting on God in the upper room before the day of Pentecost, the apostle Peter declared to the one hundred and twenty disciples gathered there that it was necessary that this number of twelve be made complete once again.

> *Therefore, of these men who have accompanied us all the time that the Lord Jesus went in and out among us, beginning from the baptism of John to that day when [Jesus] was taken up from us, one of these must become a witness with us of His resurrection.* (Acts 1:21–22)

Mobile Ministry: Apostles

Notice that these first apostles had to have witnessed the entire earthly ministry of Jesus from the time of His baptism by John through His crucifixion and resurrection. The disciples proposed two men who met the qualification, Joseph and Matthias. Then they prayed and cast lots and asked the Lord to indicate through the lot which one was His choice.

> *And they cast their lots, and the lot fell on Matthias. And he was numbered with the eleven apostles.* (verse 26)

So, Matthias became the twelfth apostle. Many people have formed the impression that this was not a valid appointment, but there is not a single sentence in Scripture that raises any doubts about its validity. On the contrary, when Peter began to make his well-known speech on the day of Pentecost, we read, *"But Peter, standing up with the eleven..."* (Acts 2:14). The other eleven were all grouped together and all identified as being the apostles. So we find that Scripture actually endorses the appointment of Matthias. Therefore, we have Jesus, the first twelve, and then Matthias, which makes a total of fourteen who were appointed apostles before the day of Pentecost.

Apostles after Jesus' Ascension

All the remaining appointments that we will consider were made after the day of Pentecost and after the ascension of Jesus. This is a very significant point. Paul spoke of these very events when he quoted from Psalm 68:18:

> *Therefore He says: "When He ascended on high, He led captivity captive, and gave gifts to men."*
>
> (Ephesians 4:8)

Notice that it was after Jesus had ascended that He gave these gifts to men. The gifts that He gave are specified after the parentheses, as we saw at the beginning of this chapter:

And He Himself gave some to be apostles, some prophets, some evangelists, and some pastors and teachers. (verse 11)

The first twelve apostles are not referred to in this list. Rather, these are apostles, prophets, and others who were appointed after the ascension. The language is absolutely clear and unambiguous.

Let's now identify the apostles who were appointed after the day of Pentecost.

Now in the church that was at Antioch there were certain prophets and teachers: Barnabas, Simeon who was called Niger, Lucius of Cyrene, Manaen who had been brought up with Herod the tetrarch, and Saul [Paul]. As they ministered to the Lord and fasted, the Holy Spirit said, "Now separate to Me Barnabas and Saul for the work to which I have called them."...So, being sent out by the Holy Spirit.... (Acts 13:1–2, 4)

This search for apostles is something like the work of a detective. It is a fascinating process of study, inference, and deduction. Notice that Paul and Barnabas were sent out by God. Then, in the next chapter of Acts, they are called *apostles.*

But the multitude of the city was divided: part sided with the Jews, and part with the apostles. (Acts 14:4)

But when the apostles Barnabas and Paul heard this... (verse 14)

Mobile Ministry: Apostles

As a result of being commissioned and sent forth by the direction of the Holy Spirit for a special task, Paul and Barnabas became apostles. I once imagined that an apostle would somehow float down out of heaven complete in every detail. He would simply appear on the scene ready to go. This idea is not scriptural. There is promotion in the ministries. Many men in Scripture did not begin as apostles, but after having proved themselves in other ministries, were promoted to apostleship. This is a very reasonable and practical way of doing things.

So Paul and Barnabas were two new apostles, in addition to Jesus and the Twelve. Next, we have reference to another two apostles. Paul wrote,

> *Greet Andronicus and Junia, my countrymen and my fellow prisoners, who are of note among the apostles, who also were in Christ before me.*   (Romans 16:7)

Here were two additional men, Andronicus and Junia, who were noteworthy apostles. I believe the words *"of note"* contain the meaning of the above verse. Not only were they apostles, but they were also distinguished, well-known apostles. They were apparently relatives of Paul who had come to Christ before Paul himself had.

Turning to 1 Corinthians 9, we find mention of more New Testament apostles:

> *Do we have no right* [authority] *to take along a believing wife, as do also the other apostles, the brothers of the Lord, and Cephas?*   (verse 5)

Cephas, we know, is one of the names for Peter. But notice that Paul included among the apostles *"the brothers of the*

Lord"—Jesus' own brothers from His earthly family. We find this fact confirmed in Galatians 1:

Then after three years I went up to Jerusalem to see Peter, and remained with him fifteen days. But I saw none of the other apostles except James, the Lord's brother.

(verses 18–19)

The language indicates that James, the Lord's brother, was recognized as an apostle. We can turn to Matthew to discover how many earthly brothers Jesus had. Here, people from Jesus' own hometown of Nazareth were commenting about His identity and family:

Is this not the carpenter's son? Is not His mother called Mary? And His brothers James, Joses, Simon, and Judas [Jude]? (Matthew 13:55)

James is best known as the author of the epistle of James, and Judas as the author of the epistle of Jude. Jude indeed identified himself as the brother of James in his letter, which begins, as usual in ancient epistles, with the person's name and qualifications:

Jude, a bondservant of Jesus Christ, and brother of James.... (Jude 1)

It is very interesting that none of Jesus' physical brothers ever claimed this relationship after the resurrection. So, while Jude called himself the *"brother of James,"* who was the elder brother after Jesus, he also called himself the *"bondservant of Jesus Christ."* James began his own epistle by writing, *"James, a bondservant of God and of the Lord Jesus Christ"* (James 1:1). As a matter of fact, Paul said in 2 Corinthians 5:16, *"Though we have known Christ according to the flesh, yet now we know Him thus no longer."* The fleshly relationships were not the important thing and were given no prominence after Jesus' resurrection and ascension. What a lesson that our present relationships with Christ are all that matter!

The other two brothers of Jesus are not as well known, but I believe that, by putting these four passages of Scripture together, it is clear that James, Joseph, Simon, and Jude were acknowledged as apostles in the early church. That gives us four more apostles. Let's now look into the cases of Titus and others.

> *Many were promoted to apostleship after proving themselves in ministry.*

> *If anyone inquires about Titus, he is my partner and fellow worker concerning you. Or if our brethren are inquired about, they are messengers of the churches, the glory of Christ.* (2 Corinthians 8:23)

The Greek word for *"messengers"* here is *apostolos*. I suppose that the *New King James* translators (and the translators of other versions, as well) had the idea that there were only twelve original apostles, and perhaps Paul, and that was the end of it. Something prevented them from using the word *apostles*, but there is no valid reason for not doing so. The passage should read, "They are apostles of the churches." They are called that because each of them was sent forth from some particular church. These men are not specifically named, but they are mentioned in the plural. The minimum plural is two, so we have Titus, who was named, and at least two more.

With regard to Titus, we see him doing the work of an apostle in the epistle that is named after him. Paul wrote to him in this way:

For this reason I left you in Crete, that you should set in order the things that are lacking, and appoint elders in every city as I commanded you. (Titus 1:5)

As we saw earlier, Titus was to perform the apostolic ministry of ordaining elders in every city. So, the above Scripture, in addition to 2 Corinthians 8:23, shows that Titus was recognized by Paul and others as an apostle. Again, putting these verses together gives us Titus and a minimum of two other apostles.

We turn to Philippians to discover still another apostle:

Yet I considered it necessary to send to you Epaphroditus, my brother, fellow worker, and fellow soldier, but your messenger [apostolos] and the one who ministered to my need. (Philippians 2:25)

"Your messenger" should be rendered "your apostle." Epaphroditus was sent forth as an apostle from the church at Philippi. The language clearly indicates that every apostle would be sent forth from a particular local congregation, and that the local congregation had various responsibilities in connection with that apostle. For instance, Paul and Barnabas were sent forth from Antioch, Epaphroditus was sent forth from Philippi, and the *"messengers"* mentioned in 2 Corinthians 8:23 were sent forth from churches whose locality was not specified.

We find two more apostles in 1 Thessalonians 1. It was quite common in ancient times for two, three, or more people to unite together in writing an epistle, with all their names as coauthors, as we see here:

Paul, Silvanus, and Timothy, To the church of the Thessalonians... (verse 1)

Silvanus is another way of saying Silas. So the three writers of this epistle are Paul, Silas, and Timothy. Notice once more what they said about their collective ministry:

Nor did we seek glory from men, either from you or from others, when we might have made demands as apostles of Christ. (1 Thessalonians 2:6)

They said, in effect, "We could have lorded it over you and made demands upon you because we were apostles, but we didn't do it." We have already counted Paul as an apostle, but here we have the addition of Silas and Timothy. If we add up all those mentioned after the ascension, we have a minimum of fourteen. There is a possibility of more, because in one case we do not know how many unnamed apostles there were.

For most people, it is an astonishing fact that fourteen people were appointed as apostles subsequent to the day of Pentecost! We can see how much traditional interpretation still dominates our thinking.

The Authority of the Apostolic Ministry

Let's examine in detail the authority of the apostolic ministry by revisiting Matthew:

And when He had called His twelve disciples to Him, He gave them power....These twelve Jesus sent out. (Matthew 10:1, 5)

It is important to emphasize that the apostolic authority comes from God Himself. Jesus gave His disciples power or authority, and then sent them out as apostles. Similarly, the Holy Spirit said to the five prophets and teachers in the church at Antioch, *"Separate to Me Barnabas and Saul for the work to which I have called them"* (Acts 13:2). After the leaders at Antioch had fasted and prayed, they laid hands on Paul and Barnabas and *"sent them away"* (verse 3), and they also became "sent forth ones" or apostles.

I think it is correct to say that God used human instruments in propelling Paul and Barnabas out into their ministries as apostles. However, they had already received their individual callings: *"Separate to Me Barnabas and Saul for the work to which I **have** called them."* They had received individual, personal callings from the Lord prior to being prayed over and sent out. What the Holy Spirit did at that point was to make their callings public and to set the seal of His authority upon them. Although the church may recognize and set its official approval upon a ministry, the ministry originates with God.

I think this truth contains a very important lesson that goes beyond apostleship. Behind the human instruments is the authority of the Spirit of God, and behind the Spirit of God is the Head of the church, the Lord Jesus Christ. So the final authority for every placement in the church is the authority of God Himself. There is an interdependence between God and human agents. As somebody said about speaking in other tongues, and this is just an example, "You cannot do it without God, and God cannot do it without you." And this is true in many ministries. We cannot do them without God, and God will not do them without us.

God has deliberately made Himself dependent on human instruments to accomplish His will. So we look at the human instrument, and we acknowledge it, but through the human instrument we must also look to almighty God, who is the final authority.

So there is cooperation between God and the church in this matter of recognizing and releasing mobile ministries. I think this is made clear in the title of the book of Acts. In the *New King James Version,* it is called "The Acts of the Apostles." Some people will claim it should have been "The Acts of the Holy Spirit." We know that the Holy Spirit was the one behind it, but if He had not found men who were willing to do it, nothing would ever have happened.

Jesus has a tremendous desire to bless, to heal, to deliver, and to bring peace, but He cannot do these things unless the members of His body, the church, make themselves available to carry it out. The church has kept the Lord Jesus Christ waiting many centuries before making itself available to do what He wants to do. My prayer and my intention is that, even through this book, we will be more fully available as instruments to Jesus Christ to affect His will. Again, we have to look beyond the instruments, who are often weak and fallible, to the God whose authority is imparted to His people. But men are the instruments of God in the earth.

It is very interesting that Paul was always extremely emphatic that his apostleship did not originate with man.

> *The church commissions apostles, but their ministry originates with God.*

Indeed, Paul's apostleship was often challenged by his contemporaries. The last person we might imagine anybody challenging would be the apostle Paul! Yet, in 2 Corinthians 10:10, Paul's critics called his bodily presence *"weak"* and his speech *"contemptible."* He was no preacher. I would imagine that Peter was a tremendous preacher, but Paul absolutely was not. Many of Paul's contemporaries in the Christian church despised and belittled him, and from time to time, he had to take a very strong stand declaring that he was an apostle—not of men, but of God. Let's look at just two examples of this. In Galatians 1:1, he described himself as

Paul, an apostle (not from men nor through man, but through Jesus Christ and God the Father who raised Him from the dead).

Notice that he was absolutely definite about this fact, saying, in effect, "No man made me an apostle. My apostleship comes from Jesus Christ and God the Father." Likewise, he wrote,

Paul, an apostle of Jesus Christ, by the commandment of God our Savior and the Lord Jesus Christ, our hope.
(1 Timothy 1:1)

We may never find a minister who is above criticism and without fault, but in the final analysis, we do not ultimately deal with the servant but with the God whom he serves. I recall leaving a pastorate in Seattle in 1964. The congregation was quite sorry to see us go. The last Sunday, quite spontaneously, one of the deacons said, "I feel that we should have Brother and Sister Prince come to the front and that we should lay hands on them, sending them off." I had not planned it; nobody had planned it. Yet I have always treasured this experience because our local congregation gave us their endorsement, laid their hands on us, and sent us forth. I felt that God wanted it done that way. Now, these were not what some would consider "outstanding" leaders; they were a rather bedraggled company of deacons, to tell the truth! They had been through the mill for about two years in the most intense problems that churches can go through. Nevertheless, they were God's instruments in that particular situation, and we respected them as such.

It could be said that the attitude of the church toward God is indicated by the attitude of the church toward the ministers whom God gives them. Actually, Christians do not honor God more than they honor the God-given ministry placed in the church. We see this principle in the book of Judges. Barak was called by God through Deborah the prophetess to deliver Israel from an invading nation. He said to Deborah, "I won't go unless you go with me." Now, that was not the manly attitude in those days. Deborah said, "If I go with you, it will not be to your glory because God will use another." And God used a woman, Jael, the wife of Heber the Kenite, to kill the leader of the enemy. (See Judges 4:4–22.) Judges contains the well-known song of Deborah after the victory had been won, including this verse:

> *The Lord identifies Himself with those who serve Him.*

> *"Curse Meroz," said the angel of the LORD, "Curse its inhabitants bitterly, because they did not come to the help of*

the LORD, *to the help of the* LORD *against the mighty."*
(Judges 5:23)

That was a strong utterance: "Curse you bitterly, Meroz."
Meroz was one of the villages of Israel. To have a curse pronounced and recorded in Scripture about a certain community is a very terrible thing. Why was the curse pronounced?
"They did not come to the help of..."—not Barak, but *"the* LORD.*"*
In other words, the Lord identifies Himself with those who
serve Him. Those who failed to respond to Barak's call and
did not come to his help had not failed Barak, but the Lord.

This is no less true in the church today. A man called
by God and functioning within His God-given ministry is
God's representative. The attitude of the believers toward
him is really the best indication of their attitude toward God.
They may use very pious language concerning God, but their
real attitude will be seen in how they deal with the ministers
whom God sends. We don't know all the plans of the Lord.
Although the apostle Paul continually had to establish his
God-given authority, God used him in a way that He used
none of the other apostles.

The Functions of an Apostle

Let's turn now to the two main functions of apostles:
(1) to establish properly ordered churches, and (2) to bring
order to churches that already exist. Titus 1:5 exemplifies
this truth in that Titus was told to set in order the existing
churches on the island of Crete by appointing elders. I would
say that the ministry of the apostle includes one or more of
the other four ministries of prophet, evangelist, pastor, and
teacher. The breadth of gifting required for an apostle to
set an island in order shows how broad the apostolic mantle

must spread. He would have to function in many different roles, indeed!

Bringing Churches into Being

As we saw, an apostle's mandate as "one sent forth" is to extend the boundaries of God's kingdom. A static apostle is a self-contradiction. The essence of the apostolic ministry is to be moving out. I do not mean to infer that an apostle should never become resident anywhere, but when he does, he functions as an elder. Peter wrote,

> *The elders who are among you I exhort, I who am a fellow elder and a witness of the sufferings of Christ.*
>
> (1 Peter 5:1)

The word translated *"fellow elder"* is a compound Greek word, the best translation of which is *co-elder.* In the government of a local church, there is no one higher than the elders. Therefore, an apostle is merely a fellow elder. This does not mean that he is without authority. If an apostle speaks out of his apostolic ministry and you fail to listen to him, you will be sorry. However, it is the kind of authority that functions by being recognized, not by being institutionalized.

New Testament apostles went where the gospel had yet not been preached, bringing people to the Lord and setting up functioning churches. In almost every place where they preached, they left established churches:

> *So when they had appointed elders in every church, and prayed with fasting, they commended them to the Lord in whom they had believed.* (Acts 14:23)

They did not leave just groups of disciples or prayer groups but established, orderly, local congregations.

However, apostles also give direction to churches that have not been birthed by their ministries. For instance, the apostle Paul wrote to the Romans, whom he had never personally met. (See Romans 1:10–11.) In that epistle, he gave them much authoritative direction and instruction. We see the same thing in Paul's letter to the Colossians, in which he gave instruction and direction to a group of believers whom he had never visited. (See Colossians 2:1, 5.)

Remember that both Peter and Paul wrote to the churches in Galatia. They had not worked together to establish those churches, but as apostles they both exercised authority over them. The point I want to reemphasize is that an apostle does have authority over local churches, primarily over churches that were brought into being directly by his ministry. Beyond that, he has authority over all churches, as the Holy Spirit directs.

> *An apostle who is resident in a local church functions as a co-elder.*

In Galatians 2, we read that Peter and John met with Paul and Barnabas to discuss the nature of the message and ministry that God had given them, and to clear up certain points of misunderstanding:

> *But on the contrary, when they* [Peter and John] *saw that the gospel for the uncircumcised had been committed to me, as the gospel for the circumcised was to Peter (for He who worked effectively in Peter for the apostleship to the circumcised also worked effectively in me toward the Gentiles)....*
>
> (verses 7–8)

Mobile Ministry: Apostles

In chapter fourteen of this book, I mentioned that I believe apostles are sent more to a section of humanity than to a geographical area. Note again that Peter had a general apostleship to the circumcision (the Jews), while Paul had a general apostleship to the Gentiles, which extended beyond churches brought into being by either Peter or Paul. Therefore, a true apostle has general authority within the universal church, whether or not he was the instrument used to bring a certain congregation into being. I think this is really common sense, but it is important to see that this is what the Scripture says.

In 1 Corinthians 12:28, we are given a list of some of the main ministries within a congregation:

And God has appointed these in the church: first apostles, second prophets, third teachers, after that miracles, then gifts of healings, helps, administrations, varieties of tongues.

It is clear that Paul was not talking about the universal church because he left out evangelists, whose main ministry is outside the local congregation. So, within the local church, there is a specific order of authority. First apostles, second prophets, third teachers, fourth workings of miracles, fifth gifts of healings. If an apostle is present, his is the senior ministry in the local church, followed by the prophet and the teacher. These three senior ministries are all ministries of the Word. The point here is that the ministry of God's Word has preeminence over all other forms of ministry. The final authority is vested in the Word of God and those who are the representatives of the Word.

Notice, also, that there are various levels of apostleship. This is so important. As Paul said, *"For I consider that I am not at all inferior to the most eminent apostles"* (2 Corinthians 11:5). He used the same term again, saying, *"In nothing was I behind the most eminent apostles"* (2 Corinthians 12:11). Earlier, we saw that Andronicus and Junia were *"of note among the apostles"* (Romans 16:7). So there are apostles who are *"most eminent"* and *"of note"* and there are apparently apostles who are "not as eminent" or noteworthy. We tend to think that every apostle has to be a Peter or a Paul, but this is not true. For example, a man may be a God-given evangelist but not operate on the scale of Billy Graham. This does not invalidate his claim to be a genuine, God-given evangelist. The same thing is true for apostles.

Discerning False Apostles

Let's consider a final crucial point as we close this chapter. Paul spoke about certain apostles who had appeared as ministers in the church at Corinth:

> *For such are false apostles, deceitful workers, transforming themselves into apostles of Christ. And no wonder! For Satan himself transforms himself into an angel of light. Therefore it is no great thing if his ministers also transform themselves into ministers of righteousness, whose end will be according to their works.*
>
> (2 Corinthians 11:13–15)

People can claim to be apostles and yet actually be the ministers of Satan, not Christ! This is a very solemn and important fact. They are not just mistaken, misguided people, but actually the ministers of Satan. We must learn a lesson in discernment—or suffer greatly for it. The claims of apostles must be tested. Recall that, in Revelation, Jesus commended the church of Ephesus for this very reason:

I know your works, your labor, your patience, and that you cannot bear those who are evil. And you have tested those who say they are apostles and are not, and have found them liars. (Revelation 2:2)

It is the responsibility of every local congregation to test apostles and to accept only those who are in line with Scripture. Does their ministry pass the test? What kind of lives are they leading? How critical it is that we discern the true ministry of the apostle in these last days!

In the next chapter, I have outlined some of the marks of a true apostle that will help us to test and receive the true office.

Chapter 17

The Marks of a True Apostle

here are seven key marks of a true apostle: (1) a heart for "regions beyond"; (2) the ability to fulfill all the special tasks of an apostle; (3) the establishment of churches that reflect the apostle's heart; (4) a desire for team ministry; (5) accountability toward the sending church; (6) signs and wonders; and (7) perseverance.

A Heart for "Regions Beyond"

A definite mark of a true apostle is that he is always aiming at the regions beyond the established church world. He desires the work accomplished in his present sphere to catapult him into the next one. A stationary apostle is a contradiction in terms! Paul wrote,

*We, however, will not boast beyond measure, but within the limits of the **sphere** which God appointed us; a **sphere** which especially includes you. For we are not overextending ourselves (as though our authority did not extend to you), for it was to you that we came with the gospel of Christ; not boasting of things beyond measure, that is, in other men's labors, but having hope, that as your faith is increased, we*

*shall be greatly enlarged by you in our **sphere**, to preach the gospel in the **regions** beyond you, and not to boast in another man's **sphere** of accomplishment.*
(2 Corinthians 10:13–16, emphasis added)

Notice that the word *"sphere"* occurs five times and the word *"regions"* once. How perfectly this fits the mind of the apostle! First, he has a sense of his sphere: the geographic and spiritual limitations of his authority. For someone with significant authority throughout the body of Christ not to have (and know) his limitations is quite dangerous. But when an apostle operates within the correct geographic spheres, God will give him splendid results, as He did Paul. The false apostle grasps for new places to exercise authority and expand his influence. The true apostle, however, carefully and faithfully fulfills God's purposes in his sphere. Then God expands him into the next sphere by the churches he has established in the present one.

This approach provides a wonderful quality control in outreach. Only a successful apostle is going to legitimately expand into a greater region. Today, we might have a false minister or apostle who wreaks havoc in his own area and simply reappears in another city to bring trouble there. Such confusion would be eliminated if a person could move on only when his present church was healthy enough to send him.

The Ability to Fulfill All the Special Tasks of an Apostle

If I am not an apostle to others, yet doubtless I am to you [the church of Corinth]. *For you are the seal of my apostleship in the Lord.* (1 Corinthians 9:2)

The believers in Corinth were the seal or attestation of Paul's apostolic ministry because they were the evidence that he could do what an apostle had to do. Paul could go to Corinth where the gospel had not been preached and bring people to salvation, have them baptized in water and in the Holy Spirit, have them enter into the exercise of the gifts of the Holy Spirit, and establish them in a local congregation with their own local elders. In other words, Paul could do the entire job, from top to bottom. The ability to do this set him apart, or established him, in apostolic ministry. Had Paul been an evangelist only, he could have brought the Corinthians to the Lord, but another ministry would have been needed to complete the job. Had he been a teacher, he might not have brought them to salvation. The ability to do all these things is the proof of apostleship.

The task of an apostle may be summed up in this way: He is the *"master builder"* who establishes and maintains church order.

> *According to the grace of God which was given to me, as a wise master builder I have laid the foundation.*
> (1 Corinthians 3:10)

The apostle is the master contractor who understands every phase of the building—foundation to roof. Bear in mind that before Paul went to Corinth, the gospel had not been preached there. There were no believers. After he preached the gospel, he helped to develop a complete, self-sufficient, self-governing local congregation. That was a supernatural task! I have worked with believers for many decades on several continents, and I can testify that only an apostle could carve out a functioning church in new territory.

The Marks of a True Apostle

The seal of apostleship is the outward authentication that can be seen by anybody who cares to look. We would have far fewer men carrying the title of apostle today if people checked on their seals before accepting their authority. We should consider visiting the church or churches planted by apostles to test the fruit of their ministries. Paul could invite those questioning his authority to check out his work—not his website! Apostles yearn to have lasting fruit. They may have small churches to display, but these will be built as by a master craftsman.

The Establishment of Churches That Reflect the Apostle's Heart

The apostle loves the local church passionately. After all, it is his supreme desire that local churches be established and fulfill their calling. I have noticed several signs of a church planted by a true apostle:

- They are missions-minded.
- They have an emphasis on prayer.
- They tend to be multiethnic.
- They have a heart for the poor.

In other words, they reflect the heart of the founding apostle, who dreams of extending God's kingdom into every area of the city and the world.

A Desire for Team Ministry

It is unscriptural to speak of an apostle working as an individual. There is no example of this anywhere in the New Testament. The true apostle is not afraid of *team ministry*, to use a phrase that has become quite popular. It is healthy for those who exert significant authority to move in strong, interpersonal relationships. Of the five main ministries listed in Ephesians 4:11, three are always mentioned in the plural—apostles, prophets, and shepherds. It is never *the* apostle, *the* prophet, or *the* shepherd or pastor. There are only two ministries that may operate in the singular: the evangelist and the teacher. What is the difference? The apostle, prophet, and pastor are concerned with church order, which is so important that God has not committed it to a single individual. This plurality is a key element to look for in apostolic ministry.

I cannot help comparing the evangelist and the apostle here. Note the story of Philip in Acts 8. One single man went down to Samaria, a very significant city of that time. He operated on his own, without a committee. There was no band, mayor, or police chief to welcome him; he really didn't have anything! He just went down to Samaria and turned the city upside down. But this first evangelist did not finish the building of the church. He brought the people into just two experiences—salvation and water baptism. He did not even bring them into the baptism of the Holy Spirit. We pick up the story in verse 14:

> *Now when the apostles who were at Jerusalem heard that Samaria had received the word of God, they sent Peter and John to them.*

There was only one evangelist but two apostles. The evangelist is God's "paratrooper," one who drops in behind enemy lines and does great damage before the enemy even knows he is there. The apostle is generally the composite of all five main ministries. He can plow up the ground like the evangelist but also finish the whole building. And because he delves into issues of order, he does his work in a team.

The Marks of a True Apostle

Accountability toward the Sending Church

An apostle is not an apostle unless he is sent forth. In order to be sent forth, you must have someone to send you. As we have seen, the local church is responsible for the apostles it sends out—for their ethics, their morals, and their doctrine. If an apostle ever goes astray, the local church is entitled to withdraw its endorsement of his apostolic ministry.

If an apostle remains within his allotted geographic and spiritual sphere, he can do tremendous good. If he is "over his head" in some situation for which he is not graced, you have a disaster. In a true apostle, a keen sense of propriety, deference, and the fear of God are balanced with apostolic confidence and boldness. Please remember that there are genuine apostles and false apostles. We must test them. Many of us cannot imagine someone in ministry being a liar, but it happens. Exaggeration, lack of financial ethics, sexual sin, and doctrinal error are all common faults within mobile ministries.

Signs and Wonders

The apostle also demonstrates his apostleship through the miraculous attestation of signs, wonders, and miracles. An apostle is more than a successful pastor or evangelist. This is an important concept to understand because the term *apostle* is sometimes applied to such men. Thank God for the successful pastoral ministry, but that, in itself, does not make one an apostle. The ministry of an apostle must include the supernatural:

> *Truly the signs of an apostle were accomplished among you with all perseverance, in signs and wonders and mighty deeds.* (2 Corinthians 12:12)

Let's look at two other translations of this verse in order to get the full impact of what it teaches:

The signs of a true apostle were performed among you with all perseverance, by signs and wonders and miracles. (NASB)

The things that mark an apostle—signs, wonders and miracles—were done among you with great perseverance. (NIV)

I think these three translations make it absolutely clear that an apostle without the miraculous is an incomplete apostle. He may be a fledgling apostle, or he may be on the way to being an apostle, but he is not a New Testament apostle.

In 1964, I was ministering in a meeting with a brother who is known by many Christians—Kenneth Hagin. He gave a prophecy that has stuck in my mind ever since. In predicting what God was going to do in the church, he said something to this effect: "God will bring forth the full stature of the apostle and the full stature of the prophet." This statement refers to a verse in the King James Version, which says, *"Till we all come...unto the measure of the stature of the fulness of Christ"* (Ephesians 4:13). Some time ago, God spoke to me very clearly that He was shortly going to manifest apostles and prophets in the body of Christ, such that it will not be necessary to label them because their ministry and their fruit will sufficiently attest to what they are.

An apostle is a master contractor who understands all phases of the building.

I find that many people have a somewhat negative attitude toward the supernatural. If someone receives a vision, then he or she is considered "kooky." Well, that makes Paul and Peter kooks. I also hear people saying that someone may have a supernatural ministry, but their character does not measure up. Therefore, by very illogical deduction, these people do not want anything to do with a supernatural ministry. It is true that one believer might work miracles, while another exhibits godly character, but why shouldn't the person with character also work miracles?

Consider those whose character we most admire in the New Testament: Jesus, Peter, John, Stephen, Philip, and Paul. Jesus and the rest of these men had tremendous supernatural ministries. Certainly, the men in the New Testament with character also worked miracles.

Purposes of the Supernatural in Apostolic Ministry

There are two main purposes of the supernatural, which reinforce the God-given ministry of the apostle:

1. To Produce Obedience

Talking about Jesus Christ, Paul said,

> ...through whom we have received grace and apostleship to bring about the obedience of faith among all the Gentiles.
> (Romans 1:5 NASB)

The apostolic ministry was given to bring about the "obedience of faith." But how was this to be accomplished?

> For I will not presume to speak of anything except what Christ has accomplished through me, resulting in the obedience of the Gentiles by word and deed, in the power of signs and wonders, in the power of the Spirit.
> (Romans 15:18–19 NASB)

Let's look at this Scripture in the *New King James Version:*

> *For I will not dare to speak of any of those things which*
> *Christ has not accomplished through me, in word and deed,*
> *to make the Gentiles obedient; in mighty signs and wonders,*
> *by the power of the Spirit of God.*   (Romans 15:18–19)

The supernatural has a very important practical purpose in causing people to come to faith in Christ as they witness the manifestation of His power and might. This truth became very clear to me when I was in East Africa ministering to young students in the college where I served as principal. Basically, the students were cooperative and willing. I did all the preaching and teaching I could. I crammed Scripture into them by every channel, and they said, "Yes sir; yes sir," but the results were disappointing. There was something missing. Eventually, I told the Lord, "I'm going to stop trying to make them what I want them to be, and I'm going to start praying for them." About six months later, a rather poorly educated young African man turned up—with a guitar that he could barely strum—and said, "I would like to preach to your students."

Now, if there was one thing my students were proud of, it was their education. I thought, *How will a man who's never gotten beyond grade five ever convince these students?* My wife Lydia said, with characteristic wisdom, "Let's pray with him and see what he's like." Praying with him was like being at the gate of heaven, so we said, "If he can pray like that, we'll let him preach."

The power of God descended, the miracles began, and those students were a totally different group of people within a few weeks. You see, there is a great difference between the soul and the spirit. I had been reaching their souls with teaching, counseling, and discipline. All these things are very good, but they go only so far. Miracles reach the _spirit_ because it is the supernatural power of the Holy Spirit that produces them. You can reason with people a long way, but you can bring them only to a certain point. Something has to happen that is totally supernatural.

This truth became especially clear to me because my whole background was reasoning. Before I became a Christian, I could understand complex books; I could read in English, Greek, Latin, or even Russian—but I could not understand the gospel! It was the most frustrating thing. I never did understand it until I had a miraculous experience. After that, I could not help but understand the gospel. So I want to point out to you that the miraculous is no superfluity.

> _The practical purpose of supernatural manifestations is to bring people to faith._

Once I was with a group of wonderful ministers in Miami where a man had been invited to speak about what he had discovered concerning water baptism. He was a fine man, and I respected his opinion. He said he had discovered that, if you teach people about water baptism—that it is the burial of the old nature and of the past—they will not have recurrent problems in their character and behavior afterward. You can deal with it once and for all. And he said they usually put believers through a six-week course and then baptized them.

It wasn't my intention to make fun of that line of reasoning, but because it was time for a question and answer period, I got up and asked, "Then how is it that, in the New Testament, they invariably baptized people the same day? In fact, with the Philippian jailer, they didn't even wait for dawn. What's the difference?" I will tell you what the difference was. There was a work of the Holy Spirit that gave instant revelations. And there is no substitute for that. It saves a lot of discouragement and frustration. Teaching the Word is essential, but a supernatural revelation of the Lord is all that is needed for water baptism.

Some men have miraculous ministries, and sometimes we tend to belittle and to depreciate them. But we better check on how much time those men spend in prayer before we criticize them.

2. To Produce Maximum Results

The second practical purpose of the supernatural is to produce maximum results in minimum time. If we look at Acts 14 again, we will see that the apostles went through a group of cities and won converts to the Lord. Then they went on, and when they returned, they appointed elders—I doubt that it was as much as six months later. In how many places could we do that today? Often, we feel it takes two to five years to produce elders. There was something at work in the New Testament that we do not often see now. In the Spirit, things could happen almost instantly—that is the supernatural. It doesn't just involve being convinced by miracles; it is a supernatural atmosphere. It is like moving into the New Jerusalem where the light is as clear as crystal—you see things instantly; there is no need to sit down and reason them out.

Take counseling, for instance. I am not a great one for counseling, and that is a weakness of mine. People do need counseling, but I get tired of listening to people's problems for two hours! I do not have that much patience. I would rather have them in a deliverance session and get the demons out. Now, deliverance is no substitute for counseling, I want you to know. Yet in certain instances, it can greatly shorten counseling. Another thing that helps in counseling is a word of knowledge. A man might be sitting there telling you his version of the story, but you just know he is lying. It would not have happened the way he is telling it. That is supernatural knowledge.

I am sure that everyone wants to be an apostle right now! So I want to tell you what is involved before you make the final decision to apply. Before you sign that apostolic application form, just listen to the job description for a moment. The Corinthian church had become tremendously knowledgeable—they believed they knew it all and had it all. So Paul told them,

Already you have all you want! Already you have become rich! You have become kings—and that without us! How I wish that you really had become kings so that we might be kings with you! For it seems to me that God has put us apostles on display at the end of the procession, like men condemned to die in the arena. We have been made a spectacle to the whole universe, to angels as well as to men. We are fools for Christ, but you are so wise in Christ! We are weak, but you are strong! You are honored, we are dishonored! To this very hour we go hungry and thirsty, we are in rags, we are brutally treated, we are homeless. We work hard with our own hands. When we are cursed, we bless; when we are persecuted, we endure it; when we are slandered, we answer kindly. Up to this moment we have become the scum of the earth, the refuse of the world.

(1 Corinthians 4:8–13 NIV)

Now you can sign on the dotted line!

Perseverance

Let's return to 2 Corinthians 12:12, where Paul described some signs of apostleship:

Truly the signs of an apostle were accomplished among you with all perseverance, in signs and wonders and mighty deeds.

An apostle must have patience and endurance. When others become discouraged, give up, and turn back, the apostle holds out. For example, when everybody else left Paul, he said, "Demas has forsaken me, and no one else is with me, but I still hold on." (See 2 Timothy 4:6–18.)

> *A true apostle has a father's heart.*

Note the words *"among you"* in 2 Corinthians 12:2, meaning that these signs had been exhibited in the church at Corinth. An apostle has the strength of character to keep on moving in a given area until signs and wonders confirm the Word in a local church. The apostle not only goes from region to region, but he can also stick it out in a given locality until things work. This trait sets a true apostle apart from a false one; a true apostle has a father's heart for every church he plants. (See 1 Corinthians 4:14–15.) He can hang on until he is no longer needed and then appoint leaders who will carry on as he would.

Many mobile ministries have endurance but never produce signs and wonders, while others emphasize the supernatural but display little patience for the nitty-gritty of being a master builder. The true apostle exhibits endurance because of his personal relationships, which ultimately produce an atmosphere for the supernatural.

The Need for Apostles Today

With all the potential for abuse, the apostolic ministry is sorely needed today more than ever. Consider the exploding growth of the church in nations like China, India, and Africa. I am personally aware of apostles planting and overseeing hundreds of churches in primitive areas that God is visiting. How can the church come into maturity without all of the five main ministries, including the apostle? As we have seen, half of the apostles mentioned in Scripture came after the ascension of Christ, meaning that the office of apostle is still in force today! The fact that there are false apostles is no reason not to have apostles, any more than the abuse of tongues is any reason not to practice true speaking in tongues. The remedy for abuse is never disuse but proper use.

In recent years, I have seen various apostolic ministries and networks arise. I am open to them all. I am sure that we are in an infant stage within this restoration of the apostolic ministry. This is a time in which motives and relationships and ways of operating are being refined. I believe we will see the pure and real apostolic ministry reemerge, especially in Third-World nations. I don't look for the Western nations to lead the way in this restoration; there is too much ego and colonial mentality still present in the West. My eye is on the emerging church in Asia and other areas experiencing the harvest. I am looking for the true apostle to emerge, and I believe he will come from a direction we don't expect.

In the late 1960s, the Lord showed me that a great harvest of young people was coming in America. I saw that God would call many of them straight from high school into ministry without attending Bible college or finding secular employment. And so it happened. I was closely associated with (and still am) some who became fivefold ministers in an organic New Testament way. I see the apostle emerging in just such a manner, and I pray for eyes to see and support him as he comes!

Chapter 18

Mobile Ministry: Prophets

e will now consider the ministry of the prophet, a ministry that runs through the entire Bible. In Acts 3:21, we read that *"God has spoken by the mouth of all His holy prophets since the world began."* There are prophets in Scripture who go back before the time of Abraham, such as Enoch, whom Jude mentioned as prophesying. (See Jude 14–15.) Abraham is also described as a prophet. The Lord said to the heathen king Abimelech, *"Now therefore, restore [Abraham's] wife; for he is a prophet, and he will pray for you and you shall live"* (Genesis 20:7).

Therefore, while the ministry of the apostle emerges only in the New Testament, the ministry of the prophet is one that extends through all the dispensations of God's dealings with His people on earth. It is of tremendous importance and interest. Far from being some strange or New Age phenomenon, the ministry of the prophet is foundational in God's interactions with man.

Let's consider for a moment what a prophet actually is. In the New Testament, the word *prophet* comes from the Greek word *prophetes,* and its literal meaning is "one who speaks forth." The prophet speaks forth on behalf of God by the

249

inspiration of the Holy Spirit. Essentially, you could call the prophet "the mouthpiece of God."

Many people have the impression that prophecy always contains the prediction of the future, but this is not correct. Any utterance given forth on behalf of God by the inspiration of the Holy Spirit is classified as prophecy. Some prophecy relates to the past, such as that recorded in the opening chapters of Genesis, where Moses described events of remote history that could not be known by natural understanding. They could have been given only by divine revelation, and therefore Moses spoke of the creation as a prophet.

Essentially, I believe that the scriptural portrayal of a prophet is of one who stands in the counsel of the Lord. Let us look at a very remarkable statement:

> *Surely the Lord GOD does nothing, unless He reveals His secret to His servants the prophets.* (Amos 3:7)

The word *"secret"* may also be translated as *"counsel"* (NASB) or *"plan"* (NIV). This is the nature of the prophetic ministry—a person who understands the inner counsel of God.

In every age, there is a specific purpose of God, and to be in line for God's blessing, you must be moving in His purpose for that time. The prophet unfolds the specific purpose and counsel of God for a particular situation or generation. All through history, God does nothing without revealing His secret counsel and purpose to His servants the prophets.

In the Old Testament

Before examining the ministry of the prophet in the New Testament, let's consider the picture of the prophetic ministry in the Old Testament. One of the great Old Testament prophets, Elijah, was catapulted onto the stage of the history of Israel. The Bible doesn't tell us anything about his background, but he suddenly appeared in a very dramatic and powerful way:

And Elijah the Tishbite, of the inhabitants of Gilead, said to Ahab [king of Israel who had been seduced into idolatry and wickedness by his wife, Jezebel], *"As the* LORD *God of Israel lives, before whom I stand, there shall not be dew nor rain these years, except at my word."*

(1 Kings 17:1)

The courage of Elijah has always been breathtaking to me. He was saying, in effect, "From now on, the fall of rain and dew are under my control, Ahab, and I'm going to decide whether or not they will come." The words by which Elijah introduced himself to Ahab contain the central thought of the prophet. He said, *"As the* LORD *God of Israel lives, before whom I stand...."* The key phrase is *"before whom I stand."* A prophet is one who stands before God.

The other phrase that is frequently used to describe what a prophet does, as we have already seen, is "to stand in the counsel of God." He stands before God, attentive, waiting to hear and deliver God's message. This is the essential requirement of the true biblical prophet: He receives the message in the presence of God and delivers it with complete authority. It is not his message, but God's, and the responsibility for its consequences and impact rest with God, not with the prophet.

The Scripture says that no rain fell on the land for three-and-a-half years. (See 1 Kings 18:1; Luke 4:25; James 5:17.) Elijah had proved his statement that he would control the fall of rain and dew! After this period of time, Elijah received a fresh commission from the Lord:

> *And it came to pass after many days that the word of the* *LORD came to Elijah, in the third year, saying, "Go, present* *yourself to Ahab, and I will send rain on the earth."*
>
> (1 Kings 18:1)

These words have always gripped me because I see in them that the prophet cannot be divorced from his message. It is not just a message, but it is a *man* with a message. God said, *"Present yourself to Ahab, and I will send rain on the earth."* This point is tremendously significant. I remember once hearing the phrase, "God uses men, not methods." God's methods are useless if He does not have the men who can follow them! I cannot imagine anybody else taking the place of Elijah, for he was absolutely characteristic of his God. He typified certain things about God by his boldness, his unwillingness to compromise, and his refusal to show any kind of respect for a wicked king. He refused to bow to Ahab. He had a message from God, and he was determined to deliver it. This is the true spirit of the biblical prophet.

The scriptural portrayal of a prophet is of one who stands in the Lord's counsel.

On the other hand, most preachers think about people's reactions to what they are going to say: "What will people think? How will they react? Will I offend them?" Biblical prophets could not have cared less how people reacted to their messages, because they were concerned primarily with delivering the pure message from God without adding to it or taking from it. They were both fearless and confrontational.

True and False Prophets

In both the Old Testament and the New, there were many false prophets. In fact, one of the interesting and important themes of the prophet Jeremiah was the false prophets of his day. The false prophets far exceeded the true prophets, as they did in the time of Ahab. Let's consider a passage in Jeremiah 23 that presents the contrast between the true and the false prophet. As we go along, you will notice the repetition of the phrase "stand in the counsel of the Lord," which corresponds to Elijah's "standing before the Lord."

> *Therefore thus says the LORD of hosts concerning the* [false] *prophets: "Behold, I will feed them with wormwood, and make them drink the water of gall; for from the prophets of Jerusalem profaneness has gone out into all the land."*
>
> (Jeremiah 23:15)

Here we see the influence of the prophetic ministry. If it is pure, it brings purity, cleansing, and healing; but if it is impure and profane, it brings uncleanness and profaneness into the whole land. Behind the profaneness and uncleanness in the United States today are false prophets who misrepresent God and His standards. The whole nation has been profaned, and in the light of Scripture, false prophets are the source.

> *Thus says the LORD of hosts: "Do not listen to the words of the prophets who prophesy to you. They make you worthless; they speak a vision of their own heart, not from the mouth of the LORD. They continually say to those who despise Me,*

*'The L*ORD* has said, "You shall have peace"'; and to everyone
who walks according to the dictates of his own heart, they say,
'No evil shall come upon you.'"*   (Jeremiah 23:16–17)

Surely, there is much of that kind of prophesying today,
compromising with evil and suggesting that God will con-
done and tolerate sin. That is false prophecy. Notice what
God said:

*For who has stood in the counsel of the L*ORD*, and has per-
ceived and heard His word? Who has marked His word and
heard it? Behold, a whirlwind of the L*ORD* has gone forth in
fury; a violent whirlwind! It will fall violently on the head of
the wicked. The anger of the L*ORD* will not turn back until
He has executed and performed the thoughts of His heart.
In the latter days you will understand it perfectly.*

(verses 18–20)

This message refers to the times in which we are living,
the latter days. God then returned to the theme of the false
prophets:

*I have not sent these prophets, yet they ran. I have not spo-
ken to them, yet they prophesied. But if they had stood in
My counsel, and had caused My people to hear My words,
then they would have turned them from their evil way and
from the evil of their doings.*   (verses 21–22)

It is not enough to be well meaning. In fact, it is extremely dangerous to be well meaning if you speak without
having a word from God.

Notice again that the mark of the true prophet is that he
stands in the counsel of the Lord. Had these prophets stood
in God's counsel, heard His words, and caused His people

to hear His words, there would have been repentance and a returning to God. So, the prophets, in a certain sense, were responsible for the condition of the nation.

> *"Am I a God near at hand," says the LORD, "and not a God afar off? Can anyone hide himself in secret places, so I shall not see him?" says the LORD; "Do I not fill heaven and earth?" says the LORD. "I have heard what the prophets have said who prophesy lies in My name, saying, 'I have dreamed, I have dreamed!'"* (Jeremiah 23:23–25)

These verses refer to the people with the super-spiritual revelations, dreams, and visions that tickle people's ears but do not have any real message of truth and repentance. I have met many such people—enticing and fascinating people, but ones who do not produce biblical results.

> *"How long will this be in the heart of the prophets who prophesy lies? Indeed they are prophets of the deceit of their own heart, who try to make My people forget My name by their dreams which everyone tells his neighbor, as their fathers forgot My name for Baal. The prophet who has a dream, let him tell a dream; and he who has My word, let him speak My word faithfully. What is the chaff to the wheat?" says the LORD. "Is not My word like a fire?" says the LORD, "and like a hammer that breaks the rock in pieces? Therefore behold, I am against the prophets," says the LORD, "who steal My words every one from his neighbor. Behold, I am against the prophets," says the LORD, "who use their tongues and say, 'He says.' Behold, I am against those who prophesy false dreams," says the LORD, "and tell them, and cause My people to err by their lies and by their recklessness. Yet I did not send them or command them;*

therefore they shall not profit this people at all," says the
LORD. (Jeremiah 23:26–32)

The requirement of the prophet is that he speak God's
word faithfully. The *"chaff"* spoken of refers to the false
prophet, the *"wheat"* refers to the true prophet.

We find in this and other passages that far more responsibility is laid at the door of the prophets of a nation for the condition of that nation than most of us realize. The true prophet
who stands in the counsel of the Lord and delivers His word
will bring people to God. Where there is not such a prophet,
the nation is deceived and led astray by false prophets.

Whatever God does among men will be revealed to
those who stand in His counsel and share His secrets. The
true prophet is the one who knows the inner motives and
purposes of God's dealings. This requires a very intimate,
personal relationship with the Lord.

"Digesting" God's Message

Jeremiah spoke from his own experience of what it means
to be a mouthpiece of God:

> *O* LORD, *You know; remember me and visit me, and take*
> *vengeance for me on my persecutors. In Your enduring pa-*
> *tience, do not take me away. Know that for Your sake I have*
> *suffered rebuke* [few true prophets escape rebuke and
> persecution]. *Your words were found, and I ate them, and*
> *Your word was to me the joy and rejoicing of my heart; for*
> *I am called by Your name, O* LORD *God of hosts.*
> (Jeremiah 15:15–16)

Notice that the prophet "digests" God's message. God
spoke something similar to Ezekiel when He handed him a

scroll containing lamentation, mourning, and woe, written on both sides, and said, *"Eat what I give you"* (Ezekiel 2:8). When Ezekiel had eaten it, he was able to deliver the message. (See Ezekiel 2–3.)

Again, the man and the message become identified with one another. The message the prophet brings goes deep into his own spirit and becomes a part of him before he can deliver it. You will find that this is true of almost all the great

> *The prophet cannot be divorced from his message.*

Old Testament prophets. In some sense or another, they had to digest or assimilate the message they had to deliver. There is a unique identification with the Lord and with His Word.

Those who do not feed and live on the Lord's Word cannot be qualified to take His message. Some people have the impression that prophecy just drops out of heaven by a sudden, startling revelation, unconnected with the Bible. This is totally wrong. Every prophet in Scripture indicated by his language and his references that he was intimately acquainted with the revelation of God's Word as it existed in his day. Any person not deeply identified with the Word is not eligible for the prophetic ministry.

Living with Aloneness

A person who takes his stand for God as a prophet will also have to sit alone at times. There is no question about it. The prophet Jeremiah said,

> *I did not sit in the assembly of the mockers, nor did I rejoice;*
> *I sat alone because of Your hand, for You have filled me*
> *with indignation.*   (Jeremiah 15:17)

In my four-and-a-half years in the British army, one of the hardest tests I went through was "sitting alone," because I simply could not identify with the things that the other soldiers were saying and doing. In view of what I knew of God, I could not associate myself with the bad language, forms of pleasure, and whole attitude toward life of my fellow soldiers. The most difficult place to sit alone is a desert, because there is nowhere else you can go; I do not really recall a more severe test than that. I can remember sitting alone many nights because God had laid His hand upon me. Those who are not willing to do this cannot pass the test.

God's Word out of God's Mouth

Now, let us see the real crux of the prophetic ministry:

Therefore thus says the LORD: "If you return, then I will bring you back; you shall stand before Me; if you take out the precious from the vile, you shall be as My mouth. Let them return to you, but you must not return to them."

(Jeremiah 15:19)

Notice that God affirmed the essence of the prophetic ministry: *"You shall stand before Me."* Then He said, in effect, "I am looking for a mouthpiece, but the one who wants to be My mouthpiece must meet the conditions. One who receives a message or a revelation cannot compromise with man. He cannot lower his standards or go beyond the lines that I have drawn. He has to wait for people to come back to him." These verses clearly express the requirements and pressures involved in being a prophetic mouthpiece.

Notice what happens when God's Word goes out of God's mouth:

Mobile Ministry: Prophets

So shall My word be that goes forth from My mouth; it shall not return to Me void, but it shall accomplish what I please, and it shall prosper in the thing for which I sent it.
(Isaiah 55:11)

Many people misquote this verse, saying, "God's Word will never return to Him void." They stand and preach an uninspired, unanointed message to a dead congregation. Then, when there is no response or reaction, they shrug their shoulders and say, "God's Word will not return to Him void." But the Scripture really says, "God's Word out of God's mouth will not return to Him void." It must be God's Word out of a mouth that has met the conditions for being a mouthpiece for God.

> *God's Word spoken through His servant by His Spirit overcomes every obstacle.*

When my word goes out of my mouth, my breath goes with it. I cannot speak without giving forth breath. Similarly, when God's Word goes out of His mouth, His breath (Spirit) goes with it. God's Word without the Spirit does not bring life, for *"the letter kills, but the Spirit gives life"* (2 Corinthians 3:6). But when God's Word proceeds from His chosen mouthpiece by the Spirit, the results are dramatic. As God promised Jeremiah, *"Is not My word...like a hammer that breaks the rock in pieces?"* (Jeremiah 23:29). God's Word in God's mouthpiece will destroy every obstacle!

In the New Testament

With this background from Old Testament prophetic ministry, let's now turn to the New Testament. We saw that there are twenty-eight people mentioned in the New Testament as apostles. There are ten listed as prophets.

And in these days prophets came from Jerusalem to Antioch [there were recognized prophets]. *Then one of them, named Agabus, stood up and showed by the Spirit that there was going to be a great famine throughout all the world, which also happened in the days of Claudius Caesar. Then the disciples, each according to his ability, determined to send relief to the brethren dwelling in Judea.* (Acts 11:27–29)

The church of Antioch accepted this prophetic revelation as authoritative and acted upon it. They did not just say, "Wasn't that wonderful? We had a revelation." They did something about it.

Notice that prophet*s* (plural) are mentioned, one of whom was Agabus. The language implies that there were at least two others besides Agabus, which gives us a minimum of three New Testament prophets so far.

Now in the church that was at Antioch there were certain prophets and teachers: Barnabas, Simeon...Lucius... Manaen...and Saul. (Acts 13:1)

Here, five people are named who were recognized in their church as having the ministry of prophets. This gives us eight prophets.

Judas and Silas, themselves being prophets also, exhorted and strengthened the brethren with many words.
(Acts 15:32)

Notice that, included in the prophetic ministry is the ministry of exhortation. And note that Silas was called a prophet. As we saw in our study of apostles, he was also designated an apostle. Here is another example of a man who was promoted in ministry. He was promoted into the apostolic ministry from the ministry of a prophet. So these two bring us to a total of at least ten recognized New Testament prophets.

Distinctions of a Prophet

Let's now consider certain distinctions between the prophet and the other mobile ministries. We saw that the apostle has a *special task*. When the Holy Spirit separated out Saul and Barnabas, He said, *"Now separate to Me Barnabas and Saul for the work to which I have called them"* (Acts 13:2). They were called to a work, and that work, as we learned in our previous study, was essentially establishing and ordering churches. On the other hand, a prophet has a *special message* received from God to be delivered at a certain time and place. This is why I take exception to the translations that use the word *messenger* instead of *apostle*. If anyone should be called "messenger," it is the prophet. Again, the apostle has the task, while the prophet has the message—not a general message for everybody, but a special message given to him directly from God to be delivered at a specific time and place.

In contrast with the prophet, the teacher may have no special message personally received from God. He expounds God's truth *generally*. Let me illustrate these distinctions by examples from both the Old and New Testaments. We'll look first at the ministry of Jonah the prophet:

And Jonah began to enter the city on the first day's walk. Then he cried out and said, "Yet forty days, and Nineveh shall be overthrown!" (Jonah 3:4)

Nineveh had precisely forty more days before God's judgment. This was a specific revelation given to one person, Jonah, about one place, Nineveh, at a specific time.

If Jonah had been an evangelist, he would have gone into that city and preached in general terms on sin and its consequences, including God's judgment on sin. Everything he said would have been true, but it would not have contained the specific revelation that judgment was less than forty days away. This revelation marked Jonah as a prophet. Had he been a teacher, he could have taught on various aspects of God's dealings and judgments, but he could not have given the specific revelation of their timing. Experience shows that people will give much more heed when, in addition to the general exposition of God's truth, there is specific revelation that brings it right down to their particular situations. Revelation gives a specific impact to the prophetic ministry and message.

> *A mark of a prophet is specific revelation.*

Now let's look at the example of John the Baptist in the first chapter of the gospel of Mark:

> *Now John was clothed with camel's hair and with a leather belt around his waist, and he ate locusts and wild honey. And he preached, saying, "There comes One after me who is mightier than I, whose sandal strap I am not worthy to stoop down and loose. I indeed baptized you with water, but He will baptize you with the Holy Spirit."* (verses 6–8)

Notice that John was more than just a preacher. He could have preached on sin and its consequences, called people to repentance, and baptized them. But he had a specific revelation with a time factor. "Immediately after me, Another is coming who is greater than I am, and He's going to be the one to baptize with the Holy Spirit." John could not have known this without a specific, individual revelation from God. That revelation lifted him out of the rank of preacher or teacher and into the rank of the prophet.

We have already looked at the passage about Agabus in Acts 11, where he predicted a famine in the near future that indeed took place in the days of the Emperor Claudius. Agabus could not have known of this impending famine except by a specific, personal revelation from God. Further on in Acts, we find another example of a supernatural revelation that was given to this fascinating man Agabus:

> And as we stayed [in Caesarea] many days, a certain prophet named Agabus came down from Judea. When he had come to us, he took Paul's belt, bound his own hands and feet, and said, "Thus says the Holy Spirit, 'So shall the Jews at Jerusalem bind the man who owns this belt, and deliver him into the hands of the Gentiles.'"
>
> (Acts 21:10–11)

Again, Agabus knew more than just a preacher or a teacher would. He had a specific revelation of what was to happen to Paul in Jerusalem, and a specific commission from the Holy Spirit to tell him what to expect. Agabus delivered his message in a dramatic way by binding his own hands and feet with Paul's belt. God often required the prophets to do more than simply give forth an utterance. In one way or another, they had to give some picture or demonstration of their message.

The Prophetic Ministry and the Spiritual Gift of Prophesying

We need to make a distinction here between the ministry of a prophet and the spiritual gift of prophesying. Let me point this out to you by contrasting two different statements in the New Testament. Ephesians 4:11 says, "[Christ] *gave some to be apostles, some prophets, some evangelists, and some pastors and teachers.*" I think it is clear from the language that not all receive the ministry of prophet. This point is also brought out in the following:

> *God has appointed these in the church: first apostles, second prophets, third teachers....Are all apostles? Are all prophets?* (1 Corinthians 12:28–29)

It is obvious that the answer to both of these questions is no. In other words, not everyone has the ministry of apostle or prophet. On the other hand, the gift of prophesying is open to all believers:

> *For you can all prophesy one by one, that all may learn and all may be encouraged.* (1 Corinthians 14:31)

The prophetic ministry is so much more than exercising a spiritual gift—it is the total man, and it is a whole way of life. As I have already said, the prophet *is* his message. A spiritual gift is exercised in a brief moment for a supernatural manifestation that comes to an end. So, in the New Testament, the gift of prophesying is made available to all believers who care to reach out for and receive it, while the ministry of a prophet is not given to all.

Another important aspect about prophecy and the ministry of the prophet in the New Testament is that it is normally intended for believers. In the Old Testament, God often sent prophets to people who were not believers. For example, many of the prophet Jeremiah's messages were addressed to the Gentile nations around Israel who did not acknowledge the God of Israel or Jeremiah as a prophet. In the New Testament, however, we read,

> *Therefore tongues are for a sign, not to those who believe but to unbelievers; but prophesying is not for unbelievers but for those who believe.* (1 Corinthians 14:22)

In the first part of this verse, Paul was not addressing the use of tongues for self-edification but as a supernatural sign intended for unbelievers. This is what happened on the day of Pentecost. The people on whom the Holy Spirit fell spoke in languages that they did not understand, but the unbelievers understood these languages, and this became a sign to them! This was not the normal use of tongues; again, it was a sign to reach unbelievers. When a believer, by the operation of the Holy Spirit, speaks a language that he does not understand but is understood by an unbeliever who is present, it brings tremendous conviction to the unbeliever. However, in the latter part of 1 Corinthians 14:22, we see that prophesying is intended for believers, which makes it somewhat different from prophesying under the old covenant.

Judging the Prophets

Moving on in 1 Corinthians 14, we find another very important feature of prophesying and prophetic ministry in the New Testament:

> *Let two or three prophets speak, and let the others judge.* (verse 29)

The words translated *"prophets"* and *"others"* are plural in the Greek. One man did not stand up and say, "I am the prophet. You all listen to me." This was not the normal pattern. In a New Testament church, there would be a group of men who were prophets. When one prophesied or gave forth a revelation, it was the duty of the others to exercise judgment on, or spiritually discern, what was being prophesied. In this way, no person, by the ministry of a prophet or the gift of prophesying, was allowed to become a dictator. Today, we see some congregations with a set prophet—one man— and everyone does what this man says. In fact, he may even appoint the apostles and determine who will marry whom. I have personally seen these specific abuses.

In the New Testament church, there is not one man who does it all. Again, no one person should be viewed as the only mouthpiece of God. The prophets should minister in a group; as we have seen, they are normally mentioned in the plural. Where one is actually ministering, the others are to exercise judgment on that particular ministry. As members of the body, believers function together and exercise checks upon one another.

Over the years, I have come to realize what a tremendously powerful instrument prophecy is. It is like a powerful car: Before you take off in it, you better be sure that the brakes, the steering, and the other safety features are in good order. If they are not, it would be better not to go for a ride! I always point out that if you encourage people to seek to prophesy, you have a scriptural obligation to ensure that there is a scriptural process for judging that prophecy. It is completely unscriptural to have prophetic ministry without its being submitted to judgment. I would rather not have prophesying or prophetic ministry if it is not judged. That is too dangerous to permit. I can recall numerous incidents where God's people have been placed in situations where they were made to feel that they were challenging God Himself if they challenged or disagreed with a particular ministry.

Years ago, in Jerusalem, there was a rather fine Pentecostal couple from the United States that was doing a good work for God. Then a Swedish lady set herself up as a prophetess. She began to prophesy over these two that they were no longer to live together as husband and wife. They became totally confused, and both of them ended up in a mental institution. This was the result of coming under a spirit of bondage to this particular woman. They were under the impression that, if they went against what she declared to be God's will, they would be resisting the almighty God.

> *Prophets are to minister in a group, with one prophesying and the others spiritually discerning the message.*

Therefore, when you see people with prophetic ministries or with the gift of prophesying, bear in mind that their ministries and prophecies are subject to judgment. One of our responsibilities is to learn how to judge. Paul said,

> *Do not quench the Spirit. Do not despise prophecies. Test all things; hold fast what is good.*
> (1 Thessalonians 5:19–21)

We see here two dangerous alternatives. One is to quench the Holy Spirit by saying, "We don't want any prophesying. We don't want any gifts. We don't want any manifestations." But the other is to accept anything that is put forth without checking it. When we were in Africa, I used to tell the people, "Not everything the missionaries have brought you is good. Some is good, and some is not good. Some of what you yourselves have is better than what the missionaries have brought you." They would look at me in some surprise because I was a missionary. I would then say, "When you eat fish, you know what to do: Swallow the flesh, and spit out the bones. Do the same with what the missionaries brought. Swallow the flesh, but spit out the bones. Don't choke swallowing some bone just because the missionary gave it to you."

The same is true today in the church. When I hear prophesying or revelation, I decide for myself whether it is flesh or bone. If it is flesh, I swallow it and am strengthened; but if it is bones, I will not choke trying to swallow it. I spit it out. This is what God's Word directs us to do.

Prophetic Ministry's Relationship to the Whole Church

In closing this chapter, let's form a picture of the relationship that prophetic ministry has to the church as a whole. As a member of the body, the prophet functions together with the other members, and he is subject to the control and discipline of the body as a whole. He is not an autocrat or a despot, and he is not outside the framework of the local church. Let's look at a beautiful picture of true prophetic ministry. The prophet Zechariah said,

> Now the angel who talked with me came back and wakened me, as a man who is wakened out of his sleep. And he said to me, "What do you see?" So I said, "I am looking, and there is a lampstand of solid gold with a bowl on top of it, and on the stand seven lamps with seven pipes to the seven lamps. Two olive trees are by it, one at the right of the bowl

and the other at its left." So I answered and spoke to the angel who talked with me, saying, "What are these, my lord?" (Zechariah 4:1–3)

Note that Zechariah was intensely interested in the meaning of the olive trees. He did not receive an immediate answer to his question. The angel first gave him further instruction, which I believe is summed up in verse 6: *"'Not by might nor by power, but by My Spirit,' says the LORD of hosts."* That is a familiar verse, and it really is the essential theme of the revelation of this fourth chapter of Zechariah—that God is going to accomplish His purposes in the world, not by force or by might, but by the tremendous power of His Holy Spirit.

Zechariah next saw a beautiful candlestick with its seven branches, and a bowl on top. I believe that, all through Scripture, a candlestick typifies the church, and the oil that feeds the candlestick always typifies the Holy Spirit. In this vision, Zechariah saw an olive tree on either side of this candlestick. There was a channel by which the oil was flowing out of the olive tree and into the candlestick. Thus, the oil was kept pure, clean, and fresh; and therefore, the light that burned was pure, clean, and bright. Zechariah came back to his question about the olive trees:

Then I answered and said to him, "What are these two olive trees; at the right of the lampstand and at its left?" And I further answered and said to him, "What are these two olive branches that drip into the receptacles of the two gold pipes from which the golden oil drains?" Then he answered me and said, "Do you not know what these are?" And I said, "No, my lord." (verses 11–13)

I believe there is a certain irony in the answer of the angel, because Zechariah himself was one of the olive trees! In a sense, the angel was making fun of him, saying, "Don't you know what these are?"

> So [the angel] *said, "These are the two anointed ones* [literally, the two sons of oil], *who stand beside the Lord of the whole earth."*   (verse 14)

These olive trees represent men who stand before God for the express purpose of receiving and carrying oil to the lampstand, the church. This is a picture of prophetic ministry.

These two olive trees are again referred to in Revelation:

> [The angel said,] *"And I will give power to my two witnesses, and they will prophesy one thousand two hundred and sixty days, clothed in sackcloth." These are the two olive trees and the two lampstands standing before the God of the earth.*   (Revelation 11:3–4)

Then, in verse 10, we read, *"These two prophets tormented those who dwell on the earth."* So, the olive trees are prophets who prophesied. Of course, there are two specific people referred to in Revelation 11 who will come in the future. But for now, we have a picture of the relationship between the prophetic ministry and the church. The prophets are like the olive trees standing on either side of the candlestick, which is the church, and out of these olive trees pure, fresh, clean oil is piped into the candlestick. Thus, through the oil, the candlestick fulfills its function of giving clear, bright light. Of course, if the source of oil is cut off, then the light of the candlestick dies.

Mobile Ministry: Prophets

The church of Jesus Christ must have a continual supply of fresh oil if it is to be the bearer of light to the world! This supply of oil comes from the olive tree, which typifies the prophetic ministry. We have here a very clear picture of the relationship between the prophetic ministry and the church. The church needs the prophetic ministry piped in continually—not just in cases of extreme emergency. The body of Christ cannot function without fresh oil—the clean, pure inspiration and revelation of the Holy Spirit from the prophetic ministry.

This truth is in line with Proverbs 29:18, which has become a great favorite of mine: *"Where there is no vision, the people perish"* (KJV). A modern reading of *"perish"* is *"cast off restraint"* (NKJV, NIV). One version says, *"are left naked."* One thing is clear. Where there is no vision, God's people are in a bad condition. They cannot live and function the way God intends without vision.

> *The church must have a continual supply of fresh oil to be the light of the world.*

The word *vision* means "direct, fresh revelation." It is not the reading or teaching of Scripture, but an immediate, fresh word from God. When Eli was high priest and Samuel was brought into the prophetic ministry, the Scripture says, *"The word of the LORD was rare in those days; there was no widespread revelation ["open vision" KJV]"* (1 Samuel 3:1). Israel had the written Scriptures, but they lacked the fresh, prophetic illumination and vision they needed. They had all the apparatus of religion: the tabernacle, the ark, the priesthood, the sacrifices, and the law of Moses. However, they were a dead, cold, backslidden people, because religion does not keep people alive. It is only fresh oil that causes the church to burn continually with a bright flame. That fresh oil comes from the prophetic revelation appropriate to a specific situation and generation. We cannot live on past revelation. Again, what Luther said was relevant to Luther's time, and what Wesley said was relevant to Wesley's time. But we cannot live today on Luther, Wesley, or any other person of the past. We must have our own direct, up-to-date, fresh oil being discharged continually into the church.

Merely having correct doctrine is not a substitute for having firsthand revelation from God. God not only has general teaching for us, which He makes available in Scripture, but He also has particular things He wants us to know at particular times. As we saw, it was necessary for Nineveh to know they had only forty days until judgment. It was necessary for Israel to know that the Messiah was just about to come. It was necessary for Paul to know what lay ahead for him in Jerusalem. These words could not be given in the general revelation of the Scriptures. They required the specific revelation of a prophetic ministry at a particular moment.

We live in days of tremendous crises, turmoil, and danger, when everything is moving with unbelievable rapidity. No natural mind can form an accurate opinion of what will be happening five years from now socially, financially, economically, or militarily. If there ever was a time when God's people needed the fresh oil of direct, divine revelation, it is now! We cannot write off this prophetic ministry, saying, "That was for bygone days. It was needed in the Old Testament and in the time of the apostles, but not today." On the contrary, it is needed today perhaps more than at any other time in the history of the church! We need to know things that do not come merely from the teaching of doctrine or by natural sources of information, and God is willing to reveal them to us.

Jesus said, concerning the end times, *"And as it was in the days of Noah, so it will be also in the days of the Son of Man"* (Luke 17:26). Think of all the evil that flourished in Noah's day. The earth was filled with violence. Every imagination and thought of man's heart was only evil continually. Everyone was corrupt. We see all these things in our modern society, too. But there is another side to the days of Noah:

> *We can receive specific direction from God in the last days through prophetic ministry.*

> *By faith Noah, being divinely warned of things not yet seen, moved with godly fear, prepared an ark for the saving of his household.* (Hebrews 11:7)

Noah needed divine revelation, explicit instruction to warn him of what was coming on the earth and to know what steps he should take to preserve himself and his family. Like Noah, we can receive specific direction and protection from God in these last days through prophetic ministry. The church is to shine at the close of this age when darkness is covering the earth and deep darkness is covering the people. (See Isaiah 60:2.) God's message to the church is *"Arise, shine; for your light has come!"* (verse 1). I believe that an essential part of this message is the full restoration of the prophetic ministry—like the olive trees feeding the oil into the candlestick. I am personally praying for and anticipating that restoration!

Chapter 19

Mobile Ministry: Evangelists

he word *evangelist* is very familiar in contemporary Christianity, yet there are very few occurrences of it in the New Testament. Basically, it is derived from a word that means "good news." So we could define an evangelist literally as "a proclaimer of good news."

Thinking about the gospel as good news always reminds me of a friend whose husband was a deacon in their church in Chicago. This lady became incurably sick with a kidney complaint, so she went to their church's bookstore to get a book on healing. After searching diligently, she came up with fourteen books on how to suffer, but not one on how to be healed! Well, I do not call that the gospel, because the gospel is good news. Eventually, she went to an Episcopal priest who was baptized in the Holy Spirit. She received the baptism of the Holy Spirit, was anointed with oil, and was miraculously healed. When she went back to her Jewish physician, who was an unbeliever and an atheist, he was compelled to acknowledge that a miracle had taken place. That is good news; that is the gospel!

The evangelist is the one who tells the good news. If someone does not tell you good news, do not let him deceive you into believing he is telling you the gospel. The gospel is the good news that God loves you and wants to forgive you, bless you, prosper you, heal you, and enable you to live with victory, joy, and inner peace. If that is not good news, I don't know what is! Much of what is passed off on churchgoing people as the gospel has little or no relation to what the New Testament calls the gospel.

The Noun Evangelist

The first use of the noun *evangelist* in the New Testament is in Ephesians 4:11, in the list of ministries that we are considering:

And He Himself gave some to be apostles, some prophets, some evangelists, and some pastors and teachers.

Second, we have the following statement made about Philip:

And [we] *entered the house of Philip the evangelist, who was one of the seven, and stayed with him.* (Acts 21:8)

Philip was called *the* evangelist, and he is the only man who was specified by name as having this ministry. The verse says that he was one of the seven, that is, the seven who were appointed as deacons, as recorded in Acts 6. So, at one time or another, Philip had two titles: deacon and evangelist. We will study the relationship between the evangelist and the deacon in a subsequent chapter.

Let's now look at the third occurrence of the word *evangelist*, which is found in 2 Timothy 4. Paul was writing to Timothy, who is mentioned elsewhere as an apostle. Some people imagine that Timothy had the ministry of a pastor, but he was not actually a pastor, nor was he apparently an evangelist. As we saw earlier, the ministry of an apostle can include all the other ministries. In this light, we read,

> *But you be watchful in all things, endure afflictions, do the work of an evangelist, fulfill your ministry.*
>
> (2 Timothy 4:5)

Timothy was not specifically an evangelist, but Paul told him that he could not entirely fulfill his apostolic ministry in his present assignment without also doing the work of an evangelist, a proclaimer of the good news.

The Verb Evangelize

We just looked at the three occurrences of the noun *evangelist* in the New Testament. However, there is a verb directly connected with it in the Greek that we could render *evangelize*. It may be translated "to proclaim good news" or "to proclaim the good news" or "to preach the gospel." Of course, it carries with it the thought of the ministry of an evangelist and the activities connected with it. It occurs about fifty times in the New Testament and therefore must have been an important part of the early church's ministry.

To begin to examine what it means to be an evangelist, let's look at the ministry of Jesus, who, again, is the perfect pattern of all the ministries. At the beginning of His ministry, Jesus was in the synagogue in Nazareth. This was His home synagogue, where He had been brought up. He stood and read the prophecy from Isaiah 61, which He then applied to Himself:

> *The Spirit of the LORD is upon Me, because He has anointed Me to preach the gospel to the poor; He has sent Me to*

*heal the brokenhearted, to proclaim liberty to the captives
and recovery of sight to the blind, to set at liberty those who
are oppressed.* (Luke 4:18)

What the *New King James Version* translates as *"preach the
gospel"* is the single word *euaggelizo* or "evangelize" in the Greek.
The verse could be rendered, "The Spirit of the Lord is upon
Me, because He has anointed Me to *evangelize* the poor," or
"...He has anointed Me to bring the good news to the poor."

The other things in that eighteenth verse are the *result*
of bringing the good news: healing the brokenhearted, proclaiming liberty to the captives, restoring sight to the blind,
and setting at liberty those who are oppressed. The good
news of the gospel brings these wonderful outcomes in the
lives of those who receive it.

But [Jesus] *said to them, "I must preach the kingdom of
God to the other cities also, because for this purpose I have
been sent."* (verse 43)

Again, in the Greek, to *"preach the kingdom of God"* means
to "bring the good news of the kingdom of God."

The Scripture says this of the first twelve disciples who
were sent out as apostles:

*So they departed and went through the towns, preaching the
gospel and healing everywhere.* (Luke 9:6)

Once more, the phrase translated *"preaching the gospel"* refers to evangelizing. Notice that healing followed the preaching of the gospel as the evidence that it really was good news!
Further on in Luke, we have another example of the use of
this same verb:

Now it happened on one of those days, as [Jesus] taught the people in the temple and preached the gospel, that the chief priests and the scribes, together with the elders, confronted Him. (Luke 20:1)

The Greek for *"preached the gospel"* means "evangelized": thus, the verse could be translated, "He taught the people in the temple and evangelized."

We can define an evangelist literally as "a proclaimer of good news."

Turning to the book of Acts, let us look at three occurrences of the word. The first speaks about Peter and John, who had come down to the city of Samaria to help conserve the results of the evangelistic ministry of Philip.

So when they had testified and preached the word of the Lord, they returned to Jerusalem, preaching the gospel in many villages of the Samaritans. (Acts 8:25)

Notice that two forms of the word *preach* occur in this verse, but in the Greek, two completely different words are used: "So when they had testified and *spoken* the word of the Lord, they returned to Jerusalem, *evangelizing* in many villages of the Samaritans." The first occurrence of *preach* is the ordinary word for "to speak," but the second is the specific word for "to evangelize," or to bear the good news. They carried the good news to the villages on their way back from Samaria to Jerusalem.

The next occurrence is during the first missionary journey of Paul and Barnabas: *"And they were preaching the gospel there"* (Acts 14:7). The Greek for *"they were preaching"* means "they were evangelizing." They were continuing to preach the gospel. Notice that the next incident recorded is the healing of a man who was born lame. (See verses 8–10.) I think that, in almost every place that this word "evangelize" is used, you will find that healing and deliverance are not far away. They are the evidence of the good news.

Third, we have the call of Paul and his companions to go to Macedonia:

> *Now after* [Paul] *had seen the vision, immediately we sought to go to Macedonia, concluding that the Lord had called us to preach the gospel to them.* (Acts 16:10)

Where the verse says *"preach the gospel,"* the Greek again is the verb "to evangelize." They were called to carry the good news to people in Macedonia who had never heard the gospel and were waiting for it.

The word is also used quite frequently in the book of Romans. Let's look at three occurrences there, starting with these two:

> *So, as much as is in me, I am ready to preach the gospel to you who are in Rome also.* (Romans 1:15)

> *As it is written: "How beautiful are the feet of those who preach the gospel of peace, who bring glad tidings of good things!"* (Romans 10:15)

"Preach the gospel" means "to evangelize," and *"Preach the gospel of peace"* means "to evangelize peace," or "carry the good news of peace." Several New Testament quotations about evangelizing are taken from the Old Testament, from the

prophet Isaiah. If there was a prophet who was specifically of the evangelistic spirit, it was Isaiah. He was the prophet above all others whose words contained the good news of the gospel in the Old Testament.

A little further on, Paul spoke about his own ministry and his desire to always reach the unreached.

> *And so I have made it my aim to preach the gospel, not where Christ was named, lest I should build on another man's foundation.* (Romans 15:20)

Again, *"to preach the gospel"* is "to evangelize." It is typical of the evangelistic ministry to desire always to reach the unreached, to bring the message to those who never have heard it. The one consuming passion of the evangelist is to get the good news out to everybody. He is a man on the move. He cannot rest until everyone has heard.

Then, in chapter one of 1 Corinthians, Paul was speaking about people who had been baptized in water, and he said that he himself did not baptize many because that was not really his job.

> *For Christ did not send me to baptize, but to preach the gospel* [evangelize]. (verse 17)

Paul left the actual baptizing of his converts to others, though he saw them baptized. His main business was to evangelize—to bring the good news.

In his second letter to the Corinthians, Paul was speaking about what he intended to do after he had finished the ministry God had given him in the area of Achaia where Corinth was situated. His aim was *"to preach the gospel in the regions beyond* [them]*"* (2 Corinthians 10:16). Once more, the thrust of the evangelist is always to go farther, to go on to where the people have not yet heard. Of course, as I have already pointed out, Paul was doing the work of an evangelist within the scope of his ministry as an apostle, and the apostolic ministry includes that of the evangelist.

The Threefold Purpose of the Evangelist

The supreme object of the evangelist is to introduce the sinner to the Savior. Having made the introduction, he does not stay on to deepen the acquaintance with Christ, but goes on to find others who have never yet been introduced to Him. Therefore, his ministry is essentially introductory.

However, according to the clear New Testament pattern, the evangelist does not merely introduce people to the Savior. He also brings them into salvation and water baptism. We may then sum up the threefold purpose of the evangelist in this way: to introduce sinners to the Savior, to bring them into salvation, and to have them baptized in water. My personal conviction is

> *The supreme objective of the evangelist is to introduce sinners to the Savior.*

that, as the church gets closer and closer to the New Testament standards, we will see those who are really called and sent as evangelists ensuring that their converts are baptized in water.

I stated earlier that many Christians today have completely strayed away from the New Testament standard of immediate baptism in water upon conversion. They will habitually hold a water baptismal service perhaps once or twice a month: "If you want to be baptized, come on Sunday night, January 25th, and we will baptize you." But as we saw, in the book of Acts, every person who was converted was normally baptized by immersion in water within a few hours of conversion. It is hard to find anybody who waited until the next day.

There was tremendous urgency in the New Testament message about water baptism. Actually, there is no authority in the New Testament to separate salvation from water baptism. Jesus said, *"He who believes and is baptized will be saved"* (Mark 16:16). He didn't say anything about the person who believed but was *not* baptized. In Matthew 28:19, when Jesus sent out His disciples, He said, *"Go therefore and make disciples of all the nations, baptizing them in the name of the Father and of the Son and of the Holy Spirit."* When Peter preached on the day of Pentecost, the people exclaimed, *"What shall we do?"* (Acts 2:37), and he replied, *"Repent, and...be baptized"* (verse 38). After people became disciples, the first thing they were to do was to be baptized. It is unscriptural to disconnect conversion and baptism in any way. Philip, our pattern for an evangelist in the New Testament, indeed had this same emphasis in his ministry.

The Nature of Evangelistic Ministry

The greater part of Acts 8 contains the New Testament description of the ministry of an evangelist, the only guide we have for it. At this time in the life of the early church, there was great persecution due to the efforts of Saul of Tarsus. With the exception of the apostles, the believers were scattered abroad to save their lives. *"Therefore those who were scattered went everywhere preaching the word"* (verse 4). Incidentally, the Greek word for *"preaching"* here is "evangelize"—evangelizing the Word, bringing the good news that is contained in the Word of God. In the midst of this persecution and evangelizing, we have the account of Philip's evangelistic ministry. Let's notice the main features of Philip as an evangelist as they are portrayed in this chapter.

His Message

First, notice Philip's *message*, which was wonderfully simple. In each verse, it is summed up in one word.

Then Philip went down to the city of Samaria and preached Christ to them. (Acts 8:5)

Then Philip opened his mouth, and beginning at this Scripture, preached Jesus to him. (verse 35)

So his message was tremendously simple: it was Jesus Christ. He was not presenting an elaborate doctrine, he was presenting a Person—the person of Jesus. He was introducing Christ to people who did not know Him.

The marvelous thing about a real, God-anointed evangelist is that you can hear him preach the same sermon twenty times and still enjoy it because the anointing of the Holy Spirit is upon him. Yet, if a teacher taught the same thing twenty times, you would probably lose interest. For example, I have heard Billy Graham preach, and I could almost preach some of his sermons for him. However, I would never get the same results, because that is not my gifting. Moreover, I still enjoy listening to him preach because this is what the Holy Spirit wants him to do. He is proclaiming Jesus Christ, and this is the essential nature of the evangelistic ministry. Billy Graham's ministry does not end at evangelism, but the basis of his ministry is certainly that of an evangelist. As such, his one aim and purpose is to present Jesus Christ to those who have never heard.

His Attestation

Now, let's look at the *attestation* of Philip, which is also very simple. Here again, today's church, for the most part, is far from the New Testament pattern. Philip apparently went down into the city of Samaria alone. The apostles went by twos, the prophets went in groups, yet here is this one man, Philip, a Jew, going alone into hostile territory. *"For Jews have no dealings with Samaritans"* (John 4:9). But Philip went down to this quite large city of Samaria and started to preach Christ. Why did the people listen? Because God bore supernatural testimony to the truth of his message. The people knew he really had something. How did they know it?

> *And the multitudes with one accord heeded the things spoken by Philip, hearing and seeing the miracles which he did. For unclean spirits, crying with a loud voice, came out of many who were possessed; and many who were paralyzed and lame were healed.* (Acts 8:6–7)

What attracted the people's attention? Miracles of deliverance and miracles of healing. When the people of Samaria saw the evidence of the power that was in the message of Philip, they listened carefully to what he had to say. It wasn't because of the advance notice that had been given in the newspapers and over the radio about the great preacher Philip coming to town. No, he did not know he was coming, and neither did they. But when he came, everybody listened because of divine attestation. In one simple word, the attestation of the New Testament evangelist is *miracles*. They are

the only authority and attestation that God has provided—
and they work!

Now, miracles do not convert people, nor do they produce
faith. What they do is to arrest people's attention and cause
them to listen to the Word of God, and faith comes by hearing the Word. If people will not
listen, then it is no use preaching
to them. The first thing you must
do is to get their attention, and this
was done by the miraculous!

*The attestation of
the New Testament
evangelist is
the working
of miracles.*

I was conducting a deliverance service with a good friend of
mine where these exact things took
place: *"Unclean spirits, crying with a
loud voice, came out of many."* A third
preacher was there, who was also
a good friend of mine. He became quite indignant and said
afterward, "Where do you ever see a service like that in the
New Testament?" The first friend and I looked at each other,
and he said, "You find it in Acts 8:7." We eventually cleared
up the misunderstanding quite satisfactorily, and that man is
still a very good friend of mine.

Much of what we consider normal by New Testament
standards is abnormal by today's standards, and much of what
most Christians today would call abnormal is normal by New
Testament standards. The attestation of the gospel, the good
news, is supernatural. It is the proof that there is good news.
The possessed are delivered, and the sick are healed. When
people see these things happening, they know it is good news.
They are not as interested in theology; they want results. This
is the way Jesus ordained the program He laid down:

And He said to them, "Go into all the world and preach the gospel [carry the good news] *to every creature. He who believes and is baptized will be saved; but he who does not believe will be condemned. And these signs will follow those who believe: In My name they will cast out demons; they will speak with new tongues; they will take up serpents; and if they drink anything deadly, it will by no means hurt them; they will lay hands on the sick, and they will recover."*

(Mark 16:15–18)

Five supernatural signs are given here: the evidence of deliverance, the evidence of the baptism in the Holy Spirit, the evidences of not being hurt by taking up serpents or drinking anything deadly, and the evidence of having the sick recover through the laying on of hands. The ministries of the first apostles are summed up in these words:

After the Lord had spoken to them, He was received up into heaven, and sat down at the right hand of God. And they went out and preached everywhere, the Lord working with them and confirming the word through the accompanying signs. (verses 19–20)

This is the New Testament pattern. God confirms His Word with signs following. If I were challenged by God to go forth again as a missionary, I would not be willing to leave my own country and preach anywhere if I did not have the assurance that God would bear supernatural testimony to the message He gave me. I would rather stay at home and send money; it would do more good. But I do believe and have proved in my own experience that, if you go and present the good news, and trust the Holy Spirit, He will confirm His Word. That's the way it should be. As it says in Hebrews 2:3–4, when the early preachers went out, God bore witness with signs, wonders, miracles, and gifts of the Holy Spirit.

Remember the young man in Africa with little education who spoke to my students? After the Lord first saved him, he was present in a campaign conducted by Brother T. L. Osborn in Mombassa. He saw the miracles that God did there and believed that if God did it for Brother Osborn, He would do it for him. He started on this principle, and it worked wonders. This was one of the reasons he had such a tremendous response from our students.

One day, this young man said to me, "Brother Prince, there's no problem about evangelizing Africa. I just walk into a village and ask if there are any sick people there. There's always somebody sick in an African village. I pray for him, he gets healed, and I have my congregation!" That is the New Testament pattern. You do not need committees, bands, choirs, or any of these things. God bless them if they are there, but we can probably do better without them because, if we have them, we tend to depend upon them. The only thing that really matters is the supernatural attestation of the Holy Spirit.

His Direction

Going on in the eighth chapter of Acts, Philip's *direction* was also supernatural, to say the least! He knew where and when to go by supernatural guidance:

Now an angel of the Lord spoke to Philip, saying, "Arise and go toward the south along the road which goes down from Jerusalem to Gaza."...Then the Spirit said to Philip, "Go near and overtake this chariot." (Acts 8:26, 29)

Notice the direction by the voice of the Spirit. Then, even better, after the eunuch had been baptized, the Spirit of the Lord caught Philip away! (See verses 39–40.) As soon as the job was complete, Philip did not even have to decide where to go; the Holy Spirit just took him. He did not have to walk or travel in the chariot; he had divine transportation.

I call the evangelist "God's paratrooper" because he suddenly dropped in on people, did his job, and got carried off again. This does not usually happen nowadays, although sometimes it still does. In any event, the evangelist is on the move. He is unpredictable; even the devil does not know where he will turn up next. In this way, he continually keeps the devil on the defensive. By and large, the church today is on the defensive, while the devil is on the offensive. But the true evangelist is on the offensive, as was Philip.

> *The true evangelist is spiritually on the offensive, keeping the devil on the defensive.*

As I once heard Charles Simpson say, all the demons in the average church know they have to be on hand at eleven o'clock on Sunday morning because that is when the pastor preaches his sermon. The demons have all ganged up on everybody who is going. They have put in their work beforehand, and there is no element of surprise. But, believe me, when Philip was moving around, the demons just did not know where to go next or when he would be there. I long to see this initiative restored to the church.

Mobile Ministry: Evangelists

His Outreach—Not the Local Church

In the list of God's giftings in the church, we may infer one final aspect of the evangelist, which I mentioned earlier.

And God has appointed these in the church: first apostles, second prophets, third teachers, after that miracles, then gifts of healings, helps, administrations, varieties of tongues.
(1 Corinthians 12:28)

The evangelist is not listed here because Paul was speaking about the local church and the ministries that function within it, while the ministry of an evangelist is to the unconverted. Now, the evangelist might have a ministry in the local church if he was a worker of miracles who had gifts of healings. In this capacity, he might train others in the local church to be evangelistic. Other than that, he would essentially have nothing to do, because all those in the congregation would already have been introduced to Jesus Christ as Savior, which is the basic outreach of the evangelistic ministry.

Chapter 20

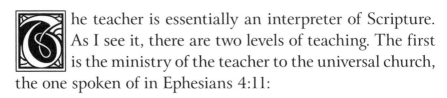

Mobile Ministry:
Teachers

he teacher is essentially an interpreter of Scripture. As I see it, there are two levels of teaching. The first is the ministry of the teacher to the universal church, the one spoken of in Ephesians 4:11:

And He Himself gave some to be apostles, some prophets, some evangelists, and some pastors and teachers.

This verse refers to the office of the teacher, one who interprets Scripture and establishes doctrine for the larger body. On the other hand, the type of teaching that is specifically for the local congregation is given by the elders of the local group. We will deal with this idea much more fully when we come to the theme of elders. However, this ministry may be seen in 1 Timothy 5 where, speaking about the ordering of a local church, Paul said,

Let the elders who rule well be counted worthy of double honor, especially those who labor in the word and doctrine.

(verse 17)

"Doctrine" is simply a noun that means teaching. This ministry is not to the universal church, but to a small group of

believers committed to the elders' care in the local congregation. So we have the teacher who ministers to the whole body in a public ministry similar to that of an apostle or an evangelist. Then we have the teacher who does not have a public ministry in the universal body, but is still responsible for teaching individuals and small groups. In this chapter, we will focus on the teacher who ministers to the universal church.

Apollos' Teaching Ministry

In looking for an example of a teacher in the New Testament, it seems that Apollos had a pure teaching ministry. There are many other men who taught, but who had another ministry combined with teaching. Apollos apparently gave himself totally to the teaching of the Word. In the book of Acts, we find the first description of Apollos' teaching ministry, which occurred in Ephesus (in modern-day Turkey):

> *Now a certain Jew named Apollos, born at Alexandria, an eloquent man and mighty in the Scriptures, came to Ephesus. This man had been instructed in the way of the Lord; and being fervent in spirit, he spoke and taught accurately the things of the Lord, though he knew only the baptism of John. So he began to speak boldly in the synagogue. When Aquila and Priscilla heard him, they took him aside and explained to him the way of God more accurately. And when he desired to cross to Achaia, the brethren wrote, exhorting the disciples to receive him; and when he arrived, he greatly helped those who had believed through grace; for he vigorously refuted the Jews publicly, showing from the Scriptures that Jesus is the Christ* [Messiah].   (Acts 18:24–28)

Let's now compare the above passage with another in 1 Corinthians 3:4–6. Apollos moved from Ephesus across the

Aegean Sea to Achaia (modern-day Greece). In Achaia, he came to the city of Corinth, where he ministered to people who had been brought to the Lord by the ministry of Paul. Now, in the church in Corinth, the same kind of rivalry developed that we see today: factions of believers were promoting the particular preachers whom they liked the best. Paul rebuked them for this, telling them that this demonstrated they were still carnal.

> *For when one says, "I am of Paul," and another, "I am of Apollos," are you not carnal?*   (1 Corinthians 3:4)

It amuses me that some theologians and Bible commentators will latch on to this statement that the Corinthian church was carnal, and then try to say that the people were carnal because they spoke in tongues. They were not carnal because of speaking in tongues, but because they were following human leaders!

The evangelist plants the seed, and the teacher waters it.

Again, this tendency is precisely what we find in the church today. Some say, "I am of Luther," others say, "I am of Calvin," and still others say, "I am of Wesley." The Word of God says, "While you speak like that, it shows you lack maturity." The mark of spiritual immaturity is hanging on to human leaders and ministers whom God has blessed and used, just as He blessed and used Paul, Apollos, and Peter. When people identified themselves within the body of Christ by the name of the particular preacher whom they were following, Paul said, "Please! There's enough of that. Grow up and stop being babies!"

Mobile Ministry: Teachers

Who then is Paul, and who is Apollos, but ministers through whom you believed, as the Lord gave to each one? I planted, Apollos watered, but God gave the increase.

(1 Corinthians 3:5–6)

The Lord gave one ministry to Paul, and another ministry to Apollos. The planting ministry of Paul was the evangelizing—the initial planting of the seed of the Word of God, or the gospel. But the seed would never have grown without subsequent watering, and so the next ministry to come along was the watering ministry of Apollos, the teacher. The evangelist plants the seed, and the teacher follows behind him and waters it. What an excellent picture of the teaching ministry!

Now let's turn back to Acts 18:24. It says that Apollos was *"born at Alexandria."* Alexandria was one of the great cities of learning in the ancient world. It had the most famous library, and the suggestion is that Apollos was a man of some educational background. He was also an *"eloquent man,"* meaning he was a very powerful speaker, and *"mighty in the Scriptures,"* meaning that he had a very thorough knowledge of God's Word. Apollos went to Ephesus, and verse 28 says that *"he vigorously refuted the Jews publicly, showing from the Scriptures that Jesus was the Christ."*

Here is a very clear picture of Apollos' public teaching ministry. Again, he had a comprehensive knowledge of the Scriptures. He was also eloquent, something of a "pulpit personality." His presentations were powerful, and he could prove the opponents of the gospel wrong in public. So he was a man with a forceful public ministry. Contrast this with the ministry of pastors or elders who may teach in small groups or churches, and who have no pulpit personality or large following, yet do tremendously valuable work on their level.

Some people expect an elder or local church pastor, since he must be able to teach, to give a tremendous sermon whenever he stands behind a pulpit. Yet this is not the kind of teaching that always accompanies a man who shares the Word in a local situation. It is unfair and unscriptural to expect your pastor or elder to preach like your favorite preacher on television or at big conferences. In fact, the teaching in your local church may be more practical and life-changing for you than that of a teacher in a mobile ministry. Since he is more in your world, he may indeed speak to the heart of your family or personal situation!

The early church did not receive a teacher unless he was recommended from his previous place of ministry.

Notice a remarkable statement in Acts 18:27: *"And when [Apollos] desired to cross to Achaia, the brethren wrote, exhorting the disciples to receive him."* The early church did not receive preachers who were not recommended from the place they had previously been ministering. This is vitally important. Adhering to this practice today would immediately cut off those who are traveling around the nation and the world without backing, and without producing any fruit, who simply make merchandise of God's people. This principle runs all through the New Testament. Any preacher who came from Asia to Achaia had to have the endorsement of the brethren in Asia, or the brethren in Achaia would not receive him. So Apollos, coming from Asia to Achaia, had a letter of recommendation, and the brethren in Achaia opened their churches to him.

And when he arrived, he greatly helped those who had believed through grace; for he vigorously refuted the Jews publicly, showing from the Scriptures that Jesus is the Christ. (Acts 18:27–28)

"Those who had believed through grace" is a rather remarkable phrase. It refers to people who had a wonderful and supernatural conversion. Perhaps they were illiterate or had no background knowledge of the Old Testament Scriptures. Remember that most of the church in Corinth was of Gentile background. Corinth was a seaport and, as such, an intersection for people of great wickedness and immorality. Then Paul arrived, and in the course of about eighteen months, he left a flourishing congregation of believers.

This was not done by the plodding method of systematically teaching a few people. This was done by a mighty impact of the Holy Spirit bearing supernatural testimony to Jesus Christ as the Savior of the world. Many of these new believers must have been swept into the kingdom of God by this supernatural touch of God. We find the same thing happening today in many parts of the world where people have a very pressing need. They have no background knowledge of the Scriptures, no education, and no ability to read or write, yet God supernaturally intervenes to save them.

I saw cases like this in Africa. One old man had never been to church in his whole life. He did not know anything whatever about the gospel. One night, he dreamed of going to the local thatched, mud-walled church and getting saved. When he awoke, he decided to go there. However, he did not feel he even had the right clothes to go to church. He had to borrow an old overcoat from somebody. Then he made his way to the church, where he was saved. Now that really was the supernatural grace of God! In some parts of the world, many are literally "believing through grace."

A missionary from South America told me of a nominal Catholic woman who had never opened the Bible, but who had a very vivid dream. She saw herself going to a certain church, and she noticed that the walls inside the church were green. The next Sunday, she thought, "I must go to this church." She went out and hired a taxi, told the driver what type of building she had seen, and said, "Take me there." Unfortunately (or so it seemed), the taxi broke down, and she could not get there.

The next Sunday, she did the same thing, and this time the taxi made it there. She went into the church, and Christ supernaturally revealed Himself to her. Afterward, she told the minister of the congregation about her dream, saying, "You know, I saw this building, and I tried to get here a week ago, but I couldn't. This time, the taxi got me here. I came inside, and I saw these green walls." The minister looked at her and said, "Are you sure you saw them green in your dream?" She said, "Yes." He replied, "No wonder you didn't get here last week. We repainted the walls this week, and last week they weren't green!" This was a supernatural revelation granted by the Holy Spirit to a woman who did not know a thing about the gospel.

During the Second World War, I was a patient in a military hospital. In the next bed was a Free French sailor. I was the only person in the hospital who spoke French, and he spoke no English, so he either spoke to me or to nobody! After a while, he asked me, "What's that book you read every day?" I said, "That's the Bible." He did not seem very interested, but he would talk to me about the Bible. One day, I said to him, "Would you like me to get you a New Testament in French?" He had never heard of the New Testament!

He did not know what it was, even though he was a good Catholic. So I got a New Testament from the British Foreign Bible Society in Cairo and gave it to him. The results were dramatic. I have never seen anything like it. In less than two weeks, he had read the whole New Testament, with the exception of the book of Revelation, and he was converted. He asked, "Why didn't they ever tell me this?" When I last saw him, sometime later, he had bought the biggest Bible he could find in French, and armed with this Bible, he was going around talking to everybody about the Lord.

For some, there must be a supernatural intervention of God in their lives, or they will not find the Lord. Those whom God cannot reach by systematic exposition, He reaches by supernatural revelation! These people are examples of those who "believe through grace," as we saw concerning the Christians of Corinth in Acts 18.

> *The teacher's gift is to make Scripture simple, real, and applicable for believers.*

The Corinthian believers knew Jesus. They knew He had saved them and baptized them in the Holy Spirit. However, as for knowing the Scripture, or knowing what grace was, or knowing any of the basic truths of the gospel, they knew virtually nothing! So God sent them a teacher, in the person of Apollos, who mightily helped them. He explained what had happened to them and filled in the gaps of their understanding. Perhaps he laid a basic doctrinal foundation in their lives. They needed the systematic exposition of Scripture, or they never would have stayed in the faith. God does the same thing today. He sends people an "Apollos" to bring them a public, systematic exposition of the Scripture so they can know what they believe and why they believe it, and how to relate one scriptural truth to another.

The mobile ministry of the teacher is the ministry to which the Lord has called me, and I vividly remember teaching the young people in America of the late 1960s and early 1970s the basic foundations of their faith. They had been sovereignly saved out of rebellion, drugs, and anarchy, but how they needed to be taught! They would sit for hours and beg for more of God's Word. In Africa, too, I have seen multitudes stand in the heat of the day and refuse to leave when I finished my message. They had traveled for days on foot in order to come, and they wanted more of the Word. I also remember a man in Moscow who had traveled for seven days and nights on a train to attend a training conference for young leaders. Can you imagine the intensity of his spiritual hunger? I have seen and experienced the power of the teaching ministry by the grace of God.

When we were on the mission field, we found that an evangelistic ministry will often come forth rapidly in someone's life after conversion. In fact, the person can be converted one week and start to act like an evangelist the next. But the ministry of a teacher usually takes much longer to develop. In most of the countries that we might describe as somewhat primitive, one of the great deficiencies is the teaching ministry. It is not difficult to get people out as evangelists, but there are sadly few teachers. This ministry is much needed today.

Teaching and the Other Mobile Ministries

Let us now see how teaching is frequently linked with some of the other main mobile ministries. In the following verse, Paul linked the ministry of the apostle and the teacher:

...to which I was appointed a preacher, an apostle, and a teacher of the Gentiles. (2 Timothy 1:11)

Apostle and teacher go together very closely as ministries of the Word. There may also be a link between prophets and teachers:

Now in the church that was at Antioch there were certain prophets and teachers. (Acts 13:1)

Further on in Acts, we read about Judas and Silas, who had come down from Jerusalem to Antioch:

Now Judas and Silas, themselves being prophets also, exhorted and strengthened the brethren with many words. (Acts 15:32)

They had a message of exhortation and teaching that went along with their ministry as prophets.

In Luke, we see the ministry of the teacher linked with that of the evangelist:

Now it happened on one of those days, as [Jesus] *taught the people in the temple and preached the gospel....* (Luke 20:1)

Jesus both taught and evangelized. So the teaching ministry is frequently joined with another ministry. This fact reinforces the concept of *team ministry*, something the church today is truly laying hold of. Apostles, prophets, exhorters, and others whose ministries are very focused and dynamic would do well to partner with teachers, who can balance their gifting and emphases. The teacher can work with an apostle plowing new ground in Africa, or an exhorter filling arenas in America, by interpreting, balancing, and applying the messages needed by these audiences that will not be given by the main leader. The teacher can preserve the results of such ministries!

The Need for Consecration and Growth

As we previously saw, however, Apollos apparently gave himself fully to the ministry of teaching. This brings up the point that the ministry of the teacher requires *consecration*. I have shocked people by a statement I sometimes make: "The friends I keep, the books I read, the food I eat—all are designed to make me the best Bible teacher I can be. Not better than someone else, but the best teacher *I* can be." Do not imagine that you can properly teach the Scriptures without a disciplined life. It will cost you something. But what a blessing to pursue what God has created you for, and this applies to whatever God has called you to do. For myself, I am a teacher. If you stand me on my head in the corner, I will start teaching! That is who I am and who God has made me to be. But I had to *give myself* totally to the development of this teaching gift, because teaching involves your whole personality: spirit, soul (mind, will, and emotions), and body. It proceeds from the whole man, and from one's whole life.

Recall that my definition of the teacher is one who interprets Scripture. The teacher's gift is to interpret and apply Scripture for others. He makes Scripture simple, real, and applicable. It is a real gift to make things simple. As a professional philosopher, I learned to make things complicated, but God had to give me the gift of making things simple. To me, if I cannot say something simply, I do not yet understand it. Oh, what a need there is for believers to truly grasp and apply the foundational truths of Scripture! This passion has consumed me for some sixty years now as I have given myself to the study and exposition of God's Word.

As I mentioned earlier, God called me to this teaching ministry through a message in tongues and interpretation in 1941: "I have called thee as a teacher of the Scriptures in truth and faith and love, which are in Christ Jesus, for many." How often I have pondered the Lord's commission to me as it has unfolded through the years. I have noticed that the progression God spoke of has come to pass in my teaching: first truth, then faith, and finally love.

In the beginning, I was totally concerned with truth, and I pursued the whole truth for the whole church. Then I began to see that I might have the truth but not have the victory in key areas of my life, such as health and finances. I laid hold of faith through the Word, as well as all the incredible blessings that God has promised in His Word. The final phase of my divine education has been in the realm of love. As 1 Timothy 1:5 says, *"The goal of our instruction is love"* (NASB). How much love has come to mean to me, even in having to give my beloved wife Ruth back to the Lord. I never knew there was so much love in the world until the body of Christ rallied around me after her passing. To this day, this love in the body of Christ brings tears to my eyes.

> *The ministry of the teacher can change history by transmitting pure Bible teaching to subsequent generations of believers.*

May I encourage the teachers to continue to grow in their gift and in its expression to the church. Do not stay just in the areas you are comfortable teaching in, but expect God to open new arenas of truth from which you can bless the church!

I recall God speaking to me in the mid-1970s as I lay on my bed in a hotel room in Atlanta: "From Cherith to Zarephath, from Zarephath to Carmel, from Carmel to Horeb, from Horeb into many lives." I recognized instantly that these were the locations of the main events in the ministry of Elijah. He was fed by ravens at the brook Cherith and by the widow at Zarephath, and then he faced down the false prophets at Mount Carmel. But at Mount Horeb, he was confronted to anoint the next kings of Syria and Israel, and the prophet Elisha who would succeed him. Recall that Elisha finished all the work that God had assigned to Elijah. God spoke to me the words "into many lives." It has been my desire both to teach others and to teach others to teach others! As Paul stated,

> *And the things that you have heard from me among many witnesses, commit these to faithful men who will be able to teach others also.*　　　　　(2 Timothy 2:2)

Paul taught Timothy, who was to teach the local elders, who were in turn to train other elders. The ministry of the teacher can change history by transmitting pure Bible teaching to subsequent generations of believers. I hope I have been successful in producing some generations of teaching behind me.

Chapter 21

Resident Ministry: Pastors

e have dealt with what I consider to be the four main mobile ministries of the church—apostles, prophets, evangelists, and teachers. In the next three chapters, we will consider the resident ministries of the local church: the elder (pastor) and the deacon.

The distinction between mobile and residential ministries is of real importance. Again, a mobile ministry can function within any sphere that God assigns. If a man is an apostle by ministry, he is an apostle whether he is in Jerusalem, Antioch, or Corinth. However, if a man is appointed an elder or pastor in Antioch, and he moves to Corinth, he will not necessarily be an elder in Corinth. He must be reappointed because the residential ministries are not automatically transferable to other locales.

I believe that the problems and challenges of each city in the New Testament were unique and that certain ministries were ordained by God to be planted in these cities. Their anointing was for the city and region in which He placed them, and not for "the ends of the earth." This is the nature of the residential ministries.

How important it is for God's people to have these ministries among them whose focus is the local congregation!

While the mobile ministries are building the corporate body, the residential ministries are pouring themselves into the families, communities, and fabric of individual cities. This is a necessary balance in the body of Christ. Some ministries must be there to stay. God's people will be insecure if leaders are always coming and going, with no one tending the flock. As we will see, the pastor/elder gives himself to their spiritual needs, while the deacon is focused on the material and practical needs. Thus, in God's program, both the ends of the earth and each city and town are cared for.

There is much confusion among believers about local church leadership, which I will address in this chapter. In fact, there are many stereotypes and traditions that I will address here that may even upset your theology!

In Philippians 1:1, we are presented with the total personnel of the local church:

Paul and Timothy, bondservants of Jesus Christ, to all the saints in Christ Jesus who are in Philippi, with the bishops and deacons.

Here are the three groups that make up a local congregation: the believers and two classes of leaders, bishops (also called overseers and elders), and deacons. There is nothing beyond them.

Different Names for the Same Leader

Let's first consider the *bishops*. The Greek word that is translated "*bishops*" in Philippians is *poimen,* and is normally translated "shepherd." Only in one place, Ephesians 4:11, is it translated "*pastors.*" Here we have to clear up some problems arising from language and translation. In the New Testament

Greek, three different words are used to describe the same office or ministry. In addition to these three words, the King James Version translates two of these Greek words by two different English words. So we have a total of five words in the King James translation, all describing one and the same office or ministry! Over the centuries, this has undoubtedly led to endless confusion among English-speaking Christians. One of my main purposes in these chapters is to clear up this confusion and therefore bring real clarity to this important residential ministry.

I have to confess that, for years, I labored under this confusion. I used to speak regularly about the pastor *and* the elders, as though the pastor and elders were distinct. It was like a flash of lightning one day when I suddenly realized that pastor and elder are just two different names for the same person or office! My study of the New Testament church order was like somebody trying to do a jigsaw puzzle with an extra piece. No matter what I did, there was always one piece there was no place for. This extra piece was the pastor as a ministry or as a person distinct from the elders. Yet this understanding of church leadership has no basis in the New Testament. *Pastor* or *shepherd* are names for the same ministry as elder. As we examine the three Greek words and the five English titles in the New Testament, it will become abundantly clear that they are all speaking about one and the same person.

The first Greek word is *presbuteros,* meaning an elder, which gives us such English words as *presbytery.* The Presbyterians are so called because they believe in the government of elders. This word is always translated as elder in the King James Version, so there's no problem about the translation there.

The next Greek word is *episkopos*. Its literal meaning in Greek is not in question: *epi* means "over" and *skopos* means "a seer"—an "overseer." However, in the King James Version, which uses older English words for some terms, the word *episkopos* is sometimes translated *"bishop."* Many people do not realize that *bishop* and *overseer* are two different ways of translating the same Greek word.

In fact, if you are interested in linguistics, *episkopos* was merely taken over into the European languages. In Danish, for example, the original word *biskof* is just *episkopos* with the first *e* dropped off and the *p* changed to a *b*. From the Scandinavian *biskof,* we get the English word *bishop* by transliteration. Yet the meaning is still that of an overseer.

The third word, *poimen,* which I already mentioned, means "shepherd" and is translated in this way many times in the New Testament. Again, only once is it translated *"pastor"* in the King James Version, but we must keep in mind that this was the word for shepherd at the time of that translation. Today, the associations of these two words are completely different from one other. Yet the fact remains that the office that is referred to acts as a shepherd. Thus, we have three different Greek words for a resident leader translated by five different English words. No wonder there is great confusion about local church leadership!

Three Greek Words	Five English Words
	elder
presbuteros	pastor
episkopos	bishop
poimen	shepherd
	overseer

Resident Ministry: Pastors

My conclusion, therefore, is that these different words all denote one and the same office or ministry. We now turn to passages in which these terms are used interchangeably:

From Miletus [Paul] sent to Ephesus and called for the elders of the church.   (Acts 20:17)

Here they are called *"elders."* Most of the rest of Acts 20 contains the address that Paul gave to these elders. He was still speaking to the elders when he said,

Therefore take heed to yourselves and to all the flock, among which the Holy Spirit has made you overseers, to shepherd ["feed" KJV] the church of God which He purchased with His own blood.   (verse 28)

They were called elders in verse 17, but in this verse, they were referred to as overseers over a flock, which is always connected with the activity of a shepherd. Then, we read, *"...to shepherd the church of God."* We have seen that the Greek word for *"shepherd,"* a noun, is *poimen.* Here, the Greek word that is translated *"shepherd"* or *"feed"* is *poimaino,* a verb. To render this verse correctly, we should say that these elders or overseers shepherd the flock, or the church.

Note again that these elders were the acknowledged leaders of the local church; there was no one above them in a local congregation. If there had been some pastor or other leader in the background, Paul's conduct would have been extremely unethical in summoning these elders to give them his instructions, while ignoring the pastor. But Paul did not do this because there was no pastor in the background to ignore. These men collectively were the local leadership of that church.

Next, let's turn to the epistle to Titus, where Paul said,

For this reason I left you in Crete, that you should set in order the things that are lacking, and appoint elders in every city as I commanded you.... (Titus 1:5)

As we have seen, one of Titus's main responsibilities was to ordain elders. Then, in the following verses, Paul went on to describe the type of person an elder should be:

...if a man is blameless, the husband of one wife, having faithful children not accused of dissipation or insubordination. For a bishop [or overseer] *must be blameless.*

(verses 6–7)

Paul was talking about an elder, but the word used here is *bishop* or *overseer*; the words are used absolutely interchangeably. An elder is a bishop, and a bishop is an elder. This is not only Paul's usage, but Peter's, as well. Turning to 1 Peter, we see that he likewise combined these ministries:

For you were like sheep going astray, but have now returned to the Shepherd and Overseer of your souls. (1 Peter 2:25)

The alternative rendering for overseer is bishop, so Jesus is the Shepherd and Overseer (or Bishop) of our souls. The same person is referred to.

In 1 Peter 5, all three concepts are joined together, and all are applied to the elders:

The elders who are among you I exhort, I who am a fellow elder and a witness of the sufferings of Christ, and also a partaker of the glory that will be revealed: Shepherd the flock of God which is among you, serving as overseers. (verses 1–2)

In verse 1, they are called *"elders"*; in verse 2, they are told to *"shepherd* [feed] *the flock of God..., serving as overseers."* We have elders (*presbuteros*) combined with feeding or shepherding (*poimaino*) and overseeing (*episkopao*, the verb form of *episkopos*). Therefore, both Peter and Paul assumed that the leaders of the local church are elders, and that they are also called shepherds and overseers. We can summarize it in this way: The qualification for leadership is to be an elder; the spiritual ministry is that of a shepherd; and the work that has to be done is overseeing. We have one person viewed from three different perspectives.

Plurality of Leadership

The next fact that we need to establish is that these resident leaders of the local church are always mentioned in the plural. There is not a single case in the New Testament where a local congregation is led by one man who is *the* pastor. The concept is not found. In fact, it is totally alien to the whole order and picture of the early church, absolutely out of line with everything that the New Testament teaches about the leadership of the local church. Instead, the New Testament picture is one of *team ministry.*

Let's look at examples of these local leaders who are mentioned in the plural: *"So when they had appointed elders in every church..."* (Acts 14:23). Notice that the church is singular, while the elders are plural. Every church had elders. Not *an* elder, *a* pastor, or *a* minister, but *elders* in every church. We have already looked at Acts 20:17, where Paul *"called for the elders of the church."* Not *the* elder, pastor, bishop, or superintendent, but *the elders* of the church. We have also noted Titus 1:5, where Paul told Titus to *"appoint elders in every city."*

It is significant that the church and the city are coextensive. In other words, they have the same boundaries or environs. Where one passage talks about ordaining elders in *every church*, another talks about ordaining elders in *every city*. We will return to this concept shortly.

We have also looked at Philippians 1:1, which speaks of *"the bishops and deacons."* There is no mention of the pastor or minister. Again, in 1 Thessalonians, we read,

> *And we urge you, brethren, to recognize those who labor among you, and are over you in the Lord and admonish you.* (1 Thessalonians 5:12)

"Those" who work among the Thessalonians are in the plural. And they do three things, which correspond to the three leadership titles: they *"labor"* (as shepherds or pastors), they are *"over"* them (as bishops or overseers), and they *"admonish"* them (as seasoned elders).

Hebrews refers three times to local church leadership, and always in the plural:

> *Remember **those who rule over you**, who have spoken the word of God to you, whose faith follow....Obey **those who rule over you**, and be submissive, for they watch out for your souls, as those who must give account....Greet all **those who rule over you**, and all the saints.*
> (Hebrews 13:7, 17, 24, emphasis added)

There is not the faintest shadow of a suggestion anywhere in the verses we have looked at that there is one man who is the ruler of a local church. It is perfectly clear in each passage that there is a plurality of leadership and ministry, or *team leadership*. Experience certainly shows that the remarkable breadth of responsibilities in pastoring God's people requires a team, and much more so than in mobile ministry. The reason is that mobile ministry is by nature more specialized than residential ministry. Residential ministry is like a doctor who has a general practice covering a broad scope of issues, while mobile ministries are like the specialized areas of medical practice. The sheer breadth of issues involved in bringing a local body of people to maturity requires a team approach. This is precisely what is pictured in the New Testament.

> *The New Testament picture of local church leadership is one of team ministry.*

Turning to Acts 15, we have the picture of key leaders meeting to discuss the conversion of the Gentiles. Again, we see a consistent thread of plural leadership on the local scene:

> *They determined that Paul and Barnabas and certain others of them should go up to Jerusalem, to the apostles and elders, about this question.* (Acts 15:2)

> *And when they had come to Jerusalem, they were received by the church and the apostles and the elders.* (verse 4)

> *Now the apostles and elders came together to consider this matter.* (verse 6)

> *Then it pleased the apostles and elders, with the whole church.* (verse 22)

> *They delivered to them* [the Gentile churches] *the decrees to keep, which were determined by the apostles and elders at Jerusalem.* (Acts 16:4)

Again, not once do we find the suggestion that one man is *the* leader of a congregation. Five times, apostles and elders are mentioned as joined together in the leadership of a local congregation.

In Acts 15:23, we have a more formal example supporting this idea, which is part of a letter:

They wrote this letter by them: The apostles, the elders, and the brethren, To the brethren who are of the Gentiles in Antioch, Syria, and Cilicia: Greetings.

This is plural local leadership. Note how consistent the New Testament is on the titles and the plural nature of residential ministry. There is little left to guesswork in this picture of leadership.

God's Original Pattern

Now, the revolutionary thing about this leadership picture is that, in any given locality, there never needs to be more than one local church, even though there may be many thousands of believers there. As we saw earlier, there was never more than one church in one city. It was never a situation where there were churches in Jerusalem, or churches in Antioch, or churches in Corinth. We see *the* church in Jerusalem, or *the* church in Antioch, or *the* church in Corinth. Yet the number of believers was very large in these cities. Historians estimate that there were at least forty thousand believers in Antioch and at least twenty-five thousand believers in Corinth, yet only one church!

One man cannot effectively serve as a shepherd to five hundred people, let alone five thousand or fifty thousand! It would be impossible for a pastor to do the job the way it should be done if he tried to oversee that number of people. The alternative is to have plurality of leaders, these elders/overseers/shepherds. That way, it does not matter how many members there are; you never have to split up the congregation. You appoint new leaders each time the congregation grows, and you keep a certain proportion between the number of leaders and the number in the congregation.

For example, suppose you need one elder for every fifty people. With a congregation of five hundred, you would need ten elders; with a congregation of five thousand, you would need a hundred elders; and with a congregation of fifty thousand, you would need a thousand elders. But you never need to divide up the congregation and make two churches in one locality simply because the church grows.

Groups of disciples transition into churches when elders are appointed for them.

Let's see this arrangement as it was applied in the church in Jerusalem. Acts 18:21–22 tells us that Paul landed at Caesarea and then went up and greeted the church. He gave his report to *the church*—not to the churches, but to one church in Jerusalem. In Acts 21:20, we can see a picture of the size of this church:

> *And when they heard it, they glorified the Lord. And they said to him, "You see, brother, how many myriads of Jews there are who have believed."*

Where some versions say "thousands," the term used by the *New King James Version* (and the original Greek) is *"myriads,"* or ten thousands. The language indicates that it must have been at least ten thousand multiplied by five, which makes fifty thousand in the one congregation in Jerusalem! Verse 22 of the same chapter says, *"What then? The assembly must certainly meet...."* This verse speaks about a very large concourse of people—multitudes, and yet one church. How could that be? Because they had elders in proportion to the number of members in the church.

I believe God does things right the very first time. This pattern may be foreign to us, but it is His pattern. I always think of Noah's ark in this connection. The ark was designed by God and built by Noah in exact agreement with God's design. It never had to be recalled, never had to go into dry dock or be modified or repaired. It was built right the first time. This is the way God works.

Consider the ministry of Jesus Christ, the perfect Apostle, the perfect Prophet, the perfect Evangelist, the perfect Teacher, and the perfect Shepherd. Jesus established this fivefold ministry from the start, and God has never had any program for ministry other than that of Jesus Christ. All we have to do is do what Jesus did—it is that simple. Jesus said,

> *Most assuredly, I say to you, he who believes in Me, the works that I do he will do also.* (John 14:12)

God started with the right pattern, which He gave to the apostles and other early leaders of the church by the Holy Spirit, and He will never accept another. We have seen many other forms and methods of ministry over the years, but they have never accomplished the job God wanted done. Why don't we fit in with God's plan instead of trying to make Him do things the way we think He ought to do them?

Let me mention two other points about the importance and necessity of elders, which we previously discussed in other contexts.

The Appointment of Elders Creates a Church

The first point is illustrated by the following verse:

And when they had preached the gospel to that city and made many disciples, they returned to Lystra, Iconium, and Antioch, strengthening the souls of the disciples, exhorting them to continue in the faith, and saying, "We must through many tribulations enter the kingdom of God."

(Acts 14:21–22)

They returned to the cities of Lystra, Iconium, and Antioch, where they had ministered within the previous year. When they left those cities after their first visit, they left behind people who were called "disciples." They did not leave churches. There is no reference to churches before this time. However, on their return trip, we read,

So when they had appointed elders in every church, and prayed with fasting, they commended them to the Lord in whom they had believed. (verse 23)

Notice the transition from being just disciples to being churches. When did this happen? When the elders were appointed. Without elders, you have amorphous groups of disciples. But as soon as the proper leaders are appointed, then each of these groups of disciples is recognized scripturally as a church. Judging by this standard, what should we think about the multitudes of denominations and congregations that are not organized around this principle?

The elders who were appointed in Lystra, Iconium, and Antioch could not have been believers for more than a year, probably less. They were not tremendous Bible students who had been through a Bible college or who had sat for fifteen years in Sunday school. They were just men who had used their time to get acquainted with God and the basic truths of His Word. When Paul and Barnabas returned, the Holy Spirit showed them the men who were to be leaders. Once again, they were probably clear choices, men who had risen up and taken responsibility naturally. Leaders always rise to the top through demonstrating initiative, responsibility, and service. In this way, the apostles simply recognized the obvious choice that God had already made.

Residential Leadership Is Fundamental

The second point may be seen in this verse:

For this reason I left you in Crete, that you should set in order the things that are lacking, and appoint elders in every city. (Titus 1:5)

Something is definitely lacking until elders are ordained. This issue of residential leadership is absolutely fundamental. It cannot be bypassed or ignored. Are we in order, or are we lacking? There is nothing more pressing than our need to embrace this biblical model of plural, "homegrown" leadership in local church bodies. I use the term *homegrown* to describe the leader whose "seminary" is the local church itself. The remarkable fact is that pastors/elders arise *out of* the churches they are to pastor.

As a recipient of a very fine education, I greatly appreciate what formal training can do. However, the skills I learned in formal education were not those I have needed in local church life. And I must say that men trained in the crucible of local church life have been the ones with the most impact in churches. Again, will we try to improve on God's methods, or will we fall in line with them?

Mobile and Residential Relationships

Let us now review the relationship between apostles and elders in a local congregation, which we have discussed to some extent in addressing the structure of the church. How do these two ministry types relate to one another? Although the apostle is primarily a mobile ministry to the whole body of Christ, even he has to have a home somewhere. He should be in fellowship with a local congregation wherever he resides. You might say he is a member by residence.

The apostle's relationship to his local church was addressed by Peter:

> *The elders who are among you I exhort, I who am a fellow elder.* (1 Peter 5:1)

As a resident of the city of Jerusalem, the apostle Peter took his position within the Jerusalem congregation as an elder together with the other elders. Since the apostolic ministry usually includes the ministries of the prophet, the evangelist, the teacher, and the elder, the apostle exercises the ministry of an elder when functioning within his home church. He is not on a higher level than the elders, for there is no individual or body over the elders. This is one of the great fundamental principles that we cannot ignore. The elders are the leaders, and you cannot get any higher than they. The moment you have anybody over the elders, then you will need to have somebody over him, and then you will need to have somebody over him, so that you will inevitably end up with some kind of bureaucracy.

Another example of mobile ministries interacting with a local congregation is the church in Antioch.

> *Now in the church that was at Antioch there were certain*
> *prophets and teachers....*   (Acts 13:1)

Five men are then listed in this verse as prophets and teachers. At this time, they were resident in Antioch, so that Antioch was their local congregation. Within this congregation, they had positions of leadership due to their ministries as prophets and teachers. But they still took their places within the congregation along with the other local leaders.

As we have seen, here is a picture of the main offices or ministries in a local congregation:

> *And God has appointed these in the church: first apostles,*
> *second prophets, third teachers, after that miracles, then gifts*
> *of healings, helps, administrations, varieties of tongues.*
>   (1 Corinthians 12:28)

The senior ministry is the apostle, followed by the prophets and teachers, but they are all co-elders. In terms of their authority outside merely local matters, their authority is ranked, but within the local church, they are equal.

This arrangement is extremely logical and practical; a very careful balance is needed, especially in the relationship between the apostles and the local elders. The apostles cannot become a group above the elders. Nevertheless, because of the apostolic ministry in certain matters, particularly those of doctrine, theirs is the highest authority.

In many things in Scripture, we must achieve a balance. I will use the relationship between husband and wife as an illustration. The Scripture says the husband is the head of the wife, but also that the husband is to cherish the wife. There are responsibilities on both sides. (See Ephesians 5:22–31.) Many marriages go wrong because one or both partners do not fulfill their obligations. A mutual fulfilling of responsibilities is required for the marriage to be successful. The wife is to submit, but the husband is to cherish. If the husband does not cherish, then the submission of the wife becomes a kind of bondage. On the other hand, the husband is to lead, but if the wife does not submit, then the husband's leadership becomes a kind of dictatorship. So for a marriage to function, both parties have to take their places and respect and acknowledge the position of the other.

> *Leaders trained in the crucible of local church life have had the most impact in churches.*

It seems to me that it is exactly the same with apostles and elders in a local congregation. The apostles are not to say, "We're a super group, and you have to do what we say because we're apostles." On the other hand, within certain spheres that are particularly under the apostolic ministry, their opinion is the most authoritative. Therefore, the other elders cannot say to the apostles, "You're just elders, and we don't need to pay any more attention to you than anybody else." Instead, they should say, "You're co-elders, but because of your apostolic ministry, we are obligated to pay attention to what you say." Likewise, in the absence of a local apostle among the elders, a senior elder should be heeded, but in either case, there should be no dictator.

The apostle's relationship to his local church was addressed not only by Peter, but also by John:

> *The elder, To the elect lady and her children...* (2 John 1)

> *The elder, To the beloved Gaius...* (3 John 1)

John was an apostle, but he took his position as an elder, just as Peter did. In the third epistle of John, however, it becomes clear that in the church situation in the city where Gaius lived, there was trouble among the elders. The trouble was due to one particular man, Diotrephes, who had a very common disease among Christians: He wanted to be lord over everybody else. He wanted to be *the one* to whom everybody else had to look to and obey, and he wanted to have the last word on everything. John was a very gracious and loving man, but the language he used about Diotrephes was pretty sharp:

> *I wrote to the church, but Diotrephes, who loves to have the preeminence among them, does not receive us. Therefore, if I come, I will call to mind his deeds which he does, prating against us with malicious words. And not content with that, he himself does not receive the brethren, and forbids those who wish to, putting them out of the church.* (3 John 9–10)

Here was a very typical church situation. Diotrephes had decided that he was going to be *the* pastor and everybody else was going to have to do what he said. As an apostle, John said, "If I come along, I'll deal with Diotrephes." Note the interplay of authority.

It is a fact that, in every aspect of the Christian life, and in every aspect of the local congregation, there is this element of authority and discipline. Where Christians refuse scriptural discipline, the result is chaos and disaster. The majority of Christians do not have the faintest concept of what it means to be under discipline. Often, when people receive the baptism of the Holy Spirit, they get a false idea of what freedom is. They say, "Now, I'm free. I can do what I like." That is not freedom but childishness!

During our ministry in Kenya, when the nation was about to obtain its independence, the Kenyans said among themselves, "When *uhuru* (independence) comes, we can ride our bicycles on any side of the road. We will travel in the buses without paying fares. We won't have to pay any more taxes." That was their idea of independence. Some Christians are just as naïve in the spiritual plane as those people were on the political level. In every area of Christian living and church life, there is authority and discipline. Remember that the first people who were ever called Christians were "*disciples*," or "ones under discipline." (See Acts 11:26.) We need to return to an understanding of a plurality of church leadership in which we can be led and instructed by godly overseers.

Chapter 22

Pastors: Ruling, Teaching, Shepherding

n this chapter, we will dig further into the work of an elder or pastor. Two of the main roles of this resident ministry are to rule and to teach, as we have seen in these and other Scriptures:

Let the elders who rule well be counted worthy of double honor, especially those who labor in the word and doctrine.
(1 Timothy 5:17)

Remember those who rule over you, who have spoken the word of God to you, whose faith follow, considering the outcome of their conduct. (Hebrews 13:7)

The third main role is that of the shepherd:

Therefore take heed to yourselves and to all the flock, among which the Holy Spirit has made you overseers, to shepherd the church of God which He purchased with His own blood. (Acts 20:28)

Shepherd the flock of God which is among you, serving as overseers, not...as being lords over those entrusted to you, but being examples to the flock; and when the Chief Shepherd appears, you will receive the crown of glory that does not fade away. (1 Peter 5:2–4)

I truly believe that the heart of a shepherd is the distinguishing mark of a true pastor/elder. This is a man who carries the people in his heart and lives continually among them as a protector and guide.

Let's look more closely at these three roles.

The Elder as Ruler

The verb "to rule" has some interesting uses in the New Testament that indicate a very definite degree of authority and discipline. In fact, a man cannot function as a true pastor or shepherd without possessing and exercising real authority in his role as a leader and protector. Let's look at a quotation about the Messiah from Micah 5:2, which we find in the New Testament:

And thou Bethlehem, in the land of Juda, art not the least among the princes of Juda: for out of thee shall come a Governor, that shall rule my people Israel. (Matthew 2:6 KJV)

The word that is translated *"rule"* is the Greek word for shepherd. The same word occurs three times in Revelation. Here is the first instance:

And he who overcomes, and keeps My works until the end, to him I will give power [or authority] *over the nations; "He shall rule* [shepherd] *them with a rod of iron; they shall be dashed to pieces like the potter's vessels."* (Revelation 2:26–27)

That fact that the reference is to a shepherd is emphasized by the use of the word *"rod."* But instead of being a wooden rod or staff, it was a rod of iron. Note that the rod is tied to breaking the nations as a potter's vessels are broken to pieces. The image of authority and discipline is very powerful in this word.

Likewise, we read this about the woman described in Revelation 12:1 as being *"clothed with the sun"*:

She bore a male Child who was to rule [shepherd] *all nations with a rod of iron.* (verse 5)

Again, we have the Messiah ruling and shepherding with a rod of iron. Third, we read of the Lord Jesus Christ,

Now out of His mouth goes a sharp sword, that with it He should strike the nations. And He Himself will rule [shepherd] *them with a rod of iron. He Himself treads the winepress of the fierceness and wrath of Almighty God.* (Revelation 19:15)

I am not suggesting that the shepherd of the church should ever rule with a rod of iron, but I am pointing out that there is a very strong inference of authority in each of these three cases in Revelation. The overall emphasis in Scripture is not so much on the sheep being in subjection to the shepherd—that is taken for granted. The real emphasis is on the shepherds not lording it over the sheep or taking their authority to excess. This is the reverse of the situation of the modern church, where the idea of anybody ruling anybody else is almost considered old-fashioned.

Yet there is a wonderful balance woven into God's original leadership plan. The men charged with the awesome responsibility to equip the saints for the work of the ministry must have the authority to do so because responsibility requires authority. Yet, according to the biblical pattern, these men are to be raised up from the very body of believers they are to lead. In this way, they already have a history and a track record with the members of the body, and they share a similarity in culture and vision. How perfect God's plan is! Authority is balanced by relationship, which is how it always should be. A shepherd who has a relationship with his followers will not abuse them. Our modern system imports into our churches virtual strangers who either wield authority outside relationship or have to fight for the minimal amount of authority to do their jobs.

The Elder as Teacher

The second aspect of the work of an elder or pastor is teaching:

Holding fast the faithful word as he has been taught, that he may be able, by sound doctrine [teaching], *both to exhort and convict those who contradict.* (Titus 1:9)

An elder is someone who has been thoroughly taught and, in turn, must be able to teach others. As we have seen, this picture is presented very clearly in 2 Timothy 2:2, where Paul was giving instructions to Timothy on how to bring forth teaching leadership in the congregation:

And the things that you have heard from me among many witnesses, commit these to faithful men who will be able to teach others also.

This is the background that the Scripture presents for an elder in respect to teaching. He must have been taught, and then he must be able to transmit the teaching he has received to other potential leaders. In this way, there is always a supply of potential teaching leadership. It never dies off but is transmitted from generation to generation.

Again, for teachers in a local body of believers, we have to get away from the picture of a "pulpit personality." In the last chapter, I used the example of Apollos to point out that, in a certain sense, the teaching ministry within the whole body demands the public exposition of Scripture in a fairly systematic way. However, for the local elder, the teaching is on a much smaller scale. It is personal counseling and the teaching of small groups. Many men who would not find themselves fully at home in a pulpit ministry can be extremely effective and much more useful in person-to-person instruction, which is desperately needed in the church today.

> *Having the heart of a shepherd is the distinguishing mark of a true pastor or elder.*

Because I am in a teaching ministry, I continually appreciate this fact. When I am out preaching, and I finish a sermon, I might have a line of fifteen or more people waiting to ask me questions. Others who are in the same type of ministry will experience exactly the same thing. Yet most of these questions should be and could be answered by any normally equipped elder. There is no need to line up and wait for some visiting preacher to answer these questions. But I have found that, in most cases, these people have no one to go to locally to get the answer to their questions. Again, this is one of the desperate needs that we should seek to supply to the church at this time.

Pastors: Ruling, Teaching, Shepherding

The Elder as Shepherd

I would now like to move on to the role of the elder as shepherd, looking at the same office but treating it now essentially as a ministry. I pointed out already that Jesus is the pattern of every ministry. Therefore, when we want a pattern of the shepherd ministry, it is good to begin with Him. The tenth chapter of John's gospel deals with the Good Shepherd. The word *good* here does not primarily mean morally good; rather, it means "efficient, capable, the one who knows his job." In His own words, Jesus set forth (as the pattern Shepherd) what a shepherd ought to do. This makes it worth studying:

> *I am the good shepherd. The good shepherd gives His life for the sheep. But a hireling, he who is not the shepherd, one who does not own the sheep, sees the wolf coming and leaves the sheep and flees; and the wolf catches the sheep and scatters them. The hireling flees because he is a hireling and does not care about the sheep. I am the good shepherd; and I know My sheep, and am known by My own. As the Father knows Me, even so I know the Father; and I lay down My life for the sheep.* (John 10:11–15)

We learn from this passage that the relationship between Jesus and the Father is parallel to the relationship between the sheep and the Shepherd: "As I know the Father and the Father knows Me, so My sheep know Me and I know them." I believe that this is the true meaning of the passage, which gives much more significance to it. The emphasis is on knowing the sheep and being known by them. It is an intimate, personal relationship.

> *And other sheep I have which are not of this fold; them also I must bring, and they will hear My voice; and there will be*

*one flock and one shepherd....My sheep hear My voice, and
I know them, and they follow Me.*   (John 10:16, 27)

Four Features of the Shepherd Ministry

We can see four features of the shepherd ministry based
on these words of Jesus. The first is *to lay down his life*. Essentially, the life of the shepherd does not belong to himself
but to the sheep. Anyone who wants to lead a self-pleasing,
self-indulgent life has no right to be in this ministry at all.
The first requirement is that he put his life on the altar for
God and for the service of God's people. A man who is not
willing to live as a servant to the people of God cannot fulfill
this calling.

Second, the shepherd is required *to know his sheep individually* in a close personal relationship.

Third, he is required *to be personally knowable*, accessible
to the sheep.

Fourth, he is required *to speak and to lead*, in other words,
to lead them by speaking. Jesus said, *"My sheep hear My voice,...
and they follow Me."* Wherever Christians are found, the need
exists for shepherds with these qualities.

When I last pastored a church, which was some time
ago, I undertook to preach on the shepherd ministry, and
I preached essentially what I am presenting now. When I
finished, I said, "I want to tell you that, officially, I am your
shepherd; I am your pastor. I have preached to you out of the
Scriptures what a pastor should be." Then I said, "I do not
want to be a hypocrite. I want to acknowledge publicly before you all that I know I am not doing what a pastor should
do. You may blame me, but at least I am not a hypocrite. One
reason why I am not doing it is that I cannot do it. There are

too many of you, and I don't have enough time to have this kind of a relationship and to offer this type of ministry."

This was not a big congregation; there were barely two hundred people in it. Yet it was absolutely out of the question for me to offer them the type of ministry that is presented in Scripture. There are many fine men who are pastors, and who are doing what they can. Yet many pastors who try to do this job end up with a nervous breakdown or a heart attack, simply because it is not possible for someone to do this type of ministry with a large number of people.

Believers must be able to go to someone for counsel who knows their personal circumstances and problems.

This truth has brought home to me very clearly that the shepherd ministry cannot take on a large congregation single-handedly. The people must be broken up into smaller groups, and each group must have one or two, or perhaps three, men who are their leaders. Then the believers can go to someone who knows them—who knows their problems, their marital and family circumstances, and their business situations. He can talk to them heart to heart and help them. I believe every Christian needs someone to whom he can go for this type of ministry. This is the great, crying need of the people of God across the nation today.

The Shepherd Psalm

Let's now look at a few other passages that address the ministry of a shepherd. Psalm 23, which is a familiar psalm to most believers, is called the Shepherd Psalm, and it speaks about what a shepherd does for his sheep. Putting himself in the place of the sheep, David said,

> The LORD is my shepherd; I shall not want. He makes me to lie down in green pastures; He leads me beside the still waters. He restores my soul; He leads me in the paths of righteousness for His name's sake. (verses 1–3)

These verses reveal two responsibilities of a shepherd: (1) to provide water and pasture, and (2) to protect, lead, and control. Again, the shepherd's rod is the mark of ruling. It is the shepherd's business to see that the sheep do not get into wrong or dangerous places, but to turn them away from danger and keep them in safety.

God's Expectations for Shepherds

There is a very powerful passage in Ezekiel where the Lord took account of the shepherds of Israel. This was a very solemn and sad accounting, and He chided them for not having done what they should have done as shepherds—which indicates that this is what the Lord expects a shepherd to do. It is a very sobering thought that, at the end of this present dispensation, there is going to be a reckoning between the Lord and the shepherds. For some professing pastors, it is going to be a very embarrassing reckoning, considering what is expected.

> And the word of the LORD came to me, saying, "Son of man, prophesy against the shepherds of Israel, prophesy and say to them, 'Thus says the Lord GOD to the shepherds: "Woe to the shepherds of Israel who feed themselves! Should not the shepherds feed the flocks? You eat the fat and clothe yourselves with the wool; you slaughter the fatlings, but you

do not feed the flock. The weak you have not strengthened, nor have you healed those who were sick, nor bound up the broken, nor brought back what was driven away, nor sought what was lost; but with force and cruelty you have ruled them."" (Ezekiel 34:1–4)

From this passage, we can see six things the Lord expects of the shepherd ministry:

1. To feed the flock
2. To strengthen the weak
3. To heal the sick
4. To bind up the broken
5. To bring back what was driven away
6. To seek the lost

With regard to ministering to the sick, let's compare this passage with James 5:14–15:

Is anyone among you sick? Let him call for the elders of the church, and let them pray over him, anointing him with oil in the name of the Lord. And the prayer of faith will save the sick, and the Lord will raise him up. And if he has committed sins, he will be forgiven.

Notice the New Testament prescription for a believer who becomes sick: *"Let him call for the elders of the church"*—in other words, the shepherds. It is the believer's responsibility to call for them, not the shepherd's responsibility to find out who is sick. Then, it is the shepherd's responsibility to minister to him, anoint him, instruct him, counsel him, and pray over him the prayer of faith. So we see that, according to the Scriptures, healing is within the ministry of the shepherd.

Another passage where there is a controversy between the Lord and the shepherds of Israel is Isaiah 56:9–10. The shepherds are referred to as *"watchmen,"* which is another title quite often used for these leaders.

> *All you beasts of the field, come to devour, all you beasts in the forest. His watchmen are blind, they are all ignorant; they are all dumb dogs, they cannot bark; sleeping, lying down, loving to slumber.*

There is irony in these verses. The one responsibility of a watchdog is to bark or give warning when a wolf approaches the flock. In Isaiah's day, the Lord said, "All My shepherds are like mute dogs. They can't bark. All they do is lie down and go to sleep." In the New Testament, Jesus referred to false prophets as *"wolves"*:

> *Beware of false prophets, who come to you in sheep's clothing, but inwardly they are ravenous wolves.*　　(Matthew 7:15)

I am afraid it is very often the case today that false prophets and false teachings come to the church, but the shepherds are mute watchdogs. They do not make a sound. They just let the enemies of the people of God come in to their midst, while they are spiritually asleep.

The Lord also spoke to Ezekiel in terms of being a watchman:

> *So you, son of man: I have made you a watchman for the house of Israel; therefore you shall hear a word from My mouth and warn them for Me. When I say to the wicked, "O wicked man, you shall surely die!" and you do not speak to warn the wicked from his way, that wicked man shall die*

in his iniquity; but his blood I will require at your hand. Nevertheless if you warn the wicked to turn from his way, and he does not turn from his way, he shall die in his iniquity; but you have delivered your soul. (Ezekiel 33:7–9)

This passage may likewise be related to the shepherd ministry. The Lord said that if a watchman is appointed by the people, and there is a danger of war, it is the watchman's business to blow the trumpet.

If war comes, the watchman blows the trumpet, and people are killed because they did not give heed to his warning, then it is the people's responsibility. But if war and danger come and the watchman does *not* blow his trumpet, then he will be held responsible for the people who are killed.

> *It is the shepherd's responsibility to warn the flock against false prophets and teachings in the church.*

We can see that there is a tremendously solemn responsibility here. God said that if the spiritual watchman fails to warn a wicked person, and he dies in his sin, the wicked person will still perish, but his blood will be required at the watchman's hand. I am sure that Paul had these words in mind when he spoke to the elders at the church at Ephesus about his own ministry among them and challenged them to walk by the same principles:

I kept back nothing that was helpful, but proclaimed it to you, and taught you publicly and from house to house, testifying to Jews, and also to Greeks, repentance toward God and faith toward our Lord Jesus Christ. (Acts 20:20–21)

Paul could honestly say that he had kept nothing back of the truth that the Ephesians needed to know. He fully declared the whole truth to them.

Therefore I testify to you this day that I am innocent of the blood of all men. For I have not shunned to declare to you the whole counsel of God. (verses 26–27)

God will hold the person who does not deliver His full truth accountable for the souls who were not warned and who did not receive the teaching that they should have received. To me, it is a very solemn thing for us to have to be able to say, "I have not shirked from declaring to you the whole counsel of God."

It is obvious from this passage that Paul must have experienced some pressure that he did not yield to. In fact, in the church today, there are many pressures that would keep a person from declaring the whole counsel of God. I know many men who know much more than they preach. The pressures that keep them from declaring what they know are various—denominational, social, or financial: "What will happen if I offend the rich members? What will happen if I go against the teaching of my denomination?" But Paul always bore in mind the fact that he was answerable primarily to God and not to man for what he preached and taught. He was responsible for declaring what he knew to be true from the Word of God and to keep nothing back. I believe that the Scripture teaches that this is included in the responsibility of the shepherd.

An Exacting Ministry

Now let us turn to the testimony of Jacob as a shepherd. I heard this preached on in the land of Israel years ago, and it made a deep impact on me. Jacob, who had served for twenty years with his uncle Laban as a shepherd, described the type of work he did and the kind of life he led:

> *These twenty years I have been with you; your ewes and your female goats have not miscarried their young, and I have not eaten the rams of your flock. That which was torn by beasts I did not bring to you; I bore the loss of it. You required it from my hand, whether stolen by day or stolen by night. There I was! In the day the drought consumed me, and the frost by night, and my sleep departed from my eyes.* (Genesis 31:38–40)

In the last part of this passage, Jacob was saying, "I couldn't even sleep at night because I was answerable for anything that might be stolen while it was under my care." This is a picture of a very exacting calling, and it is precisely what the shepherd ministry is today. I think this passage compares well with Hebrews 13:17: *"Obey those who rule over you, and be submissive, for they watch out for your souls, as those who must give account."* The leaders of the church are to diligently watch over the souls of those under their care.

The Qualifications of a Elder

What are the qualifications of an elder or shepherd? What is expected of him according to the standards of Scripture? Let's turn, first of all, to John's gospel where Jesus spoke to Peter on the shore of the Sea of Galilee. The background of this encounter, of course, is that Peter had been a disciple of the Lord and had vowed that, even if everyone else might forsake Jesus, he would never forsake Him. And Jesus had warned Peter, *"Even this night, before the rooster crows twice, you will deny Me three times"* (Mark 14:30). Peter could not believe that was true, but it turned out exactly that way. Three times, he said publicly that he did not know Jesus and had no association with Him.

This is a very, very solemn fact because, at the resurrection scene, when the angel addressed the women, the message was, *"But go, tell His disciples; and Peter"* (Mark 16:7). The indication was that Peter was no longer a disciple. Why? Because he had denied that he was a follower of Jesus. He had made the wrong confession. He had forfeited his right to the title of disciple. As you read Peter's interview with Jesus, you will find that Peter did not understand what the Lord was doing, but the Lord drew out of him the right confession three times, to make up for the three times he had made the wrong confession.

> *The shepherd is responsible for declaring what he knows to be true from God's Word, holding nothing back.*

There is a tremendous truth in this incident about right and wrong confession. Many times, if we have said or done the wrong thing, it has to be canceled by the right confession. For instance, if we have not forgiven people, we cancel that unforgiveness by forgiving them. And this is true in many other respects. So Jesus dealt with Peter on the basis of the fact that three times, he had denied Him, and He led Peter to making the right confession three times. On the basis of each confession, He charged him with the ministry of a shepherd to his sheep. Let's look at the words Jesus used. I am going to provide amplification on the words in order to bring out the exact meaning from the original Greek.

Pastors: Ruling, Teaching, Shepherding

So when they had eaten breakfast, Jesus said to Simon Peter, "Simon, son of Jonah, do you love Me [the strongest Greek word for love: passionately, totally, devotedly] *more than these* [more than the rest of the disciples, because you said that when they forsook Me, you were going to stay with Me]*?"* [Peter] *said to Him, "Yes, Lord; You know that I love You* [a much weaker word, that of a friend: "I am fond of You"]*."* [Jesus] *said to him, "Feed My lambs* [on the basis of that confession]*." He said to him again a second time, "Simon, son of Jonah, do you love Me* [passionately, devotedly]*?" He said unto him, "Yes, Lord; You know that I love You* [again, "I am fond of You"]*." He said to him, "Tend My sheep* [This is the same word we have been dealing with: to shepherd]*." He said to him the third time, "Simon, son of Jonah, do you love Me* [This time, Jesus came down to Peter's level by saying, "Are you fond of Me?"]*?" Peter was grieved because He said to him the third time, "Do you love Me?" And he said to Him, "Lord, You know all things; You know that I love You* [but again, "I am fond of You"]*." Jesus said to him, "Feed My sheep."*

(John 21:15–17)

I am somewhat amused at Peter's responses. Because Peter had always been so impetuous, he usually said a little bit more than he was entitled to say. Here, however, he was very careful to say a little bit *less*.

We see three commissions in this passage: *"Feed My lambs," "Tend* [shepherd] *My sheep,"* and *"Feed My sheep."* The instruction is not the same each time. Notice that the basic requirement for taking care of the Lord's sheep is not our attitude to the sheep, but our attitude to the Lord: "Do you love *Me*? Feed My sheep."

I have learned by experience that a sentimental love for the people of God is never going to see a person through this job. If our eyes and our minds are centered on the people, there will come a time when either they will act in such a mean and unworthy way that our love will not be strong enough, or in loving them, we will allow them to dictate to us and lead us to do things that the Lord would not have wished us to do.

> *The primary requirement of an elder is wholehearted devotion to the Lord Himself.*

I have seen so many people go astray in this type of ministry through a kind of second-rate human affection, sympathy, or emotion that simply does not stand the test of the hard times. These are times when God's people are ungrateful and critical; when they talk about you behind your back and do not appreciate anything you do for them. If there is not something higher than love for them, it will not stand the test.

What will stand the test, what will carry a man through and keep him faithful, is devotion to the Lord Himself. So the primary requirement, which is basic to all others, is real dedication to the Lord Jesus Christ. If we have that, then He says, "I'm going to commission you to be a shepherd to My sheep."

With this basis, the Scripture then lists quite a considerable number of character qualities that are required in an elder or a shepherd. Anyone who can come up with a hundred percent in these lists definitely has outstanding character. The lists are taken from 1 Timothy 3:1–7 and Titus 1:5–9, which I will summarize. I suggest that you read the King James Version and two or three other versions, and compare the words of these passages, so that you may have a pretty clear picture of the necessary qualities. I will give you my summary under three headings: personal character, family situation, and spiritual ability. This summary is intended to be just an overview. It is quite possible that you could improve upon it as you study these passages yourself.

Personal Character

The following are the positive requirements: He must be blameless. That is quite something to start with, isn't it? In other words, there must be nothing in his life that is so obvious and persistent that people would not want him to be an elder because of it. He must also be vigilant, patient, self-controlled, righteous, holy, and a lover of good.

Then there are the things that an elder must *not* be—the negatives. He must not be self-willed, covetous, greedy, quick-tempered, violent, or a drunkard.

Family Situation

The Scripture brings out several points in relation to an elder's character and his family situation:

1. He must be the husband of one wife.
2. The home and children must be under discipline.
3. He must be able and willing to show hospitality—not merely willing, but also able. You see, if the children are not under discipline, a man cannot really show hospitality. I have been to homes where you could not have an intelligent, consecutive conversation because the children were making such a noise and

fighting so continually that no one else could get more than five words in without being interrupted. A great deal depends on the whole atmosphere of the home.

4. He must be respected in the community. This is essential. The leader of the local congregation must be a worthy representative of that congregation to people who are not believers or committed Christians. I have seen it happen that a man who has been an alcoholic and a wife beater, and so on, gets wonderfully converted, and then is put into some position in the church within the next few days. This is a mistake. Thank God for his wonderful conversion, but the world cannot be expected to believe in that. The man is going to have to prove himself and his life so that he wins the respect of the community before he is put into such a position.

Spiritual Ability

An elder must be well grounded in doctrine and able to teach others. This quality reflects what we have covered in detail in other chapters of this book about apostles and elders studying and understanding the Scriptures and being able to commit this knowledge to other believers.

The Appointment of Elders

Appointing elders, therefore, combines two requirements: First, recognizing the men whom the Holy Spirit has been preparing for this ministry. Second, knowing and applying the standards of Scripture. This is not done by some dramatic prophetic revelation. It is done by the application of sanctified common sense, plus a sensitivity to the Holy

Spirit—an ability to recognize what the Spirit is doing in the lives of men and women. It is not a matter of getting a prophetic utterance that says, "Thou art an elder," or anything. That is an absolute denial of this method. If I seem to belabor this point, it is because I have actually run into situations where this very thing has happened. A man has been in a city three or four days, gone around and appointed elders, and moved on. This is contrary to what the Scripture presents. The man who makes the appointment must know the men. He must know their lives and be able to judge whether they have come up to the standards. Then he must also understand the mind of the Holy Spirit. Are these men whom the Holy Spirit has already begun to prepare for this ministry?

Appointing elders requires recognizing those whom the Holy Spirit has been preparing and applying the standards of Scripture.

It is clear from the New Testament that an elder did not fully function in a local congregation before he was specifically recognized as an elder. There are many Scriptures that emphasize this point. For instance, in James 5:14, we read, *"Is anyone among you sick? Let him call for the elders of the church."* It is obvious that every Christian was expected to know who his elders were so that he could call on them in such a situation. It is undeniable that even though a man may have all the qualifications—he may have the heart, and he may be prepared by the Holy Spirit—he cannot fully exercise this function until he is officially recognized within the body. It is recognition that gives him the final authority he needs to function in this way.

My conclusion is that we will not see valid New Testament eldership emerge in the body of Christ until we are prepared to recognize it, call it by the right name, and embrace all the things that go along with it. We are taking a vital, revolutionary step when we begin to do this, as some of us have discovered in a very direct and personal way. The more I study this area of church leadership, the more I am convinced that we cannot bypass these things. We will fail the church if we do not go through with what God has shown us to do.

Remuneration of Elders

Let us now consider a very practical question in regard to spiritual leadership. How do elders support themselves? Some people think money is not important, but I am not one of those. As a matter of fact, people talk like that only in church, not anywhere else. The Bible certainly doesn't speak that way.

Let's look at 1 Timothy 5:17–18:

> *Let the elders who rule well be counted worthy of double honor, especially those who labor in the word and doctrine. For the Scripture says, "You shall not muzzle an ox while it treads out the grain," and, "The laborer is worthy of his wages [or his hire]."*

It is perfectly clear that Paul was talking in terms of financial and material remuneration for those who have the responsibility of being elders. In the New Testament, the word *"honor"* does not just mean to bow to, or to bestow a medal, but it means something very tangible and practical. Let's look at some examples of this. After Paul and his

342

company had been shipwrecked on the Island of Malta, and a ministry of healing had broken out, the people showed their gratitude:

They also honored us in many ways; and when we departed, they provided such things as were necessary. (Acts 28:10)

It is very plain that they were *"honored"* with things that they could be provided with. In other words, they were brought provisions, such as food and clothing—everything they would need for their material and physical needs. If you have ever ministered in a more primitive society, such as some African countries, many times, when you are finished preaching, you will be given a hen, corn cobs, some coffee beans, and things like that. Those are *honors*, but they are very practical and necessary honors. In that type of society, they are things that keep you alive.

We find the same use of the word *honor* from the lips of Jesus when He was reproving the religious people of His day for their hypocrisy:

For God commanded, saying, "Honor your father and your mother."...But you say, "Whoever says to his father or mother, 'Whatever profit you might have received from me is a gift to God'; then he need not honor his father or mother." Thus you have made the commandment of God of no effect by your tradition. (Matthew 15:4–6)

People were required to support their parents and to care for them, but some were saying to their parents, with utter religious hypocrisy, "I've dedicated to the Lord what you ought to get from me, so you can't have it." That was their cop-out. Jesus said, "You hypocrites!" But notice that He talked of supporting parents financially and materially in terms of showing them honor. So the word *honor* has this connotation (not exclusively, but it is included in it) of financial and material provision. It is clear that this is what Paul intended when he said, *"Let the elders who rule well be counted worthy of double honor,"* because *"You shall not muzzle an ox while it treads out the grain,"* and, *"The laborer is worthy of his wages* [or his hire]*."*

> *The works of God will be undermined if financial provision is not made for those in full-time ministry.*

I say this with some emphasis because the works of God will surely be undermined if no financial provision is made for those who step out into full-time ministry. That would be one sure way to hold back the work of God.

Paul also dealt with this question in 1 Corinthians 9. Notice the principles involved in the following two verses; in fact, you may want to read the entire chapter for yourself:

> *Who ever goes to war at his own expense? Who plants a vineyard and does not eat of its fruit? Or who tends a flock* [Greek: who shepherds a flock] *and does not drink of the milk of the flock?...Even so the Lord has commanded that those who preach the gospel should live from the gospel.*
>
> (verses 7, 14)

No soldier who goes out to fight has to provide for his own wages. He is always paid by those for whom he fights. Similarly, anyone who owns a vineyard and puts in the work of cultivating it also eats the fruit of it. Likewise, a shepherd will not slaughter his flock, but he will at least take of its milk for his own support.

Pastors: Ruling, Teaching, Shepherding

If those who minister the gospel to the people of God devote so much time to it that they cannot also earn a living, they should be supported by the people to whom they minister. This is an ordinance of God. It is also common sense. There are certain sections of the church that boast that they do not have a paid ministry. However, I have seen that this practice ultimately undermines the efficiency of God's servants.

Now, if a man is not working full-time as an elder, then he probably would not need full remuneration. Or if a man has another source of income and is independent, then perhaps he would not need full compensation. However, if he spends a lot of time in teaching the Word, then you have to make it up to him by remuneration. The elder's remuneration should be according to the need and the amount of time he spends. The principle is clear.

Sheep Require a Shepherd

As I conclude this chapter, let me offer one more tremendously important point regarding elders. There is a principle that sheep must have a shepherd. According to the words of Scripture, in both the Old and New Testaments, sheep without a shepherd become scattered, lost, weary, sick, and a prey to wild beasts. This is a very interesting fact. You can leave cattle without anybody looking after them, but you cannot leave sheep without being looked after.

As far as I understand the New Testament, this comes down to the personal obligation of every believer: You either have to *be* a shepherd or to *have* one. Either you're exercising the ministry of a shepherd, or you must be under the ministry of a shepherd. The Scripture makes no provision for any sheep to be without a shepherd. Yet, today, if you look across this country, you will see thousands and thousands of people who have no shepherd, acknowledge no shepherd, and are not themselves shepherds. The result is that they are scattered, lost, weak, spiritually unhealthy, and a prey to all the deceivers and false prophets that feed upon the people of God when they are not protected.

Being under the ministry of a shepherd is a commitment to being a disciple. Acts 11:26 says, *"The disciples were first called Christians in Antioch."* To me, this statement is definitive. A Christian is a disciple. A person who is not a disciple is not entitled to the title Christian. A disciple is one who is under discipline. The word indicates it. Within the church, there must be discipline. It is necessary to have those who rule, and it is necessary to have those who are ruled. Divine grace is required for both. I accept it as a principle that a person who is not willing to be ruled can never qualify to rule.

> *Believers who ignore their need for discipleship become spiritually weak and vulnerable to deception.*

As we near the end of this section on the leadership of the church, I am impressed to add this thought: No one in their right mind would ever *call themselves* to a position of leadership if they truly feared God. It is a natural thing to desire position and significance, but it is a dangerous thing to enter into leadership without God's initiative.

The restoration of biblical leadership is essential today, especially in nations like China where the gospel is exploding and leaders are sorely needed. Therefore, if you are a leader, you should measure yourself by the standards of Scripture. Ask yourself the following questions: Am I walking in the sphere and responsibilities outlined for my God-given role? Will I obey *God*? If you are a member, you can ask yourselves these questions: Will I commit myself to praying that God will raise up leaders after His own heart? Will I pray that His leaders will faithfully represent Him?

As we do these things, the leadership of the local church will be able to fulfill its calling to rule, to teach, and to shepherd the flock of God.

Chapter 23

Resident Ministry: Deacons

In any given locality, the local church unfolds in its growth and development somewhat like the development of a human body out of a biological cell. The four phases that contribute to the development of a properly functioning church body are (1) the cell; (2) the appointment of elders, at which point a group of disciples becomes a church; (3) the appointment of deacons; and (4) the ministries completed through body or church member ministry. Let's look at each of these phases in a little more detail:

1. The cell is a small house meeting. It is often a church in embryonic form.

2. During a season of fellowship, prayer, study, and evangelism, the spiritual leadership of the cell becomes evident. After a time of proving themselves, these leaders are duly appointed and ordained as elders by apostles. This is the first time the word *church* may officially be used for the body of believers.

3. In order to complete the leadership, there must also be deacons. As we have seen, the deacons are responsible for the material administration of the church.

4. Every member in the congregation is commissioned to be functional. The members are to minister or serve in some capacity under the direction of the elders and deacons, and that involvement will continue to grow and be a work in progress. This diversification should eventually embrace all the gifts and ministries that God has released to the local church. At this point, you have a completed body that has developed from a cell.

The Appointment of Deacons

The administrative leadership of a local church is extremely simple: Elders minister to the spiritual and deacons minister to the material; the deacons' role is to serve. For an introduction to the responsibility of deacons, let's look again at how the first deacons were appointed:

Now in those days, when the number of the disciples was multiplying, there arose a complaint against the Hebrews by the Hellenists [Greeks], because their widows were neglected in the daily distribution. Then the twelve summoned the multitude of the disciples, and said, "It is not desirable that we should leave the word of God and serve tables. Therefore, brethren, seek out from among you seven men of good reputation, full of the Holy Spirit and wisdom, whom we may appoint over this business; but we will give ourselves continually to prayer and to the ministry of the word."

(Acts 6:1–4)

The church had run into a very real problem. It was growing fast, and the apostles were getting so busy that they needed helpers. The believers went to the apostles and said, "Things aren't working out right. Our widows are being neglected." The apostles said, "All right, we'll take steps to correct the problem."

Let me point out something about the New Testament church. The believers invariably accepted responsibility for their widows—this was taken for granted. The problem today is that the government has taken over so many functions that the church does not realize its responsibilities. I believe the church is responsible for widows, orphans, and the poor, and in some way that responsibility should be carried out.

> *Elders minister to the spiritual needs of believers, while deacons focus on their material needs.*

The twelve apostles summoned the congregation and told them to seek out seven men of good reputation, full of the Holy Spirit and wisdom, to appoint over this business. This would enable the apostles to give themselves to prayer and to the ministry of the Word—the specific ministry to which they were called. They required other ministers to focus on the daily administration of money, food, clothing, or whatever else might be necessary for people.

While elders are meant to focus on prayer and the ministry of the Word, this does not mean that deacons are unimportant people. In fact, the Scripture says that they must be of good reputation, and that they must be full of the Holy Spirit and wisdom, in order to fulfill their ministry.

> *And the saying pleased the whole multitude. And they chose Stephen, a man full of faith and the Holy Spirit, and Philip, Prochorus, Nicanor, Timon* [Timothy], *Parmenas, and Nicolas, a proselyte from Antioch.* (Acts 6:5)

Resident Ministry: Deacons

Seven men were chosen as the first deacons. Once again, we see that the leadership in a local congregation is always plural. Notice that the congregation chose the deacons, with instructions from the leadership to choose godly men. This was very practical. If the apostles had chosen the deacons, the congregation might have said, "You've put men in there who will do what you want them to do." So the apostles said, "You choose them; we'll approve them and then instruct them regarding their responsibilities." In this way, there could be no murmuring about the men who had been appointed to do this particular task.

God-Appointed versus Man-Appointed

Many churches choose pastors, deacons, and other ministry positions by a simple vote of the congregation. This is not really scriptural. It is God who makes the appointments. Jesus said to His apostles, *"You did not choose Me, but I chose you"* (John 15:16). I believe this is also true of every valid function, ministry, and appointment in the church. It is not man who makes the choice, but God, because Jesus Christ is Head over *all* things to the church, which is His body. Appointments that are not made on the authority of Jesus really have no validity. Furthermore, the appointment does not make a person anything if God has not already given him the ministry. We should simply recognize what God has chosen a person to be and then affirm this.

Here is a practical example of what I am saying: If you are in a meeting to discuss or vote on potential deacons, your purpose should not be to decide who you would like to have as a deacon, as if it were a popularity contest. Your purpose should be to decide whom God has chosen as a deacon. It is a very different attitude. The congregation should suggest the names of those whom they believe God has called to this service, and the elders should make the final confirmation and then commission them. They should do this with the public laying on of hands to establish them as deacons of the church.

> *...whom they set before the apostles; and when they had prayed, they laid hands on them* [as a seal of their approval and as a setting apart to the ministry of deaconship].   (Acts 6:6)

As we have seen, the laying on of hands is not just a formality. Something happened when the apostles, led by the Holy Spirit, prayed and laid their hands on the first deacons. Spiritual authority and power was released, which blossomed into wider ministry. This act of laying hands upon the deacons served three main purposes:

1. The apostles publicly acknowledged that they accepted these people as qualified to hold the office of deacon.
2. They publicly committed these believers to God for the task for which they had been chosen.
3. They transmitted to these people a measure of their own spiritual grace and wisdom needed for the task they were commissioned to carry out.

The Servanthood of Deacons

When my wife Ruth and I went to Pakistan, we were questioned at the immigration department. A Pakistani official asked me, "What are you?" It was a Muslim country, and I thought, *I need to be careful.* Eventually, I said, "I'm a minister."

I thought that was a pretty safe term that most people do not understand. Well, from then on, I got the red carpet treatment everywhere I went. I was sent to the head of the line, and so on. I realized later that he must have thought I was a minister of the government of the United States!

It is often like this in the church. We have moved far away from the meaning of the word *minister*, which is "servant." I often wonder how some churches would change if they realized that the word *deacon* in Greek also means "servant." In some churches, the board of deacons has a lot of authority. How would it be if they were called the board of *servants*?

> *Some churches would change dramatically if they understood that the title* deacon *means "servant."*

If you are a deacon, you are a servant of the Lord and a servant of the Lord's people. Deacons are to serve under pastors or elders. When the board of deacons runs the church, this is unscriptural, because it is putting the material above the spiritual. The people who control the finances have the last word. You can be as spiritual as you like about it, but this is what it comes down to. Consequently, in my opinion, the elders must be in control of the finances, and the deacons should do what the elders instruct them to do.

The Qualifications of Deacons

Let deacons be the husbands of one wife, ruling their children and their own houses well. For those who have served well as deacons obtain for themselves a good standing and great boldness in the faith which is in Christ Jesus.

(1 Timothy 3:12–13)

As with elders, deacons should also first be proved or tested. Nobody was put into a responsible position in the church in the New Testament without first being thoroughly tested in the practical realm. Some people who do not do well in secular occupations go on to spiritual ministry and become failures.

I have been in full-time ministry for over fifty years, and I have seen scores of people who were called into full-time service for the Lord: missionaries, ministers, pastors, evangelists, youth leaders, and so on. In all these years, I cannot recall ever seeing God promote in the spiritual someone who was a disaster with material matters. Never in my life have I seen a man who could not make it in the secular realm be called by God into spiritual service. It is contrary to His basic principles. I have seen many such men who have tried to make it, but they made a mess of things. Candidates for deacon do not need to own their own businesses, but they should be able to make things work in the material world. They should be able to administer dollars and cents and make it work with their secular employment or education.

The Promotion of Deacons

When a man becomes a deacon, it is not just to supervise the giving of charity. It is a responsible place of sharing the burden with the elders, and it is often a preparation for spiritual leadership, as we saw in the case of Philip, who became an evangelist. If a person does the job of a deacon well, he is beginning to qualify for spiritual promotion.

Most people really do not grasp the fact that there is growth and promotion in ministry. If you start in the position of a deacon, therefore, bear in mind that it can be a stepping-stone to something else. In fact, if you do not start as a servant, you will likely miss your promotion, because God only promotes people who start at the low end of the ladder. Spiritual leaders do not just appear from heaven fully formed, without any process of trial and error. This does not happen with the gifts of the Spirit, and it does not happen with the spiritual ministries. There is a process of making mistakes and of learning from these mistakes. This is how it was with God's people in the New Testament, and that is exactly how it is in the church today.

Part 5:

The Lifestyle of the Church

Chapter 24

The Daily Life of the Local Church

ome time ago, I realized that I was teaching people the initiatory experiences that bring them into the Christian life, but then I was leaving them without direction or instruction as to how to live this life after they had entered it. Therefore, in this chapter, I will endeavor to paint a picture of the lifestyle of the true local church—not its structure, administration, or titles, but its lifestyle. In other words, we will consider what "a day in the life of a true church" would look like.

Three Experiences of Initiation into the Church

We will first look at three experiences that are the gateway or entrance into the local church and into daily Christian living. Then we will look at the living itself.

Acts 2 contains the clearest account both of the initiatory experiences and the ongoing daily life of the church:

Now when [the people] *heard this, they were cut to the heart, and said to Peter and the rest of the apostles, "Men and brethren, what shall we do?" Then Peter said to them, "Repent, and let every one of you be baptized in the name of Jesus Christ for the remission of sins; and you shall receive the gift of the Holy Spirit."* (verses 37–38)

That is one comprehensive answer. It presents a unified experience of New Testament salvation that I call "the package deal": Repent, be baptized in water, and receive the Holy Spirit. As I understand the Scripture, with these three things, they got it all. I believe that God's will and His answer to the question *"What shall we do?"* have not changed in the least bit since the day of Pentecost.

1. Repent

The Scripture is quite emphatic: We must repent. The Greek tense used in Acts 2:38 means to "do a thing once and never repeat it." There is no teaching in the New Testament about continually repenting. A person who is living right should not have to keep repenting, and a person who has truly repented should not keep sinning! This word is very decisive and incisive in the Greek: Repent. Change your mind. Stop doing the wrong things; start doing the right things. Turn from the devil; turn to God. All this is included in repentance. It is not emotion; it is a decision.

2. Be Baptized

The second thing is to be baptized: *"Let every one of you be baptized in the name of Jesus Christ for* [or into] *the remission of sins."* In the early church, a person's baptism in water was the official recognition that he had placed his faith in Jesus Christ and received forgiveness of sins. It was not requisite for the forgiveness; rather, it was an indication that forgiveness of sins had been claimed by that person and had been acknowledged by the leaders of the church. In essence, water baptism is the human recognition of a person as being eligible for membership in the church of Jesus Christ.

As I mentioned earlier, every convert in the book of Acts was baptized within a few hours of conversion. In Acts 8, the eunuch on the road to Gaza saw a pool of water by the side of the road and said, *"See, here is water. What hinders me from being baptized* [right now]?" (verse 36). In Acts 16:29–33, the Philippian jailer was saved at midnight and was baptized before dawn. Note, also, the response of the new converts in Acts 2:

> *Then those who gladly received his word were baptized; and that day about three thousand souls were added to them.*
>
> (verse 41)

My comment is that people who do not get baptized may have received the Word, but perhaps they did not receive it gladly. Those who gladly receive the Word will get baptized.

3. Receive the Holy Spirit

The baptism in the Holy Spirit is divine recognition that a person belongs to God. The baptism in the Holy Spirit, in this sense, is a supernatural seal placed upon a person by the Head of the body, Jesus Christ, acknowledging that person as a member of His body. Paul said, *"In whom also, having believed, you were sealed with the Holy Spirit of promise"* (Ephesians 1:13).

Both of these recognitions should come at the outset of Christian living. A person should be acknowledged by the church in the act of water baptism, and he should be acknowledged by the Head of the church by the supernatural seal or baptism of the Holy Spirit.

Four Continuing Activities

Now, what did this threefold initiatory experience lead the new believers into? In Acts 2, we find the official New Testament declaration of daily Christian living. Notice that it begins with the phrase *"They continued."* Believers pass from the initiatory, single experiences, which do not have to be re-peated, into the continuing, daily, regular pattern of life:

They continued steadfastly in the apostles' doctrine and fellowship, in the breaking of bread, and in prayers.

(Acts 2:42)

The following are descriptions of the four basic activities of New Testament Christian living.

Activity #1: Teaching

First, there is *doctrine*, which refers to the process of teaching and being taught. The first essential for people who have come to Christ and been baptized in water and in the Holy Spirit is regular, authoritative teaching in the Scriptures. Ephesians 6:17 says to *"take...the sword of the Spirit, which is the word of God."* This directive comes before the one to *"[pray] always with all prayer and supplication in the Spirit"* (verse 18). Before you move into life in the Spirit, you must take hold of the Word of God. This is the divine order, because you are open to a whole new range of problems, temptations, and difficulties once you are baptized in the Holy Spirit. This was precisely the experience of Jesus after the Spirit came upon Him. When He was tempted by the devil, Jesus used only one weapon against the enemy. Every temptation was answered with the words, *"It is written....It is written....It is written...."* (See Luke 4:1–13.) He utilized the sword of the Spirit, which is the Word of God. Jesus is the perfect pattern of a person baptized in the Holy Spirit yet desperately needing a sound, thorough, practical knowledge of the Word of God.

There were some five hundred believers to whom Christ had appeared at one time after His resurrection. (See 1 Corinthians 15:6.) After His ascension, however, there were only a hundred and twenty praying in the upper room. (See Acts 1:15.) Apparently, three hundred and eighty of those did not hear what He said about tarrying in Jerusalem until they were endued with power from on high. The number of Jesus' disciples at this time was not very impressive by human standards, but when the Holy Spirit came, they were increased by three thousand people in one day!

The day of Pentecost would have been a disaster without systematic, practical Bible teaching!

What was the function of the disciples in the upper room? They provided the teaching and the authority that would immediately be needed by the people who came in to the church on the day of Pentecost. If the apostles had not been there ready to teach, there would have been chaos when the Holy Spirit fell that day.

This is not a theory. We saw it happen in Africa when we were missionaries. There was a sovereign outpouring of the Spirit of God, mainly on Quakers, with many hundreds receiving the baptism in the Holy Spirit. Some were actually put in prison for speaking in tongues. The American Quaker missionaries actually convinced the British authorities to imprison these humble Africans for speaking in tongues! Without sound teaching, many of those unfortunate people went off into the most fantastic errors and facets of fanaticism because they had no restraining, disciplinary, instructive influence at work. The day of Pentecost would have been a disaster without systematic, practical Bible teaching!

But God be thanked that though you were slaves of sin, yet you obeyed from the heart that form of doctrine to which you were delivered. (Romans 6:17)

The word *"form"* is from a Greek word that gives us the English word *type* and refers to a mold designed to produce a certain pattern or shape. I am no expert on molds, but whether you are casting metals or making Jell-O at home, the process is clear. First, there must be a condition (such as extreme heat) that prepares the material to make it subject to the mold. Second, there must be a mold that will produce the right shape. Spiritually speaking, salvation brings the "heat" that makes a person willing to accept a new spiritual form. The form of the mold determines the ultimate shape, and the mold is biblical teaching.

Today, we have people who have no mold and who end up like a sticky mess on a kitchen table, leaving only the mark of some undefined experience. We also have people getting into the wrong mold who end up in the wrong shape. Straightening out such people is almost impossible; they have literally had their lives formed incorrectly. Yet it is remarkable how quickly the teaching mold works. A few weeks of solid Bible teaching can produce the most wonderful change and can bring out a character and lifestyle that will withstand any test.

Speaking of the tragic situation where God's people are left without teaching, Isaiah said,

> *Therefore my people have gone into captivity, because they have no knowledge; their honorable men are famished, and their multitude dried up with thirst.* (Isaiah 5:13)

Many of God's people today are in captivity because they do not have God's kind of knowledge. I am struck by the words *"their honorable men are famished."* Even their theologians and their leading men had nothing to give, and thus the multitudes went thirsty. In Hosea, we see a similar picture:

My people are destroyed for lack of knowledge. Because you have rejected knowledge, I also will reject you from being priest for Me; because you have forgotten the law of your God, I also will forget your children. (Hosea 4:6)

Notice that the requirement of a priest is that he should know and, by implication, teach the law of God. In fact, Malachi defined this as the responsibility of the priest:

For the lips of a priest should keep knowledge, and people should seek the law from his mouth; for he is the messenger of the LORD of hosts. (Malachi 2:7)

God rejected the priests of Hosea's time because they rejected the knowledge of God's Word. This can be equally true today. A person can enter the Catholic priesthood or the Protestant ministry while rejecting the knowledge of the Word of God, but he has no priestly ministry in the sight of God.

The statement in Hosea is so tragic and so true: *"Because you have forgotten the law of your God, I also will forget your children."* In America today, we see God-forgotten children because their parents have forgotten the law of God and have not brought them up under its teaching. This is an exact fulfillment of God's judgment.

Activity #2: Fellowship

The next basic activity is fellowship. We have to understand that fellowship is actually the end purpose of the gospel, as we saw earlier when we looked at the central purpose of the local church.

God is faithful, by whom you were called into the fellowship of His Son, Jesus Christ our Lord. (1 Corinthians 1:9)

"Called into" indicates destination. Fellowship is not a means to an end—it is the end. Fellowship with God and His people is where we are heading! It even precedes praying. So many of us do not realize what the church is really all about. Paul said,

> *These things I write to you* [Timothy], *though I hope to come to you shortly; but if I am delayed, I write so that you may know how you ought to conduct yourself in the house of God, which is the church of the living God, the pillar and ground of the truth.* (1 Timothy 3:14–15)

Fellowship with God and other believers is the end purpose of the gospel of Jesus Christ.

Why did Paul write the epistle to Timothy? So that Timothy might know how to behave himself in the house of God. Paul went on to say that the church of the living God is *"the pillar and ground of the truth."* What should be happening in the church was to be no mystery to Timothy. Yet, in some churches today, it is not clear exactly what they are there for! Often, there is no fellowship at all. You cannot fellowship with the back of somebody's neck in church!

I remember preaching in a fine church one time, and at the conclusion of the service, the pastor said, "Now, don't hurry home. Stay and have fellowship. Shake hands with at least half a dozen people." I prayed silently, *God, is that the ration of fellowship Your people are living on? Shaking hands with half a dozen people before they go home?*

Again, most Christians do not even begin to realize that fellowship is the end purpose of the gospel. We go through religious procedures and rituals and ceremonies and programs and projects. These are all means, but do they bring us to the desired end?

The early church immediately entered into a life of fellowship manifested in two main areas or platforms. Fellowship needs a platform, and the early church had both a large one and a small one. The large-scale platform was the temple—the national, institutional place of worship for the Jewish people. The small-scale platform was the obvious, practical one that we find being used throughout the New Testament: the homes of believers.

So continuing daily with one accord in the temple, and breaking bread from house to house, they ate their food with gladness and simplicity of heart. (Acts 2:46)

Notice that, every day, they were in the temple, and they ate together in their homes. Breaking bread here does not necessarily mean taking the Lord's Supper, though it may have included that. It means that they shared meals together every day in one another's homes, which is remarkable.

And daily in the temple, and in every house, they did not cease teaching and preaching Jesus as the Christ. (Acts 5:42)

Again, we see that their daily ration of fellowship was centered on meetings in the temple and in the homes. The first Christians continued for a time to attend the institutional place of worship, but with two qualifications: They did not compromise their testimony, and they did not depend on the institution for their personal spiritual lives. I think this is extremely relevant for us today.

Many Christians feel led to attend churches that do not feed or support them spiritually. They may do so if they do not compromise their testimony. Second, they cannot depend on the large-scale institutional type of meeting alone for their real spiritual nourishment. These early Christians certainly did not; they had a completely different life and fellowship going on in the homes.

Remember that the word *fellowship* in Greek actually means "sharing together." The fellowship of these early Christians in Jerusalem was expressed in a very intimate kind of sharing. The main thing that we share together is the Lord Jesus Christ, but these early Christians shared practically everything.

Now all who believed were together, and had all things in common, and sold their possessions and goods, and divided them among all, as anyone had need. (Acts 2:44–45)

Nor was there anyone among them who lacked; for all who were possessors of lands or houses sold them, and brought the proceeds of the things that were sold, and laid them at the apostles' feet; and they distributed to each as anyone had need. (Acts 4:34–35)

The early Christians felt an obligation to minister not merely to the spiritual needs of their fellow believers, but also to their physical, material, and financial needs! The situation in Jerusalem was unique, for we do not read that in every city the Christians sold all their possessions. This perhaps was the wisdom and inspiration of the Holy Spirit because, in less than a generation, Jerusalem was totally desolated by the Roman armies, and Jews were not allowed to own land anywhere in that area.

So there are times of urgency when the Spirit of God will prompt us to sell out and share with everybody, but it is not necessarily a universal pattern for every situation. Without question, however, true Christians will share together with their fellow believers in every situation and need. The marvelous testimony was that there was none among them who lacked. I wonder if that could be said of all Christians today. If we shared as the New Testament believers shared, I believe it would be possible.

Another aspect about fellowship that I have discovered is that it is the place of spiritual birth. As Jesus said,

That which is born of the flesh is flesh, and that which is born of the Spirit is spirit. (John 3:6)

Jesus was speaking about two different kinds of birth: birth out of the flesh, which produces the flesh, and birth out of the Spirit, which produces the spirit. Even so, there is much in contemporary Christianity that is born out of the flesh, and all that the flesh can ever produce is flesh. Only what is born out of the Spirit will have the life of the Spirit in it.

> *If we are not in fellowship with other believers, there can be no spiritual birth.*

If we are not in fellowship, there can be no spiritual birth. So many times, we bypass fellowship and fail to produce something truly spiritual. We start a project, make a program, or appoint a committee, but what happens is flesh producing flesh! A program or a project is different from a birth. God is disciplining and dealing with many to return to the true fellowship that produces spiritual birth.

Let's look at a conspicuous example of fellowship producing spiritual life. Acts 1:14 describes the lives of the believers who were in the upper room during the time between the ascension and the outpouring of the Holy Spirit on the day of Pentecost:

These all continued with one accord in prayer and supplication, with the women and Mary the mother of Jesus, and with His brothers. (Acts 1:14)

The believers continued for ten days in close fellowship, in a fairly confined place, in prayer and supplication. That was surely a pretty searching experience. My wife Lydia defined fellowship in this way: "You're all fellows in the same ship, and you can't get off." Fellowship is not fellowship if you can back out and turn away any time you please! Fellowship demands a commitment to other people. That is where it tests you.

In fact, fellowship is compared to light:

But if we walk in the light as He is in the light, we have fellowship with one another. (1 John 1:7)

If sin or darkness enters a person's life, the first obvious result is a withdrawing from fellowship. I have learned by experience that to live in the light of fellowship is an intensely testing experience. I conducted a Bible training course years ago in Jamaica. One sister lasted just three days before she flew back home, even after paying her fare and all the expenses related to the course. There was something in those forty-five Spirit-baptized people being together that this precious soul just could not survive. After one deliverance service, another woman said, "If I could have swum, I would

370

have swum away from this island! I just could not stand the pressure with which I was being surrounded." It was the pressure of fellowship. No one was preaching at her or arguing with her, but intense fellowship generates such pressure that you either stand the fire or back out! I have seen many Christians who cannot stand the fire and light of continued fellowship. However, in real fellowship, "You're all fellows on the same ship, and you can't get off"!

Think of what must have been involved in ten days of continual prayer and supplication in the upper room. It must have tested every fiber of their being, because those apostles did not always see eye to eye with their fellow apostles. But the climax comes in Acts 2:1:

Now when the Day of Pentecost had fully come, they were all with one accord in one place.

What happened? There was a spiritual birth. What came into being was the church of Jesus Christ, born (on the human plane) during ten days of fellowship by a hundred and twenty people. In Acts 13:1–2, we see another tremendous example of fellowship as the "birthing room" of God's purposes:

Now in the church that was at Antioch there were certain prophets and teachers: Barnabas, Simeon..., Lucius..., Manaen..., and Saul. As they ministered to the Lord and fasted, the Holy Spirit said, "Now separate to Me Barnabas and Saul for the work to which I have called them."

Out of the fellowship of these five men waiting upon God with prayer and fasting was born what we call "foreign missions." This was the first occasion in which a church sent forth people specifically to bring the gospel to the unevan-gelized. On previous occasions, it had happened through persecution or seemingly by chance. Indeed, Paul's first mis-sionary journey emerged out of fellowship and prayer, not a committee. Fellowship is of primary importance. If we want spiritual birth, we have to be in the place where it occurs. Oh, how I long to see true spiritual birth rather than a dress-ing up of the flesh! However, having been a missionary on more than one field, I would say it is much easier for the flesh to sit in fifteen committee meetings than it is to have one day of fellowship. In fact, I have never been in so many committee meetings as when I was a missionary!

Committees will never produce what fellowship can.

I used to say to my fellow mis-sionaries in Africa, "All we do is scramble out of one crisis in time to tumble into the next." One day, we had a meeting to solve the various insoluble problems we faced. The meeting started at dawn and went on hour after hour. Meanwhile, all the missionaries' children were rampaging over the mission compound and getting into trouble. About mid-afternoon, my wife Lydia said to the rest, "You carry on in the meet-ing; we're going to go have a meeting for the children." And so, we had a meeting for the children! Two of the real prob-lem children received the baptism in the Holy Spirit, and one of them subsequently entered full-time ministry. It was revolutionary. We were picturing ourselves as the saviors of Africa when, in actual fact, we could not control our own children. We were neglecting the basic picture of waiting on God together in real fellowship. Committees will never pro-duce what fellowship can.

Activity #3: Eating Together

The basic form of fellowship is very simple: It is eating together. This is so simple that people overlook it. We see a picture of it in Acts when Paul spent seven days in the city of Troas:

"Now on the first day of the week, when the disciples came together to break bread, Paul, ready to depart the next day, spoke [or preached] *to them and continued his message until midnight"* (Acts 20:7). Again, the language implies it was a normal thing for them to eat together. In their homes, around their tables, they praised the Lord, prayed, and shared the Word of God.

When God opened my eyes to the fact that eating together was an activity of fellowship, I was astonished to see how much there was in the book of Acts about eating together. As a Pentecostal, I had come to think of food as a pretty unspiritual thing, and eating together as the mark of the carnal church. I had once heard a preacher say, "They have gone from the upper room to the supper room." In fact, they *did* go from the upper room to the supper room, and they continued eating together regularly. It is a remarkable thing.

There is much significance in eating together on a regular basis. We discovered this truth in Africa where, theoretically, there was no barrier between black and white. Of course, there was a very deep split that troubled my wife and me. Eventually, we decided to invite the Africans to meet in our home, which was somewhat socially revolutionary.

One of the reasons it was revolutionary was that many of the Africans at that time could not handle a knife and a fork. To have somebody in your home who sits eighteen inches away from the table and pours with perspiration when he tries to handle a knife and fork can be embarrassing.

But they were so sweet. They said, "Don't worry. We don't understand, but you'll teach us. We want to know." We discovered that this fellowship changed the whole relationship.

Later on, we would go down twice a week to eat with our students in their dining hall. We did not enjoy the food, but we found it made a completely new relationship between them and us. This is so scriptural. And, according to Eastern custom, when you eat with a person, you have committed yourself to him. You must not then be disloyal to him. It was equivalent to entering into a kind of covenant. If you partook of a man's hospitality, you put yourself under an obligation to him that only the most base and unworthy would ever violate. Part of Judas' guilt was that he first ate bread with Jesus and then betrayed Him. Psalms gives this dramatic prophecy of the betrayal of Jesus:

Even my own familiar friend in whom I trusted, who ate my bread, has lifted up his heel against me. (Psalm 41:9)

Jesus Himself referred to this passage in John 13:18, shortly before Judas left to betray Him. *"I do not speak concerning all of you. I know whom I have chosen; but that the Scripture may be fulfilled, 'He who eats bread with Me has lifted up his heel against Me.'"* Again, this is the height of treason and treachery—to eat with a man and then betray him. The purpose for which God brings His people together in fellowship around the table is that we will be loyal to one another from then onward. We will not eat together with someone, say, "God bless you, brother," and then walk out and start gossiping about him around the neighborhood. If we do, we are acting like Judas, though obviously not in the same degree.

I can picture this act of eating together including the Lord's Supper. In fact, the roots of the Lord's Supper are in the Passover meal, which was indeed a whole meal enjoyed over extended fellowship. When we take the Lord's Supper, we are renewing our covenant with Jesus and with everybody else who partakes with us. We are pledging our loyalty to Him and to one another. Severe judgments are pronounced on those who take the Lord's Supper unworthily, precisely because it is a covenant meal. (See 1 Corinthians 11:27–32.) To betray a man with whom you eat *and* take the Lord's Supper is extremely dangerous. It is like looking a man in the face, waiting until he turns around, and stabbing him in the back. That is how it is viewed by biblical standards.

We see Paul's concern that this fellowship of eating together be handled correctly:

Therefore when you come together in one place, it is not to eat the Lord's Supper. For in eating, each one takes his own supper ahead of others; and one is hungry and another is drunk. (1 Corinthians 11:20–21)

The Corinthian church was enthusiastic, but sometimes a little blunted in their perceptions. Recall that they could be happy with the Lord's blessing upon them, even when there was gross sexual immorality in their midst. (See 1 Corinthians 5:1–2.) Apparently, they also had a very strange practice in which everybody brought his own food, and one would start eating while another was hungry. One would drink too much wine while another had nothing at all to drink.

These very verses prove that the church at Corinth regularly ate together. They did not do it correctly, but at least they did come together. This was a natural form of fellowship.

Paul did not criticize the fellowship, although he wouldn't have condoned the drunkenness. He was saying, "Don't imagine that this type of fellowship, in itself, is taking the Lord's Supper." Let's have fellowship around the table, and do it as a church family, sharing as we eat together.

The first and primary outreach of the local church is prayer.

This is a totally different picture from sitting in pews and calling it fellowship. You cannot eat together with people and have the same attitude toward them. It changes you, it changes them, it changes relationships, and it changes the atmosphere. Consider this beautiful picture that gives us the "final product" of the chapter:

So continuing daily with one accord in the temple, and breaking bread from house to house [or eating their meals at home], *they ate their food with gladness and simplicity of heart, praising God and having favor with all the people.*
(Acts 2:46–47)

Here is a picture of the church walking in victory, living in the Spirit and in perfect fellowship. Where was it effective? In their homes. Every meal table became a place of fellowship, a place of prayer, and a place of praise. The unbelievers did not see them in the temple because the unbelievers did not go to the temple. They saw them in their homes, and what they saw made them want what these believers had.

There isn't much happiness in many people's homes today. A really happy home, where family members enjoy one another and praise the Lord, will stand out! People will say, "What's going on there?" If the only place you display your wares is in the church building, most unbelievers will never see what you have. In Matthew 5:15–16, Jesus said that we are not to hide our light under a basket, and the biggest basket we seem to hide under today is the roof of the church building!

Activity #4: Prayer

Fourth, while the first need of the local church is teaching, the first and primary *outreach* of the local church is prayer. After a congregation is properly taught, the ministry of prayer should emerge as believers come together in the name of the Lord Jesus Christ. It is an outreach that proceeds from the teaching.

> *Therefore I exhort first of all that supplications, prayers, intercessions, and giving of thanks be made for all men.*
> (1 Timothy 2:1)

Paul was giving instructions to Timothy about the conduct of the affairs of a local church, and he said, *"First of all...."* The primary ministry of a local congregation is offering supplications, prayers, intercessions, and the giving of thanks. God expects the church to be a center of prayer, a powerhouse from which effective intercessory prayer goes forth into the world. If the church were fulfilling this function, its relationship to the world would be very different. If you pray for people enough, they feel something in you that causes them to respond to you. If you serve them without prayer, their attitude toward you is vastly different.

> [The Lord said,] *"Even them* [foreigners and those who feel rejected] *I will bring to My holy mountain, and make them joyful in My house of prayer. Their burnt offerings and their sacrifices will be accepted on My altar; for*

My house shall be called a house of prayer for all nations."
(Isaiah 56:7)

God's house is to be called *"a house of prayer for all nations."* His people are made joyful in His house of prayer with a joy that stands the test of tribulation. There are other types of joy that Christians enter into that may not stand the test. But when we let God make us joyful in the house of prayer, we are truly established.

When I was converted out of complete ignorance to the things of God (though I had been a member of a church for twenty-five years), the thing that I liked best and never wanted to miss was the prayer meeting. This was totally alien to my natural character. I remember once, as an unbeliever, hearing about some people going to a prayer meeting. I had never been to a prayer meeting in my life and did not know what one was. However, when I understood that they were going to spend one hour in a prayer meeting, I thought, "How could people ever think of enough to pray about for one hour?" When I was saved and baptized in the Holy Spirit, I soon understood how a person could pray for long periods of time. I must say, God made me joyful in His house of prayer.

Let's return to 1 Timothy 2, where we see that the first specific topic for prayer is *"for kings and all who are in authority"* (v. 2). The first prescribed topic of prayer in the local congregation is for those who are in civil authority, not for the preachers or the missionaries or the sick. I have asked some congregations, "How many of you in the last week have even once prayed intelligently for the head of your government and its affairs?" Very rarely, you see 20 percent of the people respond. We are missing the first priority.

My dear friend, the late Don Basham, first heard me preach about this in Australia, as I asked, "How many of you pray regularly for the Queen and all the rulers of this Commonwealth?" About five out of the hundred and fifty people present rather timidly slipped their hands up, and Don was not one of them! When he heard me preach about a year later, he said, "Brother, you'll never catch me again! I was caught once, but never again. In our family, we pray for the rulers every day."

So he caught the message. Here is where the majority of professing Christians are still grossly at fault. They criticize by the hour but pray very little for the leaders they criticize. I tell people frequently, "If you would spend the time praying instead of criticizing, you would have much less to criticize." In fact, the people you criticize may be much more faithful in their jobs than you are in yours. If our rulers were not more faithful in administrating the nations than the Christians are in praying for them, we would be headed for chaos.

> *The basic requirement of effective corporate prayer is harmony among believers.*

Romans 13:1 simply states, *"The powers that be are ordained of God"* (KJV). Secular authority is ordained by God, but it is our business to see that it is directed the way God desires through our prayers. It is because of God's mercy and provision that we have secular rules and authority, without which there would be great disorder and confusion. Our responsibility is to pray for our government.

Let me say here that prayer is not a way of getting God to do what you want Him to do. Rather, it is the way to get to the place where you know God is going to do what you are asking Him to do. After coming to this place of confidence, telling Him what you desire is a small matter.

Let us also note the relationship between fellowship and prayer:

> *Again I say to you that if two of you agree on earth concerning anything that they ask, it will be done for them by My Father in heaven. For where two or three are gathered together in My name, I am there in the midst of them.*
> (Matthew 18:19–20)

Where two or three have been brought together by the Holy Spirit to meet around Christ Himself, He promises to show up on their behalf. The basic requirement of effective corporate prayer is harmony. Again, the Greek word for *agree* is *sumphano*, from which we get the English word *symphony*. It means "blending together in harmony." If two people harmonize, their prayers are irresistible.

The devil does not fear prayer meetings in the least bit, because most of the prayers that are offered never get above the ceiling! God does not even hear them, because He has strict requirements about the type of prayers He will hear. What the devil really fears is two people harmonizing. But remember that being almost in harmony is not harmony. There is nothing more grating than two instruments or voices that are almost in harmony. When we harmonize and meet the other requirements of prayer, we fulfill a necessary component of church life. Without it, we will fall short of all that God has for the church.

Chapter 25

The Corporate Gathering

hile the New Testament acknowledges the regular fellowship of believers in their homes, it never allows us to rest content with this alone. It encourages the corporate church to meet together. In this chapter, I will describe eight different purposes for which the believers in an area come together. The following points summarize and put into specific context many of the principles and truths we have been learning about the church and how we can apply them to our lives today.

Purposes for Which Believers Come Together

1. To Edify Each Other

> *How is it then, brethren? Whenever you come together, each of you has a psalm, has a teaching, has a tongue, has a revelation, has an interpretation. Let all things be done for edification.* (1 Corinthians 14:26)

The purpose of the gathering, as presented by Paul, is for all the believers to edify each other through prayer, worship, and the exercise of their particular gifts and ministries. It is all about mutual edification. Every time you gather with your fellow believers, therefore, imagine yourself as being "on duty" to encourage them. You are to draw from your spiritual gifts and your current devotional life to help build them up spiritually.

2. To Eat the Lord's Supper

The second purpose, as we have recently seen, is for the believers to fellowship around a meal and partake of the Lord's Supper together. This must be a time of corporate unity and not individual selfishness.

> *What! Do you not have houses to eat and to drink in? Or do you despise the church of God and shame those who have nothing? What shall I say to you? Shall I praise you in this? I do not praise you. For I received from the Lord that which I also delivered to you....Therefore, my brethren, when you come together to eat, wait for one another.*
>
> (1 Corinthians 11:22–23, 33)

We can see here that everyone is important. We all know the feeling of arriving late to dinner and finding out that it has already started. How honored we would feel if everyone waited to eat until we arrived. Such was to be the spirit of even huge gatherings of several thousand believers. Paul was saying, "Wait! Hold the food until every brother or sister has arrived. How can we enjoy ourselves if they are not all here?"

This was indeed a large meeting, one that could never fit in a home, for Paul said, *"Do you not have houses to eat and to drink in?"* Here we have a gathering together around a meal and the Lord's Supper that centered on the mutual affirmation and edification of the corporate body of Christ.

3. To Be Taught by Mobile Ministries

In Acts 21, Paul visited Jerusalem after many years' absence. James and the other brethren in Jerusalem said, in effect, "Now we must have a meeting and let you minister to the whole congregation."

> *And when they heard it, they glorified the Lord. And they said to [Paul], "You see, brother, how many myriads [ten thousands] of Jews there are who have believed, and they are all zealous for the law; but they have been informed about you that you teach all the Jews who are among the Gentiles to forsake Moses, saying that they ought not to circumcise their children nor to walk according to the customs. What then? The assembly must certainly meet, for they will hear that you have come."* (verses 20–22)

A mobile ministry had been directed by the Holy Spirit to the city of Jerusalem in the person of Paul, and the whole church in Jerusalem was to receive the benefit of this apostolic ministry.

It is the responsibility of the local leaders to call the entire church together and make available to them the mobile ministry. The mobile ministries of the apostle, prophet, evangelist, and teacher are to take a place in corporate gatherings as the city leadership invites them. Obviously, these ministries would impact church gatherings in a powerful way, and we need their spiritual instruction and encouragement.

The purpose of corporate gathering is for believers to edify one another.

4. To Hear First-Person Reports of Mobile Ministries

We see such a report given by Paul to his "sending church" in Antioch:

From there they sailed to Antioch, where they had been commended to the grace of God for the work which they had completed. Now when they had come and gathered the church together, they reported all that God had done with them, and that He had opened the door of faith to the Gentiles. (Acts 14:26–27)

Imagine a gathering of at least fifteen thousand people who had not seen Paul for two to three years!

As we have seen, when a local church sends out a ministry, it is answerable to that congregation. Even Paul and Barnabas as apostles had to give an account of their stewardship. It is an exciting and critical part of church life that local people be connected to world missions. The Great Commission must become part of the understanding and lifestyle of every congregation.

5. To Read Letters from Mobile Ministries

Often, Paul and the other apostles could not go to a city, but would write a letter with the directions and instructions that the particular congregation in that city needed. Fifty percent or more of the early Christians were illiterate and could not read the letter for themselves. How was it communicated to them? The letter would be the focal point of a meeting of the whole congregation. The local elders would call all the believers together and read aloud the letter slowly. No doubt, they read it out twice or three times. The people might also have had the opportunity to say, "I didn't understand that. Read it again. What did he mean?"

Sometimes, letters were shared among churches in different cities. Paul wrote to the Colossians,

The Corporate Gathering

Now when this epistle is read among you, see that it is read also in the church of the Laodiceans, and that you likewise read the epistle from Laodicea. (Colossians 4:16)

Colossae and Laodicea were neighboring cities and had similar types of problems. Paul did not want to give his advice and counsel to just one church, so he said, "When this letter arrives at Colossae, it will be read among you, and when you've finished it, send it to the church at Laodicea and let it be read there. I've also sent a letter to the church at Laodicea, so when it comes, read it, too." Paul confidently anticipated that the whole group of believers would be called together in each city to hear the letters he had written to them.

So far, we see a fascinating picture of the corporate gathering of a New Testament church. We have a gathering centered on mutual edification and the sharing of a meal that might also include the ministry, report, or instruction (even by letter) of a mobile ministry. Now, there are three other purposes for such gatherings.

6. To Settle Issues of Doctrine and Practice

An important reason they gathered together was to settle issues of doctrine and practice. Oh, how this needs to be done to settle unresolved doctrinal issues today!

The fifteenth chapter of Acts is devoted to the discussion of what Gentiles must do to be recognized as Christians. Some of the believing Pharisees were saying, "They have to become proselytes. They have to come under the law of Moses and be circumcised. If they keep the Law, then we will acknowledge their faith in the Messiah." But Paul and Barnabas said, "No, it doesn't have to be that way." So the apostles and elders, and then the whole church in Jerusalem, met to consider and settle the question.

> *Then it pleased the apostles and elders, with the whole church, to send chosen men of their own company to Antioch with Paul and Barnabas....* (Acts 15:22)

The entire congregation came together. When they arrived at a decision, they sent Paul and Barnabas to communicate it to the believers in question. They arrived at a very basic fourfold code of conduct, instead of the incredibly complex law of Moses: to abstain from things polluted by idols, from things strangled, from blood, and from fornication. That is all that would be required of Mosaic observance for Gentile believers coming to the Lord Jesus. I believe true spirituality always opts for simplicity instead of complexity. Now, let's read these beautiful verses:

> *It seemed good to us, being assembled with one accord....For it seemed good to the Holy Spirit, and to us....* (verses 25, 28)

This group of believers had arrived at absolute unanimity on what the Holy Spirit required. The principle is that matters affecting doctrine and practice relating to every believer should be settled in the entire congregation. The apostles and elders held preliminary discussions and arrived at what they considered to be the mind of the Lord, but they let it be ratified by the whole congregation.

7. To Maintain Discipline and Standards of Behavior

The church also came together in matters of discipline and standards of behavior. For example, in the case of sexual immorality in the Corinthian church, Paul felt the issue

386

could not be ignored. For the sake of preserving purity in the church, he demanded that it be brought out in front of the whole congregation:

> *It is actually reported that there is sexual immorality among you, and such sexual immorality as is not even named among the Gentiles; that a man has his father's wife! And you are puffed up, and have not rather mourned, that he who has done this deed might be taken away from among you. For I indeed, as absent in body but present in spirit, have already judged (as though I were present) him who has so done this deed. In the name of our Lord Jesus Christ, when you are gathered together, along with my spirit, with the power of our Lord Jesus Christ, deliver such a one to Satan for the destruction of the flesh, that his spirit may be saved in the day of the Lord Jesus.* (1 Corinthians 5:1–5)

Without question, Paul anticipated the whole congregation coming together as his letter was read. Judgment would be rendered so that the man might be brought to repentance and his soul eternally saved. How different it would be today if we gathered the church and dealt corporately and directly with extreme sin, especially in the lives of Christian leaders. This is part of the lifestyle of the true church.

8. To Settle Disputes between Believers

One other reason the whole local church gathers was presented by Jesus Himself:

> *Moreover if your brother sins against you, go and tell him his fault between you and him alone. If he hears you, you have gained your brother. But if he will not hear, take with you one or two more, that "by the mouth of two or three*

witnesses every word may be established." And if he refuses to hear them, tell it to the church. But if he refuses even to hear the church, let him be to you like a heathen and a tax collector. (Matthew 18:15–17)

We see again the need for a corporate gathering when someone refuses all previous steps to reconcile a dispute.

The work of the gospel can utilize buildings, but it cannot be contained by them.

As we discussed earlier, anyone who refuses to accept the decision of the local congregation in such matters is no longer to be treated as a Christian. The only way to make this effective is by having the entire church in agreement, so they all need to gather and come into the type of agreement pictured in the following verses:

Assuredly, I say to you, whatever you bind on earth will be bound in heaven, and whatever you loose on earth will be loosed in heaven. Again I say to you that if two of you agree on earth concerning anything that they ask, it will be done for them by My Father in heaven. For where two or three are gathered together in My name, I am there in the midst of them. (verses 18–20)

Notice that we move from binding and loosing to agreeing to gathering in Jesus' name. This is what happens when the church comes together in unity! We have the power to bind and loose (or forbid and permit) because we are in agreement (or harmony) as we gather around His name. Our unity enforces discipline. No rebel or rebellion can stand against the unified church.

Let's sum up the eight reasons for corporate gatherings:

1. To edify each other through gifts and ministries
2. To eat the Lord's Supper together
3. To be edified by visiting mobile ministries
4. To hear reports by mobile ministers returning to the local church that sent them out
5. To hear letters from mobile ministers read
6. To settle issues of doctrine and practice affecting all believers
7. To maintain discipline and proper standards of behavior among believers
8. To settle disputes between believers

Now, where were these meetings held? The Bible is delightfully silent about this! It just does not tell us. We know from Acts 2:46 and 5:42 that believers met in the temple. In Acts 19:9, Paul preached for a year and a half in a philosopher's school. In Acts 20:8, the believers met in an upper room. The reason why the Bible does not tell us is that it is not important. Any place that will meet the need is fine.

The first building specifically built as a church was constructed in 222 A.D., almost two hundred years after the day of Pentecost. The Jews built synagogues, and the heathen built temples, but the early Christians coming from either Jewish or heathen backgrounds did not build. This speaks to the flexibility and mobility needed for a true New Testament church. We cannot be trapped either within or by our churches. The work of the gospel can utilize buildings, but it cannot be contained by them. The daily life of the local church has to spill out past the church buildings into the everyday world.

Part 6:

The Future of the Church

Chapter 26

Your Kingdom Come

Many Christians are preoccupied with end-time questions, such as these: "What will happen to the church in the last days? What battles and confrontations lie ahead? What role will the state of Israel play?" I will attempt to address these questions in this final section on the future of the church.

First, I must establish God's goal for the present age. We will find the answer in three words from Matthew 6:10. They are part of what we call the Lord's Prayer. Most of us who have grown up with a Christian background have prayed this prayer more times than we can remember, yet we have not often realized what we were praying for: *"Your kingdom come."* The prayer goes on, *"Your will be done on earth as it is in heaven."*

So, the prayer is saying, "Your kingdom come on earth." The ultimate goal of God for the present age is the coming of His kingdom on earth under His chosen King, the Lord Jesus Christ. I believe that He will actually have an earthly kingdom and that He will reign as king. I believe this is the only solution to the problems of the world.

Some people say we are dreamers, that we're talking about pie in the sky. Yet, after all these years of human history, I think the people who can imagine that *man* can resolve his own problems are the dreamers. We are probably further away from resolving the problems of the world at this time than we ever have been. So how can anyone persuade us that it is going to change through man's efforts?

There is only one hope. It is the coming of God's kingdom on earth. Every committed Christian needs to be lined up with this hope.

> *And the world is passing away, and the lust of it; but he who does the will of God abides forever.* (1 John 2:17)

God's will is not going to change. If there has to be any change, it is in our wills. If we each align our wills with the will of God, if we make the purpose of God our purpose in life, we will be as unshakable and undefeatable as the will of God. *"He who does the will of God abides forever."* The crucial issue for every person is, Are you aligned with God's will? Is God's purpose your purpose?

For many churchgoers in this nation, this is not so. They are involved in all sorts of religious activities, but they have lost sight of the goal, the end purpose, which is the establishment of the kingdom of God on earth.

There are a great many passages of Scripture that speak about this kingdom, and I want to give two of them. The first is from Daniel 2:44. We cannot go into the background of this verse, but it is the interpretation by Daniel of a vision that King Nebuchadnezzar had. The king could not remember the vision, let alone understand it. Supernaturally, God showed Daniel what the vision was and gave him the interpretation. This verse is really the climax of the interpretation:

And in the days of these kings the God of heaven will set up a kingdom which shall never be destroyed; and the kingdom shall not be left to other people; it shall break in pieces and consume all these kingdoms, and it shall stand forever.

At a certain season in human history (and I believe it is very close), God is going to set up a kingdom that will stand forever. It will never pass away, and it will never be passed on to others. It will utterly, totally, finally, and completely destroy all rival kingdoms.

Psalm 72 is what is called a messianic psalm. In other words, its theme is the kingdom of the Messiah. I want you to notice two main aspects of the messianic kingdom in this prophetic picture. First of all, the essential requirement for peace is righteousness. The politicians and other leaders who talk about peace but bypass righteousness are deceiving themselves and others. There never can be true peace without righteousness.

Many churchgoers are involved in religious activities but have lost sight of the goal: the establishment of God's kingdom on earth.

Second, the psalm emphasizes something that I think many Christians—whether they are evangelical or full-gospel—have not adequately appreciated: God's intense concern for the poor, the needy, and the downtrodden. This is a picture of the kingdom and the King:

Give the king Your judgments, O God, and Your righteousness to the king's Son. He will judge Your people with righteousness, and Your poor with justice. The mountains will bring peace to the people, and the little hills, by righteousness.

He will bring justice to the poor of the people; He will save the children of the needy, and will break in pieces the oppressor....He shall have dominion also from sea to sea, and from the River [Euphrates] to the ends of the earth. Those who dwell in the wilderness will bow before Him, and His enemies will lick the dust. The kings of Tarshish and of the isles will bring presents; the kings of Sheba and Seba will offer gifts. Yes, all kings shall fall down before Him; all nations shall serve Him. For He will deliver the needy when he cries, the poor also, and him who has no helper. He will spare the poor and needy, and will save the souls of the needy. He will redeem their life from oppression and violence; and precious shall be their blood in His sight.

(Psalm 72:1–4, 8–14)

With some exceptions, humanity does not care for the poor. The majority of the governments in the world today do not care for the poor. In Ezekiel 16:49, God paints a picture of the sins of Sodom, and it is remarkable that homosexuality is never even mentioned. The sins of Sodom were *"pride, fullness of food, and abundance of idleness; neither did she strengthen the hand of the poor and needy."* Homosexuality arises out of these conditions, which is precisely what has happened in the United States and other Western nations. But notice that the main condemnation of Sodom was that they did not strengthen the hands of the poor and the needy. Basically, in the world today, two things are happening simultaneously: The rich are getting richer and the poor are getting poorer. Most of the political negotiations that take place are aimed to protect the rich.

Let me point out one other fact about this kingdom before we focus on three primary purposes of God that need to be fulfilled prior to the coming of the kingdom. In Psalm 92, the psalmist dealt with an issue that is very current: the rise of the wicked. I have lived for over eighty years, but never have I seen wickedness flaunt itself so openly. Why does God permit this? Does God care? This is what the psalmist said:

> O LORD, how great are Your works! Your thoughts are very deep. A senseless man does not know, nor does a fool understand this. When the wicked spring up like grass, and when all the workers of iniquity flourish, it is that they may be destroyed forever. (Psalm 92:5–7)

God permits iniquity to flourish; He allows a tremendous harvest of iniquity, and it is taking place in the world today. But His purpose is to destroy the wicked. I am impressed with how little is spoken from the pulpit about the judgment of God. If we never speak about judgment, we deprive the Holy Spirit of the opportunity to convict people. Judgment is an essential part of the revelation of the gospel. Jesus is the Savior, but He is also the Judge.

In Revelation 1:9–17, John encountered Jesus as the Judge. Now, he had known Him as the Savior. He had rested his head on Jesus' breast at the Last Supper. But when he met Him as the Judge, he fell at His feet like one who was dead! I think the church needs to get a vision of Jesus as the Judge.

Now, let us look at three purposes of God that need to be fulfilled before the coming of the kingdom.

The Gospel Will Be Preached to All the World

In Matthew 24, Jesus was asked this question by His disciples:

*What will be **the sign** of Your coming, and of the end of the age?*   (Matthew 24:3, emphasis added)

Not *a* sign or the *signs*, but *the sign*. Jesus gave a specific answer. But before He gave it, He gave a number of signs, which were indications but not *the* sign. Let us look at some of them:

For nation will rise against nation, and kingdom against kingdom. And there will be famines, pestilences, and earthquakes in various places. All these are the beginning of sorrows [or birth pangs].   (verses 7–8)

The establishment of Christ's physical kingdom on earth at the end of the age cannot be organized; it can come only by a birth. This parallels the experience of every individual who enters the kingdom of God: He must be born again; there is no other way. A birth is preceded by labor pains, and the more intense the pains, the more imminent the birth. I believe we are in the period of the labor pains of the birth of Christ's physical kingdom on earth.

Here are the labor pains that Jesus described in verse 7: Nation will rise against nation, kingdom against kingdom. The word *"nation"* in Greek is *ethnos*, so Jesus was referring to ethnic conflict, such as we saw after the collapse of the former Soviet Union. Personally, I believe the labor pains began with World War I. From that point onward, we have increasingly seen global conflict rooted in ethnic hatred. This is indeed a sign of the end of the age!

Now, going on in Matthew 24, we note the word *then*, which occurs multiple times. This indicates that a series of situations will develop, one after the other. After Jesus indicated that these events are the beginning of birth pangs, He said,

*Then they will deliver you up to tribulation and kill you,
and you will be hated by all nations for My name's sake.*
(Matthew 24:9)

I have often asked Christian groups who the *"you"* in this verse is. These words are addressed to followers of Jesus, so *"you"* is *us*!

*And then many will be offended, will betray one another,
and will hate one another.* (verse 10)

Many *Christians* will give up their faith in the face of the persecution, and they will betray their fellow believers to save themselves. This happened in the former Soviet Union and has been happening in China probably for two generations, but it will become far more widespread.

Then many false prophets will rise up and deceive many.
(verse 11)

The greatest single danger at the present time is not persecution but deception. Jesus warned us against deception more than He warned us against anything else. If your attitude is "I couldn't be deceived," then you are a candidate for deception. I have learned, from over sixty years of experience, that only one thing can keep us faithful. It is not our cleverness, our knowledge of Scripture, our ministry gifts, or our status—it is the mercy of God. Paul said, *"I give judgment as one whom the Lord in His mercy has made trustworthy"* (1 Corinthians 7:25). I regularly acknowledge to God, "God, if I am to remain faithful, it will be by Your mercy, and Your mercy only. Not by my cleverness, not by the languages I know, not by the Scriptures I can quote, not by my past experience of ministry, but only by Your mercy."

And because lawlessness will abound, the love of many will grow cold.   (Matthew 24:12)

The Greek word for *"love"* here is that famous word *agape*. It means primarily the love of the Christians. Why will the love of many Christians grow cold? Because lawlessness will abound. Looking back over the last twenty or thirty years of American history, we would have to say that lawlessness is abounding. It has abounded more and more until, as a matter of fact, there is really no force that can contain it. People blame the police, but the police can maintain law and order only if the majority of citizens are law-abiding. When that comes to an end, there is no way to maintain law. Unless we are on our guard in this atmosphere of lawlessness, the result will be that our love will grow cold.

But he who endures to the end shall be saved.   (verse 13)

Actually, the Greek is more specific. It says, "He who *has endured* to the end will be saved." You are saved now, but to remain saved, you have to endure to the end. Otherwise, you will not be saved.

That is a pretty grim picture. But the next verse is astonishing, it is so paradoxical. You would expect that Jesus would say, in this situation, "Hide yourself; keep out of sight; do everything you can to protect yourself and your family. Don't become conspicuous. Maybe you will make your way through." Actually, He said the exact opposite. In the light of this situation, here is *the sign.*

And this gospel of the kingdom will be preached [or proclaimed] *in all the world as a witness to all the nations, and then the end will come.*   (verse 14)

The final, conclusive sign is the proclamation of the gospel of the kingdom in all nations. Incidentally, it is the gospel of *the kingdom*. I find that many preachers preach the love of Jesus, but they never preach the kingdom. I heard a Romanian Christian say, "As long as we told people, 'Jesus loves you,' we were all right. When we said, 'Jesus is King,' they put us in prison." That is not a popular message.

The enemies of the apostles in Corinth criticized them, and they summed up the apostles' message in this way: First, they said, *"These [people] have turned the world upside down"* (Acts 17:6). Would they say that about you and me? Have we turned the world upside down?

Then, they said, *"These are...saying there is another king; Jesus"* (verse 7). Is that how unbelievers would sum up the message of the gospel as we proclaim it today? I think not. Mostly, we go with the approach that "God will meet your need." It is true that God will meet your needs, but the problem

> *Many preach the love of Jesus but neglect to preach the message of His kingship.*

with this is that it leaves people with the impression that God is there only to meet their needs. This is the attitude of most American Christians today. "God is a good God, and He will meet my need." The truth of the matter is, God does not exist for you; you exist for God. The most important thing is to glorify God, not to have your needs met. There has to be a different presentation of the gospel.

The sign, again, is:

And this gospel of the kingdom will be preached [proclaimed] *in all the world as witness to all the nations, and then the end will come.* (Matthew 24:14)

This is a specific answer to a specific question. My subject of study before I became a preacher was logic. To me, this is just simple logic. This is *the sign*: The gospel of the kingdom will be proclaimed in the whole world as a witness to all the nations, and then the end will come.

Let me turn to a picture of the harvest in Revelation. This is a revelation that John had concerning the result of a hundred and forty-four thousand young Jewish men going out into the world with the gospel. You may want to read the first half of Revelation 7 in order to see the context of this, but this is the fruit:

> *After these things I looked, and behold, a great multitude which no one could number, of all nations, tribes, peoples, and tongues, standing before the throne and before the Lamb, clothed with white robes, with palm branches in their hands, and crying out with a loud voice, saying, "Salvation belongs to our God who sits on the throne, and to the Lamb!"*
>
> (verses 9–10)

Notice that there are people from all nations, tribes, peoples, and tongues. Therefore, people of every tongue, tribal background, and ethnic group have to be reached with the gospel. I believe God is jealous for the glory of His Son. In the end, Jesus will not have died in vain. There will be at least one representative from every ethnic group before the throne.

However, they will never hear unless someone tells them. In a way, the number one priority for the church of Jesus Christ is proclaiming the gospel of the kingdom in all the world, to all nations. You would have to acknowledge that, in most religious groups in this nation, this has taken a very low priority. In fact, many Christians are not even aware it is on the list. We need a tremendous adjustment. We need what they used to call an "awakening." Not for the people out in the street, not for the people in the "old-line denominations," but for people like you and me. *We* need an awakening. The Bible says that a son who sleeps in harvest causes shame. (See Proverbs 10:5.) Our churches are full of sons asleep in harvest.

Israel Will Be Restored

Another thing that has to be achieved before the kingdom can come is the restoration of Israel. When I say Israel, I do not mean the church. There is probably no greater source of confusion in the church today than the misunderstanding about the identity of Israel, in which people have started to apply the name *Israel* to the church. There are over seventy places in the New Testament where the word *Israel* is used. I have investigated every one of them, and my personal conclusion is that *Israel* is never used as a synonym for the church. The truth is very simple: Israel is Israel and the church is the church. God has a plan for each, and He has enough to give to both. He does not need to rob one to bless the other.

Let's return to Matthew 24, and I will point out to you a dramatic change of focus. It's as if we have had a video screen that embraces basically the whole world. Then, suddenly, the focus changes to one very small area of the earth's surface, Jerusalem and the land of Israel.

Therefore when you see the "abomination of desolation," spoken of by Daniel the prophet, standing in the holy place (whoever reads, let him understand), then let those who are in Judea flee to the mountains. (verses 15–16)

As far as I am concerned, in the light of Scripture, there is only one holy place, and that is the temple area. Notice that it does not say to flee to the West Bank. So, our focus has suddenly changed from all nations and the whole world to the city of Jerusalem and to the Jewish people in the land.

This corresponds to a passage in Romans 11. Paul wrote this to believers from Gentile backgrounds:

> *For I do not desire, brethren, that you should be ignorant of this mystery, lest you should be wise in your own opinion* [or lest you think too highly of yourselves], *that blindness* [or hardening] *in part has happened to Israel until the fullness* [full number] *of the Gentiles has come in. And so all Israel will be saved.* (verses 25–26)

It might prove an interesting challenge for you sometime to find all the places in the New Testament where Paul said he did not want believers to be ignorant. In most cases, believers are ignorant of the very things about which Paul said they should *not* be ignorant.

Here in Romans, we see that, first of all, the full number of the Gentiles has to come in. A certain number of Gentiles elected by God for salvation has to be saved. Then all Israel will be saved. Israel is the only nation of which the Bible promises that an entire nation will be saved. However, you need to bear this in mind:

> *Isaiah also cries out concerning Israel: "Though the number of the children of Israel be as the sand of the sea, the remnant will be saved."* (Romans 9:27)

Not *a* remnant but *the* remnant. This is the remnant chosen and foreknown by God. When it says that all Israel will be saved, *"all Israel"* will be the remnant. It will be the entire nation that is left. Israel has to go through a lot before that happens, what Scripture calls *"the time of Jacob's trouble"* (Jeremiah 30:7).

It is very important for all of us to realize the special position that the Jews occupy in the purposes of God. For many Gentiles, this is a very hard fact to swallow. Most of us who are not of Jewish background have been brought up, in varying degrees, to look down on the Jewish people, to make snide remarks about them, and so forth, and even to despise them. I am not of Jewish background, and I was never an anti-Semite, but I remember that, even in my family, which was a cultivated, British family, when they spoke about the Jews, somehow there was a different tone of voice, a different atmosphere.

> *We must realize the special position that the Jews occupy in the purposes of God.*

Anti-Semitism is bred into most Gentiles. Paul said that we better be careful. He said that we are not the root, but the branches. (See Romans 11:16–24.) Remember, the branches do not bear the root; the root bears the branches. The root is Israel. There is going to have to be a tremendous change in the thinking of multitudes of Christians in this respect, because God is going to judge the nations on the basis of their attitude to the Jews. Many of you reading this may find yourselves beginning to object to this idea.

I was talking to a young man of Muslim background who was born in Algeria and who became a believer in Jesus Christ in a dramatic encounter. He started to argue with the Lord about the position of the Jews. The Lord said to him, "It's not the Jews you're against. It's Me." And that changed his whole attitude. The Jews did not choose themselves; God chose the Jews. If it had been left to the Jews, they would not have chosen themselves. You have no idea how much they would like to get away from the responsibility of being chosen. On his first day in office, one prime minister of Israel said, "We are a nation like any other nation." It sounds good, but it just is not true. They did not choose it, and we did not choose it—God chose it. If you have a problem with the Jews, your real problem is with God.

I believe that God makes the right choice—in our lives, in the church, and among the nations. If it had been left to me, I would not have made that choice. But God did not leave it to me. In fact, there are many things God did not leave to me. For example, I have been married twice, and each time, God chose my wife for me. He made wonderful choices, and I am grateful to Him. Maybe you are cleverer than I am, but I am just not a good enough judge of human nature to make the right choice.

The choice of the Jews is God's choice, and He knows what He is doing. Personally, I believe He is the only Person who can deal with the Jews. I am not saying that to be smart; I am just saying that they are not an easy people to deal with. God says, in effect, "I've accepted the responsibility, and in the end, I'll produce what I've promised." Jesus said, *"Wisdom is justified by her children"* (Matthew 11:19). In other words, what wisdom produces is the justification for wisdom's choice. God has not finished yet. Do not judge the product until it is complete.

I want to point out something to you that is extremely important for the United States of America. I am British by background, and Britain at one time had the mandate for the government of what was called Palestine. When the United Nations decided to give the Jewish people a very small strip of territory, the official reaction of the British government was to do everything short of open war to oppose it. Now, not only am I British, but I also served in the British army, and I was living in Palestine at that time, so I am speaking about something of which I was an eyewitness. There were forty million Arabs with modern armies against six hundred thousand Jews with very few military weapons. And who won?

Britain had a vast empire, but from the day it turned against the purposes of God for Israel, the British Empire fell apart and went into decline. They had given lip service to being in favor of the Jews, but it was not the way they acted. Frankly, the American government must be careful not to follow in the footsteps of Britain. They must not oppose the purposes of God for Is-

> *God will judge the nations on the basis of the way they have dealt with the Jewish people.*

rael in the peace processes. Oh, they know how to talk to Christians; they know how to use the right language. That is what politicians do—they talk to every group in such a way as to cause that group to think they are in favor of them. But when you get down to facts, it may be different.

I believe that no politician who takes a stand against Israel can ultimately prosper, and no nation that takes a stand against Israel can prosper. The Lord says,

For behold, in those days and at that time, when I bring back the captives of Judah and Jerusalem [this is the time of the regathering of the Jewish people in which we are now living], *I will also gather all nations* [goyim, meaning Gentile nations in Hebrew], *and bring them down to the Valley of Jehoshaphat* ["Jehovah judges"]; *and I will enter into judgment with them there on account of My people, My heritage Israel, whom they have scattered among the nations; they have also divided up My land.* (Joel 3:1–2)

God says He is going to judge the nations on the basis of the way they have dealt with the Jews. Whether you like it or not, this is how it is going to happen. It is in our own interest to take note of that.

Not only did they scatter them, but they divided up their land. We need to bear in mind that, above all, it is God's land: *"They have also divided up **My** land"* (emphasis added).

Let me return here to the history of the present state of Israel. I would have to say that Britain carries the main responsibility for dividing the land because, in 1919 or 1920, the League of Nations gave Britain the mandate for that territory with the specific understanding that they would create a national home for the Jewish people. In 1922, the British government, with one stroke of a pen, took 76 percent of the allotted area and made it an Arab state—originally called Trans-Jordan, now called Jordan—in which no Jew is permitted to live. That means only 24 percent was left. Then the United Nations offered to the Jews about 10 percent of the remaining 24 percent. Yet God intervened. At the present time, who knows? One thing I will tell you is that, again, God will judge all nations by the way they have related to the Jewish people.

Matthew 25:31–46 refers to the coming of the King and the kingdom. We need to understand that this is a direct reference to Joel 3:1–2. It is the same scene:

When the Son of Man comes in His glory, and all the holy angels with Him, then He will sit on the throne of His glory [His earthly throne—at this moment He is sitting on His Father's throne]. *All the nations [goyim] will be gathered before Him, and He will separate them one from another, as a shepherd divides his sheep from the goats.*
(Matthew 25:31–32)

So all nations will be gathered before the Lord Jesus when He comes as King, and He will separate them into two groups: the sheep on the right hand, the goats on the left. The basis of the division, if you will study the chapter carefully, is how they have treated the brothers of Jesus. *"Inasmuch as you did it to one of the least of these My brethren, you did it to me"* (Matthew 25:40; see verse 45). God has chosen to make the basis of His judgment the way the nations have related to the brothers of Jesus.

The judgments are appallingly severe. Concerning the sheep, it says, *"Come, you blessed of My Father, inherit the kingdom prepared for you from the foundation of the world"* (verse 34). That is the earthly kingdom of Jesus. To the goats, He says, *"Depart from Me, you cursed, into the everlasting fire prepared for the devil and his angels"* (verse 41).

In the political arena, the supreme purpose of God at this time is the regathering of the Jewish people in their own land preliminary to restoring them to Himself. A few of us, I think, can take into account the immensity of the miracle that, although the Jewish people were scattered for nineteen centuries among more than one hundred nations under every pressure to give up their identity, they remained a separate, distinct people. In the last ninety years, they have been re-gathered from more than one hundred different nations. I do not know whether you can understand what a miracle that is. It is one of the major demonstrations of the control of God over human affairs that has ever taken place in the history of this planet.

My wife Lydia was Danish. She used to say that if you were to take the Danes and scatter them among all the nations, and then come back after two hundred years, you would not find a Dane anywhere; they would all have become assimilated. The Jews were scattered for nearly two *thousand* years—and some of them for longer than that. The Jews from what is now Yemen were scattered for twenty-five hundred years, as well as some of the Jews from what is now Iraq, but they remained a separate, identifiable people and were then brought back to the land of Israel. This, in my opinion, was as great a miracle as the exodus from Egypt.

> *Now is the time of our preparation to be the bride of Christ, or we will not be ready.*

In a two-year period, four hundred thousand Russian Jews returned to Israel. The Jewish population of Israel at that time was about four million. So, 10 percent of the population were new immigrants—without resources, without finances, and often in a poor state of health—that needed to be assimilated. This would be like the United States having to assimilate twenty-seven million new immigrants in two years—and the United States has far greater resources than Israel. The American government would never even contemplate such a thing, and yet it happened in Israel. Why did it happen? Because God intended for the restoration of Israel to happen before His kingdom comes.

The Bride Will Be Perfected

Another development that will take place is the preparation of the church of Jesus Christ to become the bride of Christ. These developments are not necessarily in chronological order, but in the order that they occur in Scripture, and I think there is a certain logic to this order.

> *And I heard, as it were, the voice of a great multitude, as the sound of many waters and as the sound of mighty thunderings, saying, "Alleluia! For the Lord God Omnipotent reigns! Let us be glad and rejoice and give Him glory, for the marriage of the Lamb has come, and His wife* [the church] *has made herself ready." And to her it was granted to be arrayed in fine linen, clean and bright, for the fine linen is the righteous acts of the saints.* (Revelation 19:6–8)

We saw at the beginning of this book, in the picture of the bride from Ephesians, that when the time of the marriage supper comes, the bride will not be making herself ready. She will *already* have made herself ready. In other words, now is the time of our preparation. When the event comes, it will be too late to start preparing.

In a rather unusual set of circumstances, I became a father responsible for eleven girls, all of whom are now married. I know they were excited about their weddings. Most women are. They take a lot of time to prepare. They consider the kind of dress they will wear, they plan the ceremony, they choose the bridesmaids, and they have a rehearsal. These things are familiar to everyone. This is just a little glimpse of what it means for the bride of Christ to make herself ready.

If you are not preparing, I do not see how you can be ready. If you are not even aware that you have to prepare, how can you possibly be ready? For most women, their wedding day is the single most significant day of their lives. This is how it will be for the church, and it requires much preparation. *"His wife has made herself ready"*—not "is making herself ready," or "is making frantic, last-minute preparations," but *has* made herself ready.

What are the requirements for the bride to get ready? I want to offer three. You may recall some of these points from chapter eight. They are vitally important.

1. Total Loyalty to Jesus

This is not merely a doctrinal relationship or an intellectual relationship but a heart relationship that gives Jesus first place and will not share it with any other. A husband and wife can love one another and have a wonderful marriage, but they must be absolutely clear that Jesus has first place. You can never let the relationship with a spouse take precedence over your relationship with Jesus. Never. When Jesus is in His rightful place, other things will fall into place, and this will lead to a good marriage.

In writing to the Corinthian church, Paul said,

> *For I am jealous for you with godly jealousy. For I have betrothed you to one husband, that I may present you as a chaste virgin to Christ.* (2 Corinthians 11:2)

Remember that, in biblical culture, betrothal was somewhat like a present-day engagement, but it was totally binding, as binding as marriage. It was not something you could break, but it was not the consummation of the marriage, either. Paul spoke of *"a chaste virgin."*

First Corinthians 6 reveals the background of some of the people who belonged to the church in Corinth:

> *Do you not know that the unrighteous will not inherit the kingdom of God? Do not be deceived. Neither fornicators, nor idolaters, nor adulterers, nor homosexuals, nor sodomites, nor thieves, nor covetous, nor drunkards, nor revilers, nor extortioners will inherit the kingdom of God. And such were some of you.* (verses 9–11)

We need to bear this verse in mind. You can call fornication "premarital sex" if you like, but if you practice it, you cannot enter the kingdom of God. It rules you out unless you repent and change your lifestyle. But consider that, even with the background of some of the Corinthians, Paul said, *"I have betrothed you...as a chaste virgin to Christ"* (2 Corinthians 11:2). What a testimony to the power of the blood of Jesus! Through their faith in Jesus and the power of His blood, Paul could refer to them as a chaste virgin before Christ.

Then, he was concerned that we remain faithful to our commitment to the Bridegroom until the marriage ceremony:

> *But I fear, lest somehow, as the serpent deceived Eve by his craftiness, so your minds may be corrupted from the simplicity* [and sincerity] *that is in Christ.* (verse 3)

The danger that faces us between the time of betrothal and the celebration of the marriage supper is that our minds may be corrupted from the simplicity and sincerity that is in Jesus Christ.

I have to say that I see this happening to multitudes of believers. One of the factors is what they call New Age teaching, which has infiltrated a great deal of the church and corrupts our minds from the purity that is in Christ Jesus.

Another factor is having a whole lot of theology. Personally, I am not really in favor of so-called theology. Many people go to theological school as believers and come out as unbelievers. I believe in the systematic study of the Bible, but when people become too preoccupied with intellectual understanding and achievement, they usually lose their faith. When the church becomes preoccupied with educational achievements, it usually becomes spiritually corrupted. Harvard and Yale are two vivid examples of this because they began as Christian universities. And there are hundreds more where the same thing has happened. So, we are warned to maintain the simplicity, sincerity, and purity of our faith in Christ.

> *We must not lose the simplicity and purity of our first love for Christ and faith in Him.*

The Lord spoke to my wife Ruth and me one time and said, "You have lost the simplicity of your first faith. I want you to come back." When you are first saved, you believe that God will answer every prayer. Isn't that right? You pray for ridiculous things, and they happen. Then you become so sophisticated that you begin to reason, "Well, yes, but..." You have lost the simplicity and the purity of your first faith. Paul was saying, "I'm concerned about you because only if

414

you remain the way you started will you be fit to be the bride of Christ."

Ruth and I used this verse as one of our proclamations:

And such were some of you. But [we are] *washed, but* [we are] *sanctified, but* [we are] *justified in the name of the Lord Jesus and by the Spirit of our God.*

(1 Corinthians 6:11)

This is how you have to be in order to be part of the bride of Christ. You have to be washed, sanctified, and justified. You cannot let go of the simplicity of your first faith.

In Revelation 17 and other places, the Bible speaks very frankly and openly about a church called the harlot or the prostitute. What is the difference between the bride and the harlot? Remember that there is only one essential difference—the bride has maintained her commitment to Jesus, and the harlot has turned from Him. I would say there is a harlot church in the world today and that it is growing—a church of those who have abandoned their first commitment to Jesus and become involved in all sorts of unscriptural things.

2. A Heartfelt Yearning

The second requirement of the bride is a heartfelt yearning for the coming of the Bridegroom.

Christ was offered once to bear the sins of many. To those who eagerly wait for Him He will appear a second time, apart from sin, for salvation. (Hebrews 9:28)

To whom will the Bridegroom appear? To those who eagerly wait for Him, to those who are on their tiptoes in expectancy. He will not appear to anyone else for salvation except His church. My very good friend, Jim Croft, used to say, "When Jesus comes back, it will not be sufficient to say, 'Nice to have You back.'" He will expect more than that.

So, let me ask you, are you yearning, really longing, for the return of the Bridegroom? Are you eagerly waiting—not just waiting, but *eagerly* waiting?

3. Proper Clothing—Righteous Acts

The third condition, as we saw earlier, is to have the proper clothing. Everybody knows that, for the bride, her attire is one of the most important features. Many years ago, a couple from a totally nonreligious background got saved. In those days, they used to bring people to our swimming pool to get baptized. The wife appeared in a knit bikini for her baptism. Some people would have been shocked, but I thought, "How wonderful to have somebody who doesn't know you shouldn't do religious things that way." So we provided her with alternative attire. But what we must realize in terms of our relationship with Christ is that we will need to be wearing more than a "bikini" to marry our Bridegroom. In other words, for our bridal attire, we must have a record of righteous acts.

> *"Let us be glad and rejoice and give Him glory, for the marriage of the Lamb has come, and His wife has made herself ready." And to her it was granted to be arrayed in fine linen, clean and bright; for the fine linen is the righteous acts of the saints.* (Revelation 19:7–8)

It is the things you have done for the Lord that will become your attire. Now, be honest, some of you at the moment have only a small amount of material. You need to change.

In Jesus' messages to the seven churches in Revelation 2–3, there is one thing that He said to every church: *"I know your works."* He did not say, "I know your doctrinal statement," or "I know your denominational position," or "I know your theological background." He said, "I know what you're doing." And this is what is going to provide your marriage garment. It is not going to be doctrine, but the things you have done for Him.

It is not always easy to serve the Lord; sometimes, the pressures are great. But the next time you are really, honestly serving the Lord, and you feel all these pressures coming against you— and I want you to know they come against me just as much as against anybody else—just bear in mind that it is all part of providing your wedding gown. You will feel different about it then.

> *Praying "Your kingdom come" means a commitment to being aligned with everything involved in the coming of the kingdom.*

Let's summarize, then, the three major purposes of God that have to be fulfilled before the end of the age and the coming of the kingdom.

First, the gospel has to be proclaimed to all nations. I believe this is the responsibility of the entire church. No Christian is exempt in this area. It is not the job of a few professionals or missionaries. There are many different responsibilities in the overall task, and every committed Christian has his part.

Second, Israel has to be restored, first to the land and second to God.

Then you shall dwell in the land that I gave to your fathers;
you shall be My people, and I will be your God.

(Ezekiel 36:28)

Bear in mind that the purpose of restoring the Jewish people to their land is to restore them to their God. All the rest—the political and military negotiations and interchanges—is just part of the process.

There is a reason why Israel has to be regathered. God is going to deal with them not merely as a group of individuals, but also as a nation, because He made a covenant with them as a nation. In order to deal with them as a nation, therefore, He has to regather them in one place. The only place will be the place He originally gave them to live in.

Third, as we have just discussed, the bride must be prepared for her Bridegroom.

I invite you to consider how much you are really connected with the purposes of God. The next time you pray, *"Your kingdom come,"* bear in mind that it is a commitment to be aligned with everything that is involved in the coming of the kingdom.

Chapter 27

A Glorious Church

he Scripture says that the church for which Jesus will be coming will be a glorious church. Yet many people associated with the church today have no concept of what this means. The Greek word for *glory* is *doxo*, from which we get the English word *doxology*, meaning "that which ascribes the glory to God."

I came to New Testament Greek by way of classical Greek, and I was a student and a teacher of the philosophy of Plato. One of the basic concepts of Plato's philosophy is summed up in this word *doxo*. In Plato's writings, *doxo* means "that which seems to be, that which appears, or opinion." This definition is very different from the way the word is used in Scripture. While I was studying philosophy, I decided that I would read the gospel of John in Greek. What really puzzled me was John's use of *doxo*. I thought to myself, *How could it be that Plato used the word to mean "that which seems to be, that which appears," whereas John used it for "glory"?*

Some years later, when I was wonderfully born again, I suddenly understood the New Testament's use of the word *doxo*. The reason for the difference in translation is that God's glory is His presence manifested to man's senses. It is the visible, tangible presence of God; it is that which appears or that which is seen. When I saw this, I realized how the word had come from the meaning of "that which appears" to "glory." The *glory of God* is what appears or is manifested to the senses of man.

Speaking to the Jewish council in Acts 7:2, Stephen said, *"The God of glory appeared to our father Abraham when he was in Mesopotamia."* Abraham knew God by His visible glory. This encounter changed Abraham's life, motives, and ambitions, to the extent that he forsook all to go to the land that God had promised him.

When the Scripture speaks about a glorious church, therefore, it means a church that is filled with the glory of God. It is a church that has within it the manifest, visible, tangible, personal presence of almighty God. It does not refer to a church that is living on naked faith without any manifestation, but a church that has entered into a relationship with God where His visible, personal, tangible presence is with His people.

A church that is permeated with the presence of God attracts people. When people sense it, they will say, "What is here? I've never felt anything like this. It's different. What do these people have that I don't?"

That is the glory of God, and it is awesome. When the glory of God was revealed to Israel, the people bowed with their faces to the ground:

> *When Solomon finished praying, fire came down from heaven and consumed the burnt offering and the sacrifices, and the glory of the LORD filled the temple. The priests could not enter the temple of the LORD because the glory of the LORD filled it. When all the Israelites saw the fire coming down*

and the glory of the LORD above the temple, they knelt on the pavement with their faces to the ground, and they worshiped and gave thanks to the LORD, saying, "He is good; his love endures forever."   (2 Chronicles 7:1–3 NIV)

God's presence was so powerful that no one could remain standing. This is the kind of church for which Jesus is coming.

Christ...loved the church and gave Himself for her, that He might sanctify and cleanse her with the washing of water by the word....   (Ephesians 5:25–26)

Jesus redeemed the church by His blood so that He might sanctify it by the pure water of His word. The blood and the water of the Word are both needed to make the church ready for the coming of the Lord. I always honor the blood of Jesus. His blood paid the redemptive price by which we are bought back out of the hand of the devil. Then, after we have been redeemed by the blood, it is the purpose of God that we should be sanctified and cleansed by the washing of the water by the Word. His purpose is clear:

...that He might present her to Himself a glorious church, not having spot or wrinkle or any such thing, but that she should be holy and without blemish.   (verse 27)

Therefore, here are three signs that identify the church that Jesus will come for:

1. It is to be glorious.
2. It is to be marked by the manifest presence of God in its midst.
3. It is to be spotless, holy, and without blemish.

I am deeply concerned about the present state of the so-called charismatic movement—although I think that, in some ways, it is at a charismatic standstill! If it is moving, I am not sure which way it is going. It's been my observation that many charismatics pay very little attention to Scripture—the majority of them not having read the Bible through from beginning to end. There are truths in the Bible that they do not know are there. While it is exciting to have the gifts of the Holy Spirit and to experience the manifestations, there is no substitute for knowing the Word of God and apprehending God's promises. The promises are breathtaking, such as this one: that we *"may be partakers of the divine nature, having escaped the corruption that is in the world through lust"* (2 Peter 1:4).

> *A glorious church has with it the manifest, visible, tangible, personal presence of almighty God.*

Let me ask you this: How far along are you in being a partaker of the divine nature? How much have you really escaped the corruption that is in the world through lust? Jesus is going to work out these things in His church, His bride.

Only through the washing of water by the Word can we become sanctified. I would recommend to you who are leaders that you do something about this. I can remember when, in the Pentecostal movement in this country, if you got fifty people together for a Bible study, it was a large number of people, but we did take time for the Word. In most Pentecostal congregations, every Wednesday night was a Bible study night. What has happened to Bible study? In most of the places I go to now, no time is given for Bible study at all. The leaders are responsible both to teach the Bible and, even more importantly, to teach people how to study the Bible for themselves and to give them a love for the Bible. I feel so sorry for Christians who live on the spiritual equivalent of the kind of diet that is popular today: chips and fast food. There is no fast food in God's kingdom!

> *This is He who came by water and blood; Jesus Christ; not only by water, but by water and blood. And it is the Spirit who bears witness, because the Spirit is truth.*
>
> (1 John 5:6)

The blood is Jesus' redeeming sacrifice, but the water is the regular cleansing and sanctifying of the Word of God. The two have to go together. Without the blood, we have no access, we have no life. But without the Word, we are not cleansed; we are not sanctified; our impurities are not washed away.

In addition to receiving life and cleansing through the blood and the water, the church needs to be built. In Ephesians 4:11, we have seen the means by which the church will be made ready for the coming of the Lord—by the five main body-building ministries we have addressed in prior chapters: apostles, prophets, evangelists, shepherds (or pastors), and teachers. In the next two verses, we see the purpose for which these ministries were given:

> *For the equipping* [or perfecting] *of the saints for the work of the ministry, for the edifying of the body of Christ, till we all come to the unity of the faith and of the knowledge of the Son of God, to a perfect man, to the measure of the stature of the fullness of Christ.* (verses 12–13)

These building ministries are given until we all come into the unity of the faith through acknowledging Jesus Christ. Unity will not come by sitting and discussing doctrine. If there is one thing for sure, discussing doctrine does not unite Christians! The only way in which we will be united is by coming together around the headship of the Lord Jesus Christ in His supreme authority over every aspect of the church. You see, the doctrine of salvation is meaningless without the person of the Savior. The doctrine of healing is meaningless without the Healer. The doctrine of deliverance is meaningless without the Deliverer. The baptism in the Holy Spirit is meaningless without the Baptizer.

When we acknowledge the Savior, we believe in salvation. When we acknowledge the Healer, we believe in healing. When we acknowledge the Baptizer, we believe in the baptism in the Holy Spirit. When we acknowledge the Deliverer, we believe in deliverance from evil spirits. In every case, the road to unity is not the road of doctrinal disputation and discussion but the acknowledgment of the Lord Jesus Christ in His glory.

As we acknowledge Christ in all that He is to the church, we are brought into the unity of the faith, *"to a perfect man, to the measure of the stature of the fullness of Christ."* The key word here is *"fullness."* Until the church of Jesus Christ demonstrates Christ in all His fullness—in every aspect, every grace, every gift, every ministry—the church is not fulfilling its calling. At the present time, we manifest to the world a pathetically small part of the totality of Jesus Christ. There is much of Jesus that the church is incapable of demonstrating to the world, but God is going to bring us into that place where the corporate body of Christ will fully reveal the totality of Jesus.

For this reason I bow my knees to the Father of our Lord Jesus Christ, from whom the whole family in heaven and earth is named, that He would grant you, according to the riches of His glory, to be strengthened with might through His Spirit in the inner man [the Spirit is the one who ministers the glory and makes it available], that Christ may dwell in your hearts through faith; that you, being rooted and grounded in love, may be able to comprehend with all the saints what is the width and length and depth and height.... (Ephesians 3:14–18)

None of us can comprehend this individually; it is only as we come together with our fellow believers that we are able to comprehend the totality of Jesus Christ—the width, the length, the depth, and the height. Paul went on to say,

...to know the love of Christ which passes knowledge; that you may be filled with all the fullness of God. (verse 19)

This is a tremendous statement: The church of Jesus Christ is going to be the dwelling place of all the fullness of God! The totality of God, in all His nature, in all His power, and in all His aspects, will be manifested in the church. There is only one other place in Scripture that I know of where the phrase "the fullness of God" is used, and that is in Colossians 2, where it says of Jesus, *"For in him dwells all the fullness of the Godhead bodily"* (verse 9). In Christ, God was manifested totally, not partially. When the Holy Spirit has completed the work of forming the body of Christ, the fullness of God will be manifested in the church, as well. Never imagine that this can happen to you alone. You are just a little unit on your own. It is only as you come together into the unity of the faith and the acknowledgment of Christ that you will be able to comprehend with all believers the width, the length, the depth, and the height, and thus be filled with all the fullness of God. This is the purpose of God for the church.

God is going to manifest Himself in such a way that the whole earth will fear before Him and will see His glory:

> *So shall they fear the name of the LORD from the west, and His glory from the rising of the sun; when the enemy comes in like a flood, the Spirit of the LORD will lift up a standard against him.* (Isaiah 59:19)

The second half of this verse relates to our situation. The truth is, our enemy the devil *has* come in like a flood. He has infiltrated every area of our national life: politically, socially, and educationally, including the schools, the colleges, the universities, and the seminaries. Every aspect of national life in this country has, in the past few decades, been systematically infiltrated by the enemy's forces.

> *As the night gets darker and darker, the children of God are going to shine like stars in their glory.*

Not only has he come in like a flood to the world, but he has also come in to the church. This is the fulfillment of the prophecy of Joel, in which the people of God and their inheritance are desolated, much like an invading army of insects desolates the land. (See Joel 1:4.) The church has been invaded through the centuries by God's great army of judgment: the chewing locust, the swarming locust, the crawling locust, and the consuming locust. But God says that, at this time, His Spirit will move among us. *"When the enemy comes in like a flood, the Spirit of the* LORD *will lift up a standard against him."*

The standard that the Spirit of God will lift up is just one Person, and that is Jesus Christ. The Holy Spirit does not lift up a human personality; He does not exalt a doctrine or an institution. He has come to the church to do one primary thing, to lift up Jesus. In John 16:13–14, Jesus said, *"When He, the Spirit of truth, has come,...He will glorify Me, for He will take of what is Mine and declare it to you."* The ministry of the Holy Spirit within the church is to reveal, uplift, magnify, and glorify Jesus Christ.

The church must acknowledge and worship the Lord Jesus Christ. The Scripture says that through faith in Jesus Christ, we are the children of Abraham. (See Galatians 3:7.) God said to Abraham, "Your children are going to be like the stars of the sky." (See Genesis 5:15.) Normally speaking, when the sun is shining, or even at night, when the moon is shining, we do not pay much attention to the stars. But when the sun has set, and the moon is not shining brightly, and when every natural source of light has been extinguished, the stars shine brighter in the pitch darkness. This is precisely how it is going to be at the close of the age, as darkness covers the earth and deep darkness the people (see Isaiah 60:2); as the night gets darker and darker, the children of Abraham, through faith in Jesus Christ, are going to shine out like the stars in their glory. (See Philippians 2:14–16.)

Here is a glimpse of the bride coming forth in her glory:

Who is she who looks forth as the morning, fair as the moon, clear as the sun, awesome as an army with banners?

(Song of Solomon 6:10)

When the church manifests the glory of Christ, the world will recoil in amazement; it never will have seen a church like this. Who is this coming forth like the morning? After a night of darkness, the church will be like the rising of the sun. The bride of Christ will be as beautiful as the moon.

The responsibility of the moon is to reflect the light of the sun, and the moon appears in phases—quarter, half, three-quarter, and full moon. It waxes and wanes, as the church of Jesus Christ has waxed and waned. Yet, when the church ultimately comes back to full moon, it will fully reflect the glory of the Son. That is what the world is going to see—a full-orbed church, completely reflecting the glory and brightness of the Son.

And the church will be as clear as the sun. Although it will be as the moon, it will have the righteousness and the authority of the Son of Righteousness, Jesus Christ, applied to it, and it will be as awesome as an army with banners. Who has seen a church that is awesome to the forces of evil and darkness, sin and Satan? A church is coming forth that is going to cause the forces of Satan to tremble and flee.

God has shown me through experience that there is one message the devil fears more than any other. It is the message of what the church is going to be, and what it is going to do to him. The devil fights against this truth more than any other truth.

This is a picture of the church as God intends it to be. Take time to let God challenge you with His plan for the church and His plan for your individual life. He is coming back for a glorious church, and a glorious church He will have!

About the Author

erek Prince (1915–2003) was born in Bangalore, India, into a British military family. He was educated as a scholar of classical languages (Greek, Latin, Hebrew, and Aramaic) at Eton College and Cambridge University in England and later at Hebrew University, Israel. As a student, he was a philosopher and self-proclaimed atheist. He held a fellowship in ancient and modern philosophy at King's College, Cambridge.

While in the British Medical Corps during World War II, Prince began to study the Bible as a philosophical work. Converted through a powerful encounter with Jesus Christ, he was baptized in the Holy Spirit a few days later. This life-changing experience altered the whole course of his life, which he thereafter devoted to studying and teaching the Bible as the Word of God.

Discharged from the army in Jerusalem in 1945, he married Lydia Christensen, founder of a children's home there. Upon their marriage, he immediately became father to Lydia's eight adopted daughters—six Jewish, one Palestinian Arab, and one English. Together, the family saw the rebirth of the state of Israel in 1948. In the late 1950s, the Princes adopted another daughter while he was serving as principal of a college in Kenya.

In 1963, the Princes immigrated to the United States and pastored a church in Seattle. Stirred by the tragedy of John F. Kennedy's assassination, he began to teach Americans how to intercede for their nation. In 1973, he became one of the founders of Intercessors for America. His book *Shaping History through Prayer and Fasting* has awakened Christians around the world to their responsibility to pray for their governments. Many consider underground translations of the book as instrumental in the fall of communist regimes in the USSR, East Germany, and Czechoslovakia.

Lydia Prince died in 1975, and Derek married Ruth Baker (a single mother to three adopted children) in 1978. He met his second wife, like his first, while he was serving the Lord in Jerusalem. Ruth died in December 1998 in Jerusalem, where they had lived since 1981.

Until a few years before his own death in 2003 at the age of eighty-eight, Prince persisted in the ministry God had called him to as he traveled the world, imparting God's revealed truth, praying for the sick and afflicted, and sharing his prophetic insights into world events in the light of Scripture. He wrote over forty-five books, which have been translated in over sixty languages and distributed worldwide. He pioneered teaching on such groundbreaking themes as generational curses, the biblical significance of Israel, and demonology.

Derek Prince Ministries, with its international headquarters in Charlotte, North Carolina, continues to distribute his teachings and to train missionaries, church leaders, and congregations through its worldwide branch offices. His radio program, *Keys to Successful Living* (now known as *Derek Prince Legacy Radio*), began in 1979 and has been translated into over a dozen languages. Estimates are that Derek Prince's clear, nondenominational, nonsectarian teaching of the Bible has reached more than half the globe.

Internationally recognized as a Bible scholar and spiritual patriarch, Derek Prince taught and ministered on six continents for over seven decades. In 2002, he said, "It is my desire—and I believe the Lord's desire—that this ministry continue the work, which God began through me over sixty years ago, until Jesus returns."

Self-Study Bible Course
(updated & expanded edition)
Derek Prince

If you have questions about God and the Bible, here is the help you need. In this Bible study course, you will find answers to questions such as, "How can I have victory over sin?" and "How can I receive answers to my prayers?" Even if you have never read the Bible before, you will find this systematic study guide easy to use and helpful. Or, if you have been a believer for many years, you will find a new ease in conversing with God, fellowshipping with Christians, and witnessing and winning souls. As you explore in depth topics such as healing and guidance in the pages of this expanded edition, you will experience important changes in your life and discover an intimacy with God that you may have never known before.

ISBN: 0-88368-750-X • Workbook • 216 pages

www.whitakerhouse.com